Black Feminist Criticism

THE ATHENE SERIES
An International Collection of Feminist Books
General Editors: Gloria Bowles and Renate Duelli-Klein
Consulting Editor: Dale Spender

The ATHENE SERIES assumes that all those who are concerned with for-
mulating explanations of the way the world works need to know and appreciate
the significance of basic feminist principles.

The growth of feminist research has challenged almost all aspects of social
organization in our culture. The ATHENE SERIES focuses on the construction
of knowledge and the exclusion of women from the process — both as theorists
and subjects of study—and offers innovative studies that challenge established
theories and research.

ON ATHENE — When Metis, goddess of wisdom who presided over all
knowledge was pregnant with ATHENE, she was swallowed up by Zeus who
then gave birth to ATHENE from his head. The original ATHENE is thus the
parthenogenetic daughter of a strong mother and as the feminist myth goes, at
the "third birth" of ATHENE she stops being Zeus' obedient mouthpiece and
returns to her real source: the science and wisdom of womankind

Volumes in the Series
MEN'S STUDIES MODIFIED The Impact of Feminism
on the Academic Disciplines
edited by Dale Spender

MACHINA EX DEA Feminist Perspectives on Technology
edited by Joan Rothschild

WOMEN'S NATURE Rationalizations of Inequality
edited by Marian Lowe and Ruth Hubbard

SCIENCE AND GENDER
A Critique of Biology and Its Theories on Women
Ruth Bleier

WOMAN IN THE MUSLIM UNCONSCIOUS
Fatna A. Sabbah

MEN'S IDEAS/WOMEN'S REALITIES
Popular Science, 1870-1915
edited by Louise Michele Newman

BLACK FEMINIST CRITICISM
Perspectives on Black Women Writers
Barbara Christian

NOTICE TO READERS
May we suggest that your library places a standing/continuation order to receive
all future volumes in the Athene Series immediately on publication?
Your order can be cancelled at any time.

Also of Interest
WOMEN'S STUDIES INTERNATIONAL FORUM*
Editor: Dale Spender
*Free sample copy available on request

Black Feminist Criticism

Perspectives on Black Women Writers

Barbara Christian
University of California, Berkeley

Pergamon Press

New York • Oxford • Toronto • Sydney • Paris • Frankfurt

Pergamon Press Offices:

U.S.A.	Pergamon Press Inc., Maxwell House, Fairview Park, Elmsford, New York 10523, U.S.A.
U.K.	Pergamon Press Ltd., Headington Hill Hall, Oxford OX3 0BW, England
CANADA	Pergamon Press Canada Ltd., Suite 104, 150 Consumers Road, Willowdale, Ontario M2J 1P9, Canada
AUSTRALIA	Pergamon Press (Aust.) Pty. Ltd., P.O. Box 544, Potts Point, NSW 2011, Australia
FRANCE	Pergamon Press SARL, 24 rue des Ecoles, 75240 Paris, Cedex 05, France
FEDERAL REPUBLIC OF GERMANY	Pergamon Press GmbH, Hammerweg 6, D-6242 Kronberg-Taunus, Federal Republic of Germany

Copyright © 1985 Pergamon Press Inc.

Library of Congress Cataloging in Publication Data

Christian, Barbara, 1943-
   Black feminist criticism.

   (The Athene series)
   Includes index.
   1. American literature--Afro-American authors--
History and criticism--Addresses, essays, lectures.
2. American literature--20th century--History and
criticism--Addresses, essays, lectures. 3. Afro-
American women authors--Addresses, essays, lectures.
4. Feminism and literature--Addresses, essays,
lectures. I. Title. II. Series.
PS153.N5C47 1985 810'.9'9287 84-22805
ISBN 0-08-031956-4
ISBN 0-08-031955-6 (pbk.)

Printed in Great Britain by A. Wheaton & Co. Ltd., Exeter

Contents

Acknowledgments

"Alice Walker: The Black Woman Artist as Wayward" first printed in *Black Women Writers: A Critical Evaluation 1950-1980*, ed. Mari Evans, reprinted by permission of Doubleday.

"Alternate Versions of the Gendered Past: African Women Writers vs. Ivan Illich," first printed in *Feminist Issues*, reprinted by permission of *Feminist Issues*.

"The Contrary Black Women of Alice Walker: A Study of Female Protagonists in *In Love and Trouble*," first printed in *The Black Scholar*, reprinted by permission of *The Black Scholar*.

"Creating a Universal Literature: Afro-American Women Writers," first printed in *KPFA Folio*, reprinted by permission of KPFA Pacifica.

"The Dynamics of Difference," first printed in *The Women's Review of Books*, reprinted by permission of *The Women's Review of Books*.

Introduction of Afro-American Section," first printed in *Women Poets of the World*, eds. Bankier and Lashgari, reprinted by permission of MacMillan.

"Nature and Community in the novels of Toni Morrison," first printed in *The Journal of Ethnic Studies*, reprinted by permission of *The Journal of Ethnic Studies*.

"Paule Marshall: A Literary Biography," first printed in *Dictionary of Literary Biography of Afro-American Writers*, reprinted by permission of University of North Carolina Press.

"Ritualistic Process and the Structure of Paule Marshall's *Praisesong for the Widow*" first printed in *Callaloo*, reprinted by permission of *Callaloo*.

"Testing the Strength of the Black Cultural Bond," first printed in *In These Times*, reprinted by permission of *In These Times*.

Introduction

Black Feminist Process: In the Midst of . . .

I am sprawling at the low table I work at, surrounded by books and plants, a pad and pencil in front of me. Brow knit, sometimes muttering, sometimes reading or staring out the window, I am engrossed. My 10-year-old daughter touches me.

"Come play a game," she implores.

"I'm working," ending the discussion, I think. Her skeptical face bends down.

"You're not teaching," she retorts, "You're just reading a story."

I see an image from Foucoult's "Fantasia of the Library," at the center of which is a European male reader, surrounded by books, which comment on books, his posture rapt. Not too long ago I'd read Marcelle Thiebaux's commentary on Foucoult's "Fantasia," in which she proposed replacing the male reader with a woman reader. She reminds us that her reader would occupy a different space; her reading would be seen as time away from her main work. Interruptions would be normal and she would likely be reinterpreting the book she is reading without even being aware of it, reinventing herself in the midst of patriarchal discourse, as to who she is supposed to be.

Quite true, I think, but most of my black sisters *and* brothers would not even have gotten in the library, or if some of them did, like the parlour maid in *Jane Eyre*, they'd be dusting the books. *Their* libraries in Alexandria and elsewhere had been burnt long ago in the wake of conquest and slavery.

Not wishing to prolong the discussion by reminding my daughter that 100 years ago, I would not even have been conceived of as a reader, might in fact have been killed for trying, I notice the Nancy Drew book she has in her hand, her finger still tucked in her place. She's probably solved the mystery already.

"Why are you reading?" she presses.

I know the words that come to my mind—"If I don't save my own life, who will?"—are triggered by the Walker essay I'd been reading and the book under her arm. I dodge her question.

"That would involve a long discussion. I'm working."

But her comment has set my mind on a different track. She knows it, sees the shift, and pulls out her now-constant refrain.

"I'm old enough to know." As indeed she is.

I remember as a young girl in the Caribbean gobbling up Nancy Drew books, involved in the adventures of this intrepid white teenage girl, who solved mysteries, risked danger, was central to her world. I know their pull for a young girl—the need to see oneself as engaging the dangerous world in a fiction protective enough to imagine it, the need to figure out the world, the need to win. And I remember the privileges of Nancy's world—pretty, intelligent, well taken care of, white, American, she had winning allies. What girl actually lives in that universe? What black girl protagonist competed with her? My daughter has read about Harriet Tubman, Mary McLeod Bethune; she has even met Rosa Parks. Historical personages, they are still too awesome for her.

Alice Walker notes in her essay that when Toni Morrison was asked why she wrote the books she did, she replied because she wanted to read them. And Marcelle Thiebaux makes the same comment in the *lit crit* language of our day: "The only possible library for a woman is one invented by herself, writing herself or her own discourse into it."

My daughter is waiting for an answer. If I'd been reading a how-to manual, a history book, or even a cookbook, she'd have accepted the answer about work.

Leaving momentous questions aside, I respond: "I enjoy it."

Abandoned for the moment by her friends, having solved the Nancy Drew mystery, she sees a long boring afternoon ahead. She asks one of her whoppers:

"What good does it do?" Knowing that the reading will turn into writing, she looks at the low table, books, pen, and pencil: "What *are* you doing?"

A good question, I think. But she is not finished. Knowing she's got me in the grip of a conversation, she rallies:

"Why is it that you write mostly about black women's books? You read lots of other books. Is it because you like what they say best?"

Art is not flattery, I think, trying to remember if I'd read that in the Walker essay.

What my daughter was asking is not a new question. It's one I often ask myself. What is a literary critic, a black woman critic, a black feminist literary critic, a black feminist social literary critic? The adjectives mount up, defining, qualifying, the activity. How does one distinguish them? The need to articulate a theory, to categorize the activities is a good part of the activity itself to the point where I wonder how we ever get around to doing anything else. What do these categories tell anyone about my method? Do I do formalist criticism, operative or expressive criticism, mimetic or structuralist criticism (to use the categories I'd noted in a paper by a feminist colleague of mine)? I'm irked, weighed down by Foucoult's library as tiers of books written on epistomology, onotology, and technique peer down at me. Can one theorize effectively about an evolving process? Are the labels informative or primarily a way of nipping the question in the bud? What are the philosophical assumptions behind my praxis? I think how the articulation of a theory is a gathering place, sometimes a point of rest as the process rushes on, insisting that you follow. I can see myself trying to explain those tiers of books to my daughter as her little foot taps the floor.

"Well, first of all," I say, having decided to be serious, "I'm a reader," stressing my activeness, as I try to turn her comment, "You're just reading," on its head. As I state that simple fact, I think of the many analyses of the critic's role that bypass reading and move immediately to the critic's role as performer, as writer. I continue, "Reading is itself an involved activity. It's a response to some person's thoughts, and language, even possibly their heart."

When I read something that engages me, my reaction is visceral: I sweat, get excited, exalted or irritated, scribble on the edges of the paper, talk aloud to the unseen writer or to myself. Like the Ancient Mariner, I waylay every person in my path, "Have you read this? What about this, this, or this?" This reaction is no news to my daughter. She and her friends get that way about Michael Jackson, TV shows, stickers, possibly even Judy Blume. But that response, of course, is not so much the accepted critical mode, despite Brathes's *plaisir*. It's too suspect, too subjective, not grounded in reality.

Still, when I read much literary criticism today, I wonder if the critic has read the book, since so often the text is but an occasion for espousing his or her philosophical point of view—revolutionary black, feminist, or socialist program. The least we owe the writer, I think, is an acknowledgment of her labor. After all, writing is intentional, is at bottom, work.

I pause, trying to be as clear as possible to Najuma in my description of what I am doing.

"Right now," I say, "I'm listening to the voice, the many voices created by Alice Walker in this book and looking at the way she's using words to make these voices seem alive, so you believe them." (Aha, I think, formalist criticism, expressive criticism, operative criticism.) My daughter does not know these referents.

"Why," she inquires, "So you can write something?" She is now focused on the pencil and pad, which may take my attention away from her.

I try again, this time using a comparison. "Everybody wants to be understood by somebody. If you want somebody to know you, who you are, what you think and feel, you've got to say something. But if nobody indicates they heard you, then it's almost as if you never said anything at all. African people are wise when they say 'speech is knowledge.'"

My last sentence tells me my teaching instinct has been aroused. I'm now intent on her understanding of this point, the Nancy Drew book still in my mind.

"If black women don't say who they are, other people will and say it badly for them," I say, as I remember Audre Lorde's poem about the deadly consequences of silence. "Silence is hardly golden," I continue. "If other black women don't answer back, who will? When we speak and answer back we validate our experiences. We say we *are* important, if only to ourselves." Too hard for her, I think, but she's followed me.

"Like when you and your friends talk on the phone about how politicians don't understand what it means to be a mother?" she quips. "Then, why don't you just call Alice Walker on the phone and tell her what you think about her book?"

She has seen Alice. She's flesh and blood—a pretty brown-skinned woman with a soft voice. But I'm not finished.

"I am a black woman, which means that when I read I have a particular stance. Because it's clear to me that black people, black women, women, poor people, despite our marvelous resilience, are often prevented from being all they can be, I am also a black feminist critic."

I think of literary criticism as a head detaching itself from the rest of a body, claiming subjectivity only in one part of the brain. "Everybody has a point of view about life and about the world, whether they admit it or not," I continue.

"Then," she ventures, "why do you have all these other books around you?" (questioning my definite point of view). "And why can't you just tell Alice Walker what you think?"

While she's talking, she notices, on the low table, Paule Marshall's essay, "Poets in the Kitchen." Seeing that our discussion is getting her nowhere, she changes the subject.

"Isn't it funny," she says, "that whenever your friends come over, whether you're cooking or not, you all end up in the kitchen?"

"That's what Paule is talking about." I shift back to our original conversation. "That's why I need all these other books. She's telling us how she learned about language and storytelling from her mother and her mother's friends talking in the kitchen" (rather than just in Foucoult's library or Rochester's drawing room, I think).

"Are your friends poets too?" she smiles, amused by the thought. "They're in the kitchen because they're used to it," says Najuma as her face shows that she's begun thinking about the delights of food.

Yes, I think, but it's also because communities revolve around food and warmth, at least until they generate enough surplus to have women or blacks or some other group do it for them and they can retire to the library. (Ah, Marxist criticism?)

"That's true, Najuma, sometimes, we are forced to be there. But even then, human beings often make an opportunity out of a constraint. If we don't recognize what we're doing, the value of what we are doing . . . ? That's part of what a writer does. And as a critic (I now use the ponderous word), I call attention to the form, show how it comes out of a history, a tradition, how the writer uses it. If we, and others don't understand Paule's form, that it *is* a form, we can't even hear what she's saying or how meaningful it is."

My being from the Caribbean helps me to recognize that people invent their own forms. I think of Ellison's discussion of the mask Afro-Americans use, of Elaine Showalter's analysis of the double-voiced discourse of women. But I've lost her— my daughter's face puckers. Wondering if interrupting me has been worth it, she looks out the window.

Of course, I think, following my own train of thought, it's even more complicated than that. For in illuminating her kitchen poets, Paule is also calling attention to the constraints imposed on them. In denying her expression as art, those who control the society can continue their cultural hegemony. What's published or seen as central has so much to do with the cultural reproduction of the powerful.

But Najuma has interrupted my thoughts. Intently she asks: "Why do you write it down, why not just tell Alice about her book?" Writing, she knows, is even more private than reading, which separates her from me and has many times landed her in bed before she wanted to go.

I smile. Barthes' comment, "Writing is precisely that which exceeds speech" comes to mind. I pause. "Well," I say, again searching for a clear way out. "Writing is another way of ordering your thoughts. You write things differently from the way you say them, if only because you can look back at what you write, at what other people have written, and can look forward to what you may write. A blank piece of paper is an invitation to find out what you think, know, feel, to consciously make connection."

Medium criticism, I think. Is she going to ask about tape recorders or TV shows? No, I've lost her. But if she had asked, I'd remind her that tape recordings are transcribed and edited; even TV shows, as instant as they seem, are based on scripts.

Seeing her perplexity, I try again. "Sometimes," I say, "I haven't the slightest idea what I'm thinking. There's so much rushing through my mind. Don't you feel that way sometimes?" I ask as I look at her stare out the window. "Writing helps to form that chaos, (I change the word) all that energy."

I can see she's heard me.

"But what good is it besides knowing a little better what you are thinking. Who cares?"

"Hmm," I mutter, "if you don't care, who will?" But I refrain from this flippant comment and decide to take a leap. "Najuma, do you know why you worry about your kinky hair? Why there are so many poor people in this rich country? Why your friends sometimes tease you about reading too much?"

She pauses, then surprises me: "For the same reason, my school wasn't sure that a jazz class, instead of classical music, would be good music training," she says imitating a grown-up's voice.

˒ She does notice things; I feel triumphant: "And that has to do with ideas," I continue, "and how they affect consciousness." Does she know the meaning of that word? I use it so often; do I know what it means? "People *do* things, one of which might be writing, to help themselves and other people ask questions about who they are, who they might be, what kind of world they want to create, to remind ourselves that we do create the world." (I am now being carried away by my own rhetoric.) "I teach too, go to conferences, support organizations I believe in, am a mother," I emphasize, as I begin to worry about whether I've exalted writing too much.

But the writing point holds her: "So," she says, "writers tell people what to do?"

My mind winces "Well, not so much as they ask questions, try to express reality as they see it, feel it, push against what exists, imagine possibilities, see things that might not yet exist," I say, as I think of Wilson Harris's discourse on vision as a historical dimension.

"Anyway," she says, clearly wanting to end this too serious conversation, "I know what a critic is, because I saw it in the newspaper. You say what's good and what's bad," she says in triumph, knowing that I will finally agree with her.

"Literature is not a horse race," I mutter, as I remember Doris Lessing's response to such a statement. Foucoult's library looms again.

Calmly I state: "First you've got to know what it *is* you're reading. What the writer, the person speaking, is doing, which may be unfamiliar since no two of us are, fortunately, alike. Remember how you told me that I didn't understand your way of dressing, that it had a way of its own?" (I see her combining colors I wouldn't even dream of, but when I calm down, they certainly do make their own statement.)

"Then, how do you judge what's good or bad," she says, "since everybody has their own way?"

From the past, I hear R. P. Blackmur's words, "the critic will impose the excellence of something he understands on something he doesn't understand." All those texts from Plato and Aristotle through Northrop Frye, the rationalist critics, the structuralists begin to fall on me. I relax by breathing deeply.

"You play the piano," I remind her. "Sometimes, something you're learning doesn't sound quite right at first, until you begin to see the way it's put together, how it works, what it's trying to do. Then you hear it, something new perhaps, something you just didn't know about before. It sounds beautiful. Writing is like that too. It's got its own workings. At least you need to understand the workings before you can say whether it's done well, which is not the same, I think, as whether you like it or not." I think of the Latin American writers whose work I find beautiful but whose tradition I know little about.

"There's no absolute way to tell what's good or bad," I continue, wondering how I got into this conversation. "I try to hear a writer's voice, or more precisely the one she's gotten on the page in comparison to the one she might have in her head. Then I try to situate that in a tradition that has evolved some approximate ways of how that gets written down best." My thoughts go faster than my speech. I think the best writers are often the ones that break the tradition to continue it. Baraka's comment on art, "hunting is not those heads on the wall," though male, is true.

"In any case," I emphasize, as she retreats to the kitchen, this conversation having become too heavy for her, "every critic knows one thing— writing is a complex activity. That's one of the reasons, I suppose, why we too must write." By now, I'm talking to myself. "And oh, how we write, as we invent our own vocabularies of mystification. Sometimes, things ought to be switched around and writers should get a chance to judge us."

Munching an apple, Najuma passes through the room, sweetly ending the conversation: "It sounds to me like too much work. Why don't you get involved with the airlines, so we can travel free." For her, traveling is the most pleasurable activity humankind has invented. "Or if that's too much, try gardening," she continues, compromising on my fetish for plants. "At least you'd look like you're having fun," she concludes as she turns to her collection of airline flyers.

"But I do have fun doing this," I respond, though, humbled again by the terror of the blank page in front of me, it's a mystery to me why.

1 Images of Black Women in Afro-American Literature: From Stereotype to Character (1975)

This essay was originally written for inclusion in an anthology on Afro-American literature to be published by the University of Ibaden Press. Its editor, Adam David Miller, believed that Africans wanted to know more about the literature of their brothers and sisters here in North America. We agreed, without realizing the importance of our decision, that the inclusion of an essay on Afro-American women writers was critical to the anthology. Such inclusion was by no means usual in 1975.

For me, this essay was an extremely important one, since it was my first attempt to organize the research I had been doing on Afro-American women writers. It is actually the first sketch of my book, Black Women Novelists, The Development of a Tradition *(1892-1976), which I finished in 1979.*

It is interesting for me to note what I selected for use in that book, since the scope of this essay was far too ambitious. In it, I look at Afro-American poets as well as fiction writers, at male writers' treatment of women, as well as female writers. More important is what was missing in the essay. Although it does indicate that the concept of images was one of my major concerns, it does not demonstrate the depth of historical investigation and analysis necessary for the establishment of my thesis—that a tradition of Afro-American women writers existed. Instead, the essay is organized around a few women writers, chosen rather quixotically, according to historical epoch. There is, for example, little discussion of Jessie Fauset or Alice Walker. Still, the sections on Paule Marshall and Toni Morrison are clearly the kernel of the work I would do on these writers in Black Women Novelists.

Since this present collection of essays does not include any excerpt from that book, "Images . . ." is necessary background for the essays that follow. It shows how far literary criticism on black women writers has come in a decade. By now, most of the writers I mention have received some degree of attention from an emerging group of black feminist critics. As importantly, this essay's omissions illustrate how significant the few historical

*books on Afro-American women published since 1975 have been
to the development of this new body of criticism.*

(1)

Until the 1940s, black women in both Anglo- and Afro-American
literature have been usually assigned stereotyped roles—their images
being a context for some other major dilemma or problem the society
cannot resolve. Throughout the novels of the slavery and reconstruction
periods, Anglo-American literature, particularly southern white literature, fashioned an image of the black woman intended to further create
submission, conflict between the black man and woman, and importantly, a dumping ground for those female functions a basically Puritan
society could not confront.

The mammy figure, Aunt Jemima, the most prominent black female
figure in southern white literature,[1] is in direct contrast to the ideal white
woman, though both images are dependent on each other for their
effectiveness. Mammy is black in color, fat, nurturing, religious, kind,
above all strong, and as Faulkner would call Dilsey, enduring. She relates
to the world as an all embracing figure, and she herself needs or demands
little, her identity derived mainly from a nurturing service. She must be
plump and have big breasts and arms—she is the mammy in the unconscious of the South, desired and needed since ideal white women would
have to debase themselves in order to be a mother. In contrast, the white
woman was supposed to be frail, alabaster white, incapable of doing hard
work, shimmering with the beauty of fragile crystal. These images are
dependent on one another, since the white woman could not be ornamental, descriptive, fussy, if she nursed and brought up children. In the
mythology of the South, men did not fight duels or protect the honor of a
woman who was busy cooking, scrubbing floors, or minding children,
since the exclusive performance of this kind of work precluded the
intrigue necessary to be a person as ornament. In other words leisure time
on one's pretty hands made one weak enough to need protection.

The image of the ideal white women tries to deny the gross physical
aspects of being female, gross from the southern point of view. In
contrast, all the functions of mammy are magnificently physical. They
involve the body as sensuous, as funky, the part of woman that white
southern America was profoundly afraid of. Mammy, then, harmless in
her position as a slave, unable because of her all-giving nature to do harm
is needed as an image, a surrogate to contain all those fears of the
physical female.

One could analyze the other prominent black female images in white
southern literature, the concubine, in much the same way. Even the
conjure woman is a reservoir for fears—fears, in this case, of the unknown

spiritual world, so that particularly in New Orleans, the center of Catholicism in the South, Marie Laveau, the great voodoo mambo, could emerge as one of its most powerful citizens for half a century.

During the same period, Afro-American literature moved in a different direction. While southern white literature had focused on the mammy as the dominant black female image, with some glimpses at the concubine and the conjure woman, black literature centered mainly on the image of the tragic mulatta. Such novels as *Clotell* (1850) by William Wells Brown and Frances Harper's *Iola LeRoy* (1892), the first published novel by a black woman, set the stage for this heroine as a lasting image in black literature for decades to come.[2]

The tragic mulatta theme reveals the conflict of values that blacks faced as a *conquered* people. In her very being, the mulatta called up the illicit crossing between cultures. She is American in that she emerges out of the sexual relationship between a black slave mother and a white slave master, a sexual relationship denying the most basic philosophical concept of slavery—that blacks were not human beings. Do humans mate with nonhumans, and if they do, what is the product, human or nonhuman? As the white slave master entered the bodies of countless black women, he knew of her being, her humanness. His mind could attempt to deny it for economic and social reasons, but he knew in his loins her humanness.

Therefore, the plight of the mulatta arose as reading material for the ears of white folks. And we cannot forget that the first black novels were written for a white audience, since black people, according to the laws of many states, were not permitted to read or write. White audiences lapped up the stories of mulattos and their tragedies in the ironic way that the guilty and powerful always delight in looking obliquely at their guilt. The existence of the mulatta, who combined the physical characteristics of both races, denied their claim that blacks were not human, while allowing them the argument that they were lifting up the race by lightening it. Most, though, knew that in lightening the black race they were also darkening the white race, hence the laws against miscegenation in so many southern states.

In this devious circle of logic, the mulatta becomes the vehicle for cultural transference as well, since in literature, she is usually the house slave, much to the chagrin of the white mistresses who had to face their husbands' promiscuity in their most intimate slaves. By living in the Big House, the slave saw the master's way of life, its comforts and pleasures but also its disharmony and deceptiveness and could relate either to the power inherent in the master's position by identifying with him or by rejecting him in fury. In either case, however, the die is cast, for the mulatta may be light but never white and hence could not have the power or the pleasures of the Big House no matter how much she identified with her master. If independence were a virtue, as it was among white slave masters, the mulatta who identified with that spirit was in deep trouble. If refinement were a goal of life, the leisure necessary for such a quality was simply not obtainable to the slave.

Hence, the tragedy of the mulatta. The alienation that was an essential part of her being was complicated by the knowledge she represented to the black slave. To the black field slave mother, whose mulatta baby is taken away from her at an early age to be raised in the Big House, the child itself must have called up mixed emotions within her. For the black slave man who knows his lack of power to prevent the union between slave woman and master, this child must have represented his powerlessness. The birth of such a child heightened the emotional pain of being a slave. And on the practical level, the black field slave must have wondered about the loyalty of the mulatta. Is she loyal to her father or to her mother?

"Softly speak," the spirituals say, "softly speak of freedom." But what does freedom mean? The lot of the tragic mulatta challenges the easy definition of that dream. *Clotell* and subsequent novels of that gender present the mulatta as a person worthy to be free—because she is beautiful, courageous and refined: beautiful because she represents those qualities of white standards of beauty, denied automatically to the darky; refined because she has learned the manners and customs of the Big House; courageous because she knows and relates to the code of conduct defined by the South. And in order to refute the slaveowners' argument that black people are inferior, writers like William Wells Brown present heroines who say, "See, I can be like you and even be better than you by your very own standards."

It is important that the mulatto woman rather than the man is the one more often chosen in literature to project this argument since until recently in America, the women of any group represented the body of ideals that the group measured itself by. Woman, because she bears and raises children, has, for better or worse, embodied those intangibles of a culture deemed worthy to be passed on more than any code of law or written philosophy. And of course woman in white culture is not as powerful as man, so to pose the existence of a mulatto slave man who embodies the qualities of the master is so great a threat, so dangerous an idea, even in fiction, that it is seldom tried.

The image of the mulatta is a stereotype that reaches a peak in the essence of mulattas presented by Jean Toomer (himself a black man who could pass as white) in *Cane* (1923), a work principally about physical, cultural, and emotional miscegenation, and in the novels of Nella Larson, such as *Passing* (1929).

Before we move from the images of black women projected in slavery and reconstruction literature, we must look at the images fashioned by another tradition, the oral tradition, the witnessing of black people as seen through narratives and songs. The slave narrative as a genre has tended to be represented by those extraordinary slaves, usually men such as Frederick Douglass, who escaped from bondage. Yet there are many narratives of slaves, and of women slaves, who considered themselves the common folk and remained in slavery most of their lives.[3]

As would be expected, within the genre, the image of mammy persists. She is there as cook, housekeeper, nursemaid, seamstress, always nurturing and caring for her folk. But unlike the white southern image of mammy, she is cunning, prone to poisoning her master, and not at all content with her lot. It is interesting and ironic that Sojourner Truth, the flamboyant orator who advocated the abolition of slavery and fought for women's rights, would fit the stereotype, at least the physical stereotype, of the mammy southern gentlemen wanted to perceive as harmless. Sojourner Truth is not the only mammy who fought to protect her own children or who rose up against slavery. Mammies kicked, fought, connived, plotted, most often covertly, to throw off the chains of bondage. Mammy saw herself as a mother, but to her that role embodied a certain dignity and responsibility, rather than a physical debasement, doubtless a carry-over from the African view that every mother is a symbol of the marvelous creativity of the earth.[4] Mammy is an important figure in the mythology of Africa. The way in which this theme of African culture is distorted by the white southern perspective testifies to its inability to relate femaleness and femininity, as countless southern belles in antebellum American movies illustrate.

The tragic mulatta also appears in slave narratives. And indeed, she is tragic, as are almost all of the accounts. The contrast of comic darky and tragic mulatto developed in the literature of that period certainly does not stand the test of reality. There is little romanticism in the accounts mulattas give of their lives. There are tales of mulattas who as mistresses were abused and sold, their children scattered to the ends of the land, tales of mad mulattas who hated their fathers if they were acknowledged by them at all. There were sullen, cynical mulattas reared to be sold as high class courtesans. The narratives abound with tales of woman—be she field nigger or house nigger, mulatta or darky—as breeder, nurser, nurse maid, concubine, whipping block, put on the rack of everlasting work and debasing servitude.[5] And in the tales of these women, be they yaller or chocolate, the trivial underscores the abuses they faced: having to sleep outside the mistress's door so that little sexual relationship with one's husband was possible, having to take care of mistresses' children so that one's babies were born dead, time after time. The list of trivia goes on — trivia to the minds of the slavemaster — near death, in a particularly female way, for these slaves. The narratives are particularly poignant in the equalization of abuse they suggest, for the advantages that the mulatta might have because of her link to the master were easily offset by the disadvantages of alienation and frustration.

The narratives tend to focus on the relationship between slave and master, but the worksongs give us another view of how the slave woman viewed herself and was viewed by others. Since music is usually so intensely personal and need not be sanctioned by a publisher in order to be heard and spread, the songs about and by women tend to peer into the relationship between the black man and woman in their identity as man and woman. Courting, lovemaking, success and disappointment in love, all these aspects appear in the songs. Some men revel in their women. "Pretty Girl" is representative of this group:

> Rubber is a pretty thing.
> You rub it to make it shine.
> If you want to see a pretty girl,
> Take a peep at mine, take a peep at mine.
>
> Talking about a pretty girl
> You jus' ought-a-see mine.
> She is not so pretty
> But she is jus' so fine.
>
> She gives me sugar,
> She gives me lard,
> She works all the while
> In the white folks' yard.[6]

And at the same time, there is often the recurring theme that:

> De woman am de cause of it all,
> De woman am de cause of it all,
> She's de cause of po' Adam's fall
> De woman's de cause of it all.[7]

The songs also mirror the tingling clash between the dark woman and the yaller woman, often in a humorous tone:

> De mulatto gal got yaller skin, yaller skin,
> De mulatto gal got yaller skin, yaller skin,
> De mulatto gal got yaller skin, yaller skin,
> De mulatto gal got yaller skin,
> Den she got a devilish grin, daddy.
>
> De chocolate gal got greasy hair, greasy hair,
> De chocolate gal got greasy hair, greasy hair,

De chocolate gal got greasy hair, greasy hair,
De chocolate gal got greasy hair,
She is de gal can cuss and rare, daddy.[8]

Yet within the confines of their own space, threatened as it was by a more powerful society with different standards, there does not emerge a hard and fast line about the value of a woman simply because she has got some white blood. Unlike the literary products of the day, the heroines of these songs might or might not be cinnamon, coffee, chocolate, or yaller:

If 'twant for de ter'pin pie
And sto-bought ham,
Dese country women
Couldn't git nowhere.

Some say, give me a high yaller,
I say, give me a teasin brown,
For it takes a teasin brown
To satisfy my soul.

For some folkies say
A yaller is low down,
But teasin brown
Is what I's crazy about.[9]

Almost always the substances of the worksongs about or by women are sifted through the cry of hard times and how that affects relationships: The men who caught trains and left for whatever reasons, the lack of money, the pervasive sense of danger, the need for a woman to be independent of men, an independence imposed rather than desired, all shape the songs and give even the gayest song an undertone of plaintiveness. Slave narrative and worksong alike project black women as caught in the vise of hard times, their spirits occasionally rising to the heights of heroism but more often tempered by the nibbling need to always be practical.

(2)

There is no single face in nature, because every eye that looks upon it, sees it from its own angle. So every man's spice-box seasons his own food.[10]
Zora Neale Hurston, *Dust Tracks on the Road*

Zora Neale Hurston arrived in New York City with her own unique spicebox, at a time when the Harlem Renaissance was just beginning to swing. In the decade preceding her arrival, blacks had migrated in large numbers from the rural South to cities like New York. Out of that great migration emerged Harlem, the mecca of the black world in the twenties, where jazz and urban blues, a new race pride, and a wealth of black literature blossomed. Black women, of course, had made that migration to the city looking for a new life and found that the substance remained the same, though the apparel looked different. Instead of being house-keepers, cooks, and cotton pickers, they became domestics, garment factory workers, prostitutes—the hard bottom of the labor market.[11]

The literature had yet to catch up with the new reality. The women in *Cane* (1923) that you remember are the southern women who do not speak but are spoken of, tragic mulattas whose existences were meta-phors for the blend of sweetness and madness Toomer tasted in the South. Jessie Fauset's women in her novels such as *The Chinaberry Tree* (1931) were genteel ladies whose conflicts about color and class tended to be closer to fairytale than anyone's imagined or factual reality. Nella Larsen's characters in *Quicksand* (1928) and *Passing* (1929) are again mulattas plagued by the tragedy of shade. A literature of the tragic mulatta emerged—stereotype par excellence.

In the journey from this image of the tragic mulatta to a more varied, more complex view of the black woman as she appears in American literature, Zora Neale Hurston's work is transitional. Her autobiography, *Dust Tracks On The Road* (1942), told in the roving conversational tone Zora developed, breaks down stereotype and paints a canvas of multi-colors that reflects Zora's mental and emotional life. Born in Eatonville, Florida, a black town founded and governed by black men, Zora tells us about the store porch where people gathered and performed lying ses-sions, where they whispered about those who dabbled in hoodoo, about who was courting who, in a speech that was to hold wonder for her most of her life. Her wanderings in Eatonville, Washington, D.C., Barnard in New York, the South, and the West Indies chart the intellectual and artistic development of this black woman with a richness of detail not seen before in the literature.

In her novels, Hurston incorporates the complexity of character into a marvel of a tale, for she is foremost a storyteller, attempting and sometimes succeeding to capture the gestures and tones of the folk on Joe Clarke's store porch. Her heroines are not the women of New York City—they move in that mythology of the South, the roots still for the race, the place where the black culture of the previous century had reached a particular peak, though that culture was now undergoing changes in the North.

Zora's urbaneness, her sophistication did not lead her down the path to genteel literature. Her roots were so strong that the "city-fying" gave her skill, articulation, and discipline as she pursued her double role as anthropologist and writer. In her autobiography as woman, she is inde-pendent, flamboyant, humorous, and always dedicated to the work she *must* do. And as a woman, her work collided with the view of woman held high in the general society. Men could not, would not accept, she tells us, that they *and* her work were the important things to her. It had to be one or the other. For Zora Neale Hurston, nothing was ever this or that; there were too many spice boxes around to make it that clear cut. So she is a controversial figure on every issue except one, the wonderful richness and beauty of black folk culture.

Her works exude this feel for variedness—her characters move in their own space, pinching bits of their spices, applying sage or basil to different types of menus as only they can. *Their Eyes Were Watching God* (1937), her most acclaimed novel, has the Hurston blend of complexity of character within the frame of a good story.

Janie, the heroine of this tale, in some ways fits the outlines of the conventional tragic mulatta. Her grandmother Nanny tells the budding Janie how she was raped by her master and ran off with her child when threatened by her mistress. When Nanny's child, (Janie's mother) is seventeen, she is also raped and goes slightly out of her mind leaving Nanny to bring up Janie. So Janie's birth and the birth of her mother are results of rape, the genesis of the mulatto in southern literature. The outline has been drawn, but within it a portraiture begins that is Janie's and hers alone. Searching for a center, a means to clarity and harmony, Janie wanders through two unhappy marriages, one with an old man who is jealous of her youth and beauty, the other with Jody Stark, the black entrepreneur who creates a town partly to establish Janie as its queen, seated on the porch, aloof and apart from everyone. The mulatta usually sits there, regal in her imitation of the white folks' ways, content that she has gotten to the peak of colored society. But Janie cannot stand this isolation. She wants to know herself, and she wants to know her husband, a desire he perceives as a threat. When he dies, she falls in love with Tea Cake, a man younger than she, who is interested not in her money or in her long black hair but in her essence. Their love story forms the hard kernel of this book, romantic in its abandon, but tingling with a poignancy borne of a dream dreamt so long that it had to come true. That Janie must kill Tea Cake because he is mad with rabies leads us back to the stereotype of the tragic mulatta, except that to Janie, her life has not been tragic but rich:

> She pulled her horizon like a great fish net. Pulled it from around the waist of the world and draped it over her shoulder. So much of life in its meshes. She called in her soul to come and see.[12]

Such a tale could be schematic or trite in its romanticism, but it is Zora Neale Hurston's precise grasp of black peoples' ways, their speech, and wisdom that gives the novel earth's rich feel:

> Man know all dem sitters-and-talkers goin tuh worry they guts into fiddle strings till dey find out whut we been talkin' about. Dat's all right Pheoby, tell 'em. Dey goin tuh make 'miration 'cause mah love didn't wok lak they

love, if dey ever had any. Then you must tell 'em dat love ain't somethin' lak uh grindstone dat's de same thing everywhere and do de same thing tuh everything it touch. Love is lak de sea. It's uh movin' thing, but still and all, it takes its shape from de shore it meets, and it different with every shore.[13]

Zora Neale Hurston also grasped in her works a theme of black folklore, the delving into the nature of man, the nature of woman, and how these two natures blend or conflict. She delighted in the folk's continuous interest, whether devastatingly cynical, tender, or humorous, in the push and pull of human sexual relationships. Woman, viewing and viewed, is part of the theme of *Their Eyes Were Watching God*, as if the writer were illuminating one part of a canvas in order to give meaning to the entire painting. The novel begins:

Ships at a distance have every man's wish on board. For some they come in with the tide. For others they sail forever on the horizon, never out of sight, never landing until the Watcher turns his eyes away in resignation, his dreams mocked to death by Time. That is the life of men.

Now women forget all those things they don't want to remember, and remember everything they don't want to forget. The dream is the truth. They act and do things accordingly.[14]

Throughout the novel, as Janie tells her story to Phoeby, her friend, observances about black women, almost adage-like, probe not only Janie's nature but the condition of all black women. So Nanny tells Janie when she becomes a woman that

Honey, de white man is de ruler of everything as fur as Ah been able tuh find out. Maybe it's some place off in de ocean where de black man is in power, but we don't know nothin' but what we see. So de white man throw down de load and tell de nigger man to pick it up. He pick it up because he have to but he don't tote it. He hand it to his womenfolks. De nigger woman is de mule uh de world so fur as Ah can see. Ah been praying fuh it toh be different wid you. Lawd, Lawd, Lawd![15]

And Zora puts in print conversations held usually within the confines of one's own circle:

She (Janie) took a room at the boarding house for the night and heard the men talking around the front.

"Aw you know dem white mens wuzn't goin' tuh do nothin' tuh no woman dat look lak her."

"She didn't kill no white man, did she? Well, as long as she don't shoot no white man she kin kill jus' as many niggers as she please."

"Yeah de nigger women kin kill up all de mens day wants tuh, but you bet' not kill one uh dem. De white folks will sho hang you if yuh do."

"Well you know whut de say 'uh white man and uh nigger woman is the freest thing on earth.' Dey do as de please."[16]

Part of the workings of the novel tests such adages, since we know Janie's story as the characters within the book do not. We, the readers, can judge the truth of these sayings. But we know, even as we read the words, that they were not created by Zora Hurston. We have heard them or perhaps even spoken them ourselves and are now being confronted with them in stark relief, set aside from the particularity of our own lives.

Zora Neale Hurston, in her life and in her work, moved the image of the black woman beyond stereotype, as she sought the ever-evolving ways of the folk. She grafted onto the nineteenth century mode, a new way of looking at the mulatta and the southern black woman, preparing the way for different spiceboxes in the twentieth century.

In 1946, five years after Zora Neale Hurston published her autobiography, a newcomer, Ann Petry, published *The Street*. Along with Hurston's work, this novel functions as a transition from the tragic mulatta pattern and/or the rural southern woman as heroine to a more contemporary view of the black novel. As Hurston's novels had emphasized complexity of character, so *The Street* drew the outlines of the urban black woman's existence. Petry's novel belonged to the new black literary approach of the day, pioneered and symbolized by Richard Wright. In many ways *The Street* is akin to *Native Son* (1941) and its relentless presentation of the dreary despair of the inner cities and the illumination of the causal relationship between social and personal crime. As Bigger Thomas typified an alienated black male created partially by the concrete plantations of the North, so Lutie Johnson in *The Street* is the lost black female, alone and struggling. Both characters become literary types used so often by writers in later years that they have become stereotypes.

Lutie Johnson of *The Street* combines some of the characteristics of the various black female stereotypes of the previous century. She is a domestic working in the rich white folks' home, northern style. She is a mother struggling to protect her child, not only from overt physical danger, but also from the more hidden patterns of castration and debasement sketched by the concrete plantations of the North. She is a "brown, good-looking girl," plagued by the sexual advances of men, both black and white, who would use her as a sexual object in much the same way the black female slave was used. She is struggling to survive, working overtime, no longer bearing the legal status of the slave, but a slave nonetheless in the framework of society.

The novel also portrays the fragmentation of the black community which was more prevalent in the concrete plantations of the North than in the rural southern town. Here, husbands leave their wives not because they are sold or had to leave town, but because they are unable to be a man in their own eyes (i.e., find a job, protect their women and children). The apparel may be different, but the substance remains the same. Here, the spiritualists are not conjure women revered by both the master and the slave, but commercial salesmen selling powders and herbs to the highest bidder. In the North, one's child would not be sold into slavery, but might be taken away to jail or reform school. The lack of money becomes the jailer; hidden and overt racism becomes the lock. And the alienation of people, one from the other, separated by concrete and the ache to survive, strangles friendship and family ties. Everyone suspects each other as slaves were expected to. The apparel changes but the substance remains the same, except for one important factor. One was told one was free, and therefore part of the mind believed this, incorporating the attitudes of a free person into one's value systems. Frustration and confusion about who one really was further intensified an already harrowing situation.

It is on situation, setting, and environment that this novel focuses. Lutie Johnson might be one of any hundreds of thousands of black women who lived in Harlem in 1946, women whose hope for a better life was the only thing that kept them going. Lutie is seldom further delineated as a particular person, with a particular make-up. Her plight is actually the major character of the novel, a plight that can only lead to crime and tragedy. To some, this novel is unbelievable precisely because it is so grim and Lutie so alone. Yet it is as horribly true as the treatment of black slaves in southern plantations.

The Street marks a change in setting and tone in the literature of the black woman. It brings the literature into the twentieth century, for the concrete plantation became the dwelling place of more and more blacks in this century. After the publication of this novel, the black city woman could not be forgotten. The particular brand of slavery under which she exists meant that new changes in the literature would have to occur.

(3)

The poet has always been a synthesizer and a thermometer, whether she is aware of it or not. Somehow, poets allow the facility of sensing the present, a facility we all originally have, to have its own way, in spite of the world's attempt to divide time into past, present, and future. Most of us, for lack of time and stubbornness, live within the forms of the past as we dream about the possibilities of the future. Poets sense the present, and keep reminding us that the present is both past and future as it is now.

Gwendolyn Brooks' work springs from her abiding with the present. She synthesizes the work of the poets of her tradition, both Afro- and Anglo-American, and tests the temperature of the waters of our time. Her poetry (1946-present) and her only novel *Maud Martha* (1953) are Chicago, Cottage Grove, the Mecca or to put it more generically, are urban. And yet her work does not sacrifice the harshness of setting to the inner realities of her characters, who may be hampered by the environment but are not completely made of or by it. One feels both the lyricism, a soul-singing that is found in Zora Neale Hurston's work, and the harsh cutting edges of Petry's *The Street*. The major characters in her work, whether verse or fiction, are in process, flowing in and out of themselves and the world around them. We feel this process because Gwendolyn Brooks is so much in the present, sensing, perceiving, and translating those perceptions into precise words. The words become the perceptions:

> Abortions will not let you forget.
> You remember the children you got that you did not get,
> The damp small pulps with a little or with no hair,
> The singers and workers that never handled the air.
> You will never neglect or beat
> Them, or silence or buy with a sweet
> You will never wind up the sucking-thumb
> Or scuttle off ghosts that come
> You will never leave them, controlling your luscious sigh,
> Return for a snack of them, with gobbling mother-eye.[17]

Her language may not have the "hip" sound of the stereotyped ghetto mother, and some may say that we don't talk this way. Perhaps that is why some people find Gwendolyn Brooks's poetry distant at first. It is not dramatic, in the sense of being flamboyant; rather it strives always for the way we would put it, if we had the time, had all words at our disposal, could caress each perception as it happened.

Details are crucial to Gwendolyn Brooks's work, not the tedious details of legal documents but those we see but do not necessarily register as we live our lives, the details that often determine why we feel this emotion now and cannot exactly understand why. Her characters (for there are characters in her poetry) are intense perceivers. Often these perceivers are women trying to know themselves, exhausted by the seeming trivia of the commonplace yet finding truths through continuously experiencing everyday life. There are few grand topics in her works, as we have come to recognize them. Her themes are commonplace and therefore great, as birth and death are, as growing old or losing a man is. And always the tone is understated, dramatic because it *is* muted.

The women that we remember from her poetry are not so much complex as they are distinct. Maude, Sadie, Cousin Vit, Pearlie May Lee, Maude Martha, Mary, the Shakedancer's daughter, even as general a name as "the mother" are distinct, one from another, in the way that they comment on our perceptions that we may have forgotten we had or may have had not the time or patience to really crystallize into permanence.

These characters are thinking and feeling people, as black women always have been, despite the clay stereotypes in which we are perpetually cast.

As part of the dominant colors of the fabric of Gwendolyn Brooks's works, the impact of racism, subtle or hidden is also woven. Her earlier works do not address this theme as directly as do the later pieces. Yet in the earlier works it is there as part of the larger theme of her works—the perceptions of her characters. Because her characters are black, their perceptions are about birth and death, common to all human beings. Because they are black, their perceptions are about racism and its ramifications to nonwhites. Because they are black, their experience of and expression of their reality is culturally distinct; therefore their perception is as strong a statement about their condition as any manifesto. Here is a section from *Maud Martha*. Maud Martha has come to work as a maid at the home of the Burns-Coopers:

> The two of them, richly dressed, and each with that health in the face that bespeaks, or seems to bespeak, much milk drinking from earliest childhood, looked at Maud Martha. There was no remonstrance; no firing. They just looked. But for the first time she understood what Paul endured daily. For so—she could gather from a Paul-word here, a Paul-curse there—his Boss! When, squared upright, terribly upright, superior to the President, commander of the world, he wished to underline Paul's lacks, to indicate soft shock, controlled incredulity. As his boss looked at Paul, so these people looked at her. As though she were a child, a ridiculous one, and one that ought to be given a little shaking, except that shaking was not quite the thing, would not quite do. One held up one's finger (if one did anything), cocked one's head, was arch. As in the old song one hinted, "Tut, tut! now now! come come!" Metal rose, all built, in one's eye.
>
> I'll never come back, Maud Martha assured herself when she hung up her apron at eight in the evening. She knew Mrs. Burns-Cooper would be puzzled. The wages were very good. Indeed, what could be said in explanation? Perhaps the hours were long. I couldn't explain my explanation, she thought.
>
> One walked out from that almost perfect wall, spitting at the firing squad. What difference did it make whether the firing squad understood or did not understand the manner of one's retaliation or why one had to retaliate?
>
> Why, one was a human being. One wore clean nightgowns. One loved one's baby. One drank cocoa by the fire—or the gas range—come the evening, in the wintertime.[18]

The human correlative of such an abstract sociological concept as racism gives this passage and much of Gwendolyn Brooks's work its impact. Her perceivers think tangibles. In all their muted glory, they defy abstraction.

Gwendolyn Brooks published her first book of poetry, *A Street In Bronzeville*, in 1945. Since then, many black women writers have emerged, each with her particular focus, style, and world view. I cannot comment on every significant black woman writer of that time. Instead I will try to give a sense of that richness and diversity in the spectrum by concentrating on the works of three black women writers: Paule Marshall, Nikki Giovanni, and Toni Morrison.

The works of these writers cannot be discussed without some understanding of dominant literary themes in contemporary Afro-American literature. The period 1945-1975 is such a rich one that it would take many books to fully cover it. I will only sketch certain characteristics that are particularly relevant to the images of black women projected in Afro-American literature.

It is safe to say that in the genre of the novel from 1945-1960, four novelists dominate: Richard Wright, James Baldwin, Chester Himes, and Ralph Ellison. In Wright's major works, such as *Native Son* or *The Outsider*, black women are seldom seen except in the role of a slightly outlined mama or as a victim, like Bessie in *Native Son*, whose fate is given little thought by the society around her. In *Black Boy*, we do get glimpses of Wright's grandmother and mother, both long-suffering, fanatically religious women whom the author remembers primarily as being in pain. Ellison's major work, *Invisible Man*, again projects the black woman in the solo role of mammy. Mary, the woman who rescues our nameless narrator from illness, disappears from the book after she nurses him back to health.

Baldwin's novels present women in more diverse roles. Ida in *Another Country* is a perceptive person, though she shares with many of Baldwin's other women that grating quality that some call the "sapphire," named after Sapphire in the "Amos and Andy" series. Baldwin's 1973 book, *If Beale Street Could Talk*, has a black woman as its central character. However, this novel appears at the end of this thirty-year period and has yet to have its impact. Chester Himes's women veer toward another stereotype, the sex kitten, women created and used for sex, as in *Pinktoes*. Himes pushed his characterizations of women to the heights of caricature, perhaps a caricature intended as a comment on the stereotype itself.

In effect, the black women that appear in the novels of these four literary giants come painfully close to the stereotypes about the black woman projected by white southern literature in the latter part of the nineteenth century. Perhaps images do inform reality.

The poetry of the sixties reflects the growing need to include women as central figures in literature, since much of it is socio-political in nature.

Poetry advocating nationhood, by writers such as Imamu Baraka and Don Lee, assume that there have been wedges placed between black men and women and that work must be done to remove these wedges. Because of this, black women are often idealized in this poetry, saluted as queens, as Mothers of the Universe, or exhorted to change their ways (i.e., stop being Sapphires or loose women) in order to deserve these titles. A different stereotype begins to emerge: the idealized black woman poised on a pedestal somewhat in reaction to the previously projected stereotypes. Black women become symbolic holders of the moral condition of blacks in much of the nationalist poetry. In some ways, though, this kind of stereotype assumes the existence of Sapphire, Aunt Jemima, the black mammy, the sex kitten, and the evil woman—images germinated in the white southern mythology and enhanced and enriched by film, television, and social programs even up to the present.

This is not to say that one of the thrusts of contemporary male Afro-American literature was to denigrate the black woman. Rather, the black woman herself had to illuminate her own situation, reflect on her own identity and growth, her relationship to men, children, society, history, and philosophy as she had experienced it. And during these explosive years some black women writers began to project the intensity, complexity, and diversity of the experience of black women from their own point of view.

Certain trends do characterize the writings of black women writers during this period. The image of the tragic mulatta no longer dominates the literature and is replaced by a diversity of physical and psychological types. The role of mammy is carefully and continually moved from the level of stereotype to that of a living human being with her own desires and needs. The relationship between black men and women is also scrutinized, often in less generic and more particular terms, with special emphasis placed on the societal forces that strain marriage. And most importantly, black women themselves are projected as thinkers, feelers, human beings, not only used by others, but as conscious beings. There are many black women, these voices say. They have culture, race, sex, sometimes situations in common, but they are not just push button automatons who scream when given this cue, cuddle up when given that smile. They are not just stereotypes, for stereotype is the very opposite of humanness; stereotype, whether positive or negative, is a byproduct of racism, is one of the vehicles through which racism tries to reduce the human being to a nonhuman level.

(4)

Paule Marshall is supremely devoted to the creation of character. In her work and in her lectures on the craft of novel writing she emphasizes the necessity she feels to create distinct human beings who are affected by culture and society, but who also affect these two important elements. She consistently delves into the psychology of her characters, why they act as they do, as well as into the psychology of the place and time within which they exist. The essential aspects of her work—descriptions of characters and settings, storyline and themes—are all integrally related to her characters. The black women in her books are particularly complex, or at least rounded out. Daringly, she presents women who seem at first to be familiar types—the domineering mother, the prostitute, the martyred mother—only to investigate their personalities so thoroughly that the stereotype is forever broken in the mind of the reader.

Such are the people in Paule Marshall's first novel: *Browngirl, Brownstones* (1959). The central figure in this work about West Indian immigrants in New York is Selina, who as a first generation American woman must reconcile her West Indian heritage with the new world culture within which she is living. But Selina is not only type, she is an honest, sensitive young girl who struggles to understand her strong, practical, and difficult mother as she loves her marvelous dreamer father. Both mother, Silla, and father, Deighton, at first seem to be types: the mother, materialistic, bitter, set on owning a house at all costs; the father, dreaming about imagined triumphs, an artist lacking a form. But almost immediately, stereotype is dispelled by the space Paule Marshall somehow creates for them.

Because the domineering mother has been so much a part of black mythology, at least in terms of white society, Paule Marshall's development of the character of Silla is particularly instructive. We first see her as Selina looks at a family photograph taken many years before:

The young woman in the 1920's dress with a headband around her forehead could not be the mother. The mother had a shy beauty, there was a girlish expectancy in her smile.[19]

A few pages later we see Silla Boyce as she is now:

Silla Boyce brought the theme of winter into the park with her dark dress amid the summer green and the bright-figured housedresses of the women lounging on the benches there. Not only that, every line of her strong-made body seemed to reprimand the women for their idleness and the park for its senseless summer display. Her lips, set in a permanent protest against life, implied that there was no time for gaiety. And the park, the women, the sun even gave way for her dark force; the flushed summer colors ran together and faded as she passed.[20]

Paule Marshall's descriptions of her characters are particularly important as a technique, for they not only give us visual pictures but suggest questions, probe inner tensions. The question, subtly posed to the reader by the juxtaposition of these two descriptions, is one of the themes of the novel. How does Silla Boyce, the woman with the shy beauty and girlish expectations, become this dark foreboding force? And what are the ramifications of this change, if indeed the change is complete?

The struggle between Silla and Deighton, as seen by Selina, is an intense and harrowing one. Their differences: the mother's desire for security, symbolized by the possession of a brownstone, the father's need for creativity, beauty, meaning in his life, set them in life-long conflict. And their backgrounds illuminate the reasons for the intensity with which they view each other. Deighton had come from the town scene in Barbados, where his wit and the adulation of his mother had given him a sense of worth. Silla, in contrast, came from the harsh countryside, from cutting cane, and knowing how it was to starve. Their respective descriptions of their past life in Barbados is one contributing factor to their final confrontation, a confrontation that ends in tragedy. Deighton describes his youth in Barbados in this way:

> ". . . I's a person live in town and always had plenty to do. I not like yuh mother and the mounts of these Bajan that come from down some gully or up some hill behind God's back and ain' use to nothing. 'pon a Sat'day I would walk 'bout town like I was a full-full man. All up Broad Street and Swan Street like I did own the damn place."[21]

Silla's experience is quite different:

> "Iris, you know what it is to work hard and still never having to work for next skin to nothing. The white people treating we like slaves still and we taking it. The rum shop and the church join together to keep we pacify and in ignorance. That's Barbados. It's a terrible thing to know you gon be poor all yuh life, no matter how hard you work. You does stop trying after a time. People does see you so and call you lazy. But it ain laziness. It just that you does give up. You does kind of die inside."[22]

In the end, we know that Silla is the defeated one, left without the love and appreciation she desires, not giving herself the opportunity to fully develop that "odd softness" that stood out so in the old photograph and sometimes peeps out from behind her perpetual rage. She is defeated, except that at least Selina, her daughter, begins to understand her mother's need for independence:

> Quickly Selina found her coat and, putting it on, stared at her mother's bowed face, seeing there the finely creased flesh around her eyes, the hair graying at her temples and, on her brow the final frightening loneliness that was to be her penance. "Mother," she said gently, "I have to disappoint you. Maybe it's as you once said: that in making your own way you always hurt someone. I don't know. . . . Everybody used to call me Deighton's Selina but they were wrong. Because you see I'm truly your child.

Remember how you used to talk about how you left home and came here alone as a girl of eighteen and was your own woman? I used to love hearing that. And that's what I want. I want it!"[23]

Silla's pained eyes searched her adamant face, and after a long time a wistfulness softened her mouth. It was as if she somehow glimpsed in Selina the girl she had once been. For that moment, as the softness pervaded her and her hands lay open like a girl's on her lap, she became the girl who had stood, alone and innocent, at the ship's rail, watching the city rise glittering with promise from the sea.[24]

Both Silla and Deighton are trapped by the conditions of their world. The world will not give Deighton, a black man, the sense of dignity and worth he desires, unless he perverts his nature and becomes a money-grubbing businessman; it will not allow him imagination. Since Deighton cannot seek the security she needs, the dreams he had set in motion when he courted her, Silla must pursue them herself, ruthlessly, with no holds barred. She ends up partially hating herself and Deighton for her having to do it at all. Yet these people are caught not only by the circumstances of their worlds. It is their personal responses to their conditions that make their story what it is.

Browngirl, Brownstones is also about the culture from which its characters spring and how this culture mediates between them and their world. In her next book, *The Chosen Place, The Timeless People* (1969), Paule Marshall investigates the cultural levers even more, while maintaining the rich comprehensiveness of her characters. Stereotyped forms are cracked, new forms are sculpted to become characters who instruct us about their particular lives and therefore about the general themes of the culture. In Paule Marshall's books, characters and culture transform each other. And the women, who tend to be her central characters, give voice to that continual transformation.

(5)

it's funny that smells and sounds return
so all alone uncalled unheeded
on a sweaty night as i sit around
with coffee and cigarettes waiting

sometimes it seems
my life is a scrapbook[25]

Nikki Giovanni is as close to a superstar poet as any black woman poet has been in this century. At 30 she has published three books of poetry: *Black Feeling, Black Talk, Black Judgement, Re:Creation,* and *My House,* a book of poetry for children, *Spin A Soft Black Song,* edited an anthology of black women poets, *Night Comes Softly,* and written an autobiography, *Gemini*. She has read her poetry on a solo, mass-distributed album, *Truth Is On Its Way*. She has appeared on countless television talk shows, particularly *Soul*, interviewed such literary figures as James Baldwin and Yvestenschko, and has written articles for popular magazines, black and white alike. She is a popular poet in the sense that Aretha Franklin (a favorite singer of hers) is a popular singer; Nikki's books sell well.

What accounts for this poet's popularity in a country where poets are usually read primarily in the colleges? Or to be more precise, what are the societal forces that have created a phenomena such as the contemporary popular black poet? Poets like Nikki Giovanni and Don Lee, her male counterpart, sprang out of the cultural-political atmosphere of the sixties when a more intense race pride manifested itself in black America. That pride had always been there, but at certain times in history such as the 1920s and the 1960s it erupted with more force and flair. The rhetoric of the sixties, a political nationalistic rhetoric, is preceded by a language of protest, revolt, self and cultural investigation that fostered a linguistic correlative to the changing mood in the inner cities of America. Poets broadcasted that change as they helped to make it. In the late fifties, poets like Bob Kaufman, Ted Joans, and the ever-enduring Langston Hughes were not only writing their poems to be printed, but spoke them at church gatherings, in coffee houses, at political rallies, wherever they might be heard. The oral tradition was revitalized.

The oral rendering of poems, though not immediately heard by as many people as read the printed word, set up a new chain of vibrations and created another kind of audience different from the audience who read poetry. And in the case of television, perhaps even more people heard the word than read it. Not only was the craft of poetry writing important to the oral performance, but also the way the poem was spoken, the flair and personality of the poet, so that the message be gotten across in as engaging a manner as possible. The new poetry sound, released by this revival of the oral, lent itself well to emotionally involving the audience in the message the poet was sending. In the sixties that message was generally of a political-cultural nature. Social questions, political comment, and cultural insight meshed with sound to elicit audience response—if not action.

Nikki Giovanni began her career as an oral poet. Charming, petite, articulate, her image as well as her poetry communicated the message. Her first book, *Black Feeling, Black Talk, Black Judgement* (1968), first published by a black press, Broadsides, was celebrated for its hard hitting nationalistic language:

Nigger
Can you kill
Can you kill
Can a nigger kill
Can a nigger kill a honkie
Can a nigger kill the Man
Can you kill nigger
Huh? Nigger can you
Kill[26]

It is the rhythm the poem is written in as well as the controversial thoughts that elicit the audience's response, for it is the rapping style of the sixties associated with the language of the ghetto stylized by the politicos of the period. Social protest in poetry has become associated with this rapping style, a style that is named after Rap Brown, one of the political spokesmen of that period.

A distinctive quality of Nikki's poetry is her sense of humor, her sense of irony about the political rhetoric of the day:

one day
you gonna walk in this house
and i'm gonna have on a long African
gown
you'll sit down and say "The Black . . ."
and i'm gonna take one arm out
then you—not noticing me at all—will say
"What about this brother . . ."
and i'm gonna be slipping it over my head
and you'll rap on about "the revolution . . ."
while i rest your hand against my stomach
you'll go on—as you always do—saying
"i just can't dig . . ."
while i'm moving your hand up and down
and i'll be taking your dashiki off
then you'll say—"What we really need . . ."
and i'll be licking your arm
and "The way i see it we ought to . . ."
and unbuckling your pants
"And what about the situation . . ."
and taking your shorts off
then you'll notice
your state of undress
and knowing you you'll just say
"Nikki,
isn't this counterrevolutionary . . .?"[27]

You can hear the audience roar with laughter at the end of the poem.

As a woman poet, Nikki Giovanni expresses her particular view of what it is to be black and to be a woman. All of her work peaks at this point of juncture, as she traces her own girlhood in poems like "Nikki Rosa," her coming to age, her growing understanding of her parents, her own motherhood, her loves and disappointments in love. Particularly in these poems, the rapping style is underlined by the rhythms of the popular music, rhythm 'n' blues:

> i wanta say just gotta say something
> bout those beautiful outasight
> black men
> with they afros
> walking down the street
> is the same ol danger
> but a brand new pleasure[28]

And when she addresses herself to the problems of the black woman she puts all her poetic force, rap, and rhythm into illuminating the situation:

> it's a sex object if you're pretty
> and no love
> or love and no sex if you're fat
> get back fat black woman be a mother
> grandmother strong thing but not woman
> gameswoman romantic woman love needer
> man seeker dick eater sweat getter
> fuck needing love seeking woman[29]

"Woman Poem" is often anthologized and is as popular a poem today from printed as well as oral response as any poem written about black women during the last ten years. Again, it is the style, a putting together of the facts we all know in a voice that sounds familiar even as it changes from type to type.

Because the oral poet must register his/her message immediately, Nikki Giovanni's poetry is dynamic, dramatic, headed almost always for a punch line. And the advantages of this style carry with it some disadvantages—particularly the paring away of any factor that will not elicit an immediate response. Sometimes depth, precision, hard strategy is sacrificed to drama, whim, technique. But then the poet has got her audience's ear. Now they might want to go deeper with her or others, since they have at least begun to listen.

Giovanni's poetry is also urban, in the sense that the fast talk, the setting, the conflicts and confrontations feel like Harlem, the South Side of Chicago, Detroit, the glamorous though harsh, swinging inner cities of the North. And her words emphasize their glamour, their vibrancy instead of their horror or death-anguish. In some ways she idealizes their inhabitants, making them feel magnificent in their fine clothes and hip talk and therefore capable of stronger action.

Giovanni's poetry is often discussed in terms of its social themes, but especially with the publication of *My House* (1972) her poetry becomes more personal, even more impressionistic. Her view of her mother in the poem "Mothers" is one of the most touching poems in the book:

i remember the first time
i consciously saw her
we were living in a three room
apartment on burns avenue

mommy always sat in the dark
i don't know how i knew that but she did

that night i stumbled into the kitchen
maybe because i've always been
a night person or perhaps because i had
wet the bed
she was sitting on a chair
the room was bathed in moonlight diffused
through thousands of panes landlords who
rented
to people with children were prone to put
in windows
she may have been smoking but maybe not
her hair was three-quarters her height
which made me a strong believer in the
Samson myth and very black[30]

Many of her personal poems are pieces written to her women friends. They are sympathetic listeners as she talks to them about her feelings and thoughts. While her woman poems celebrate friendship, her love poems to men waver between grief and ecstasy and always ask that awful question:

and i'm asking you baby please
please somehow show me what i need
to know so i can love you right
now[31]

As a popular poet, Nikki Giovanni has been consistently asked about the women's liberation movement, its relationship to black women, and about women and their sense of the world. In *Gemini*, her autobiography, there are two sections that come as close to synthesizing her many comments as any two I could find. I think it is important that these two comments appear in an essay called *Gemini: A Prolonged Autobiographical Statement On Why* she decided to become a writer.

And sometimes you say, that's all right; if he takes advantage of me, so what? At nineteen that's cool. Or maybe at twenty-three. But around twenty-five or thirty you say, maybe men and women aren't meant to live with each other. Maybe they have a different sort of thing going where they come together during mating season and produce beautiful useless animals who then go on to love, you hope, each of you . . . but living together there are too many games to be gotten through. And the intimacies still seem to be left to his best friend and yours. I mean, the incidence is too high to be ignored. The guy and girl are inseparable until they get married; then he's out with his friends and she's out with hers or home alone, and there's no reason to think he's lying when he says he loves her. . . . She's just not the other half of him. He is awed and frightened by her screams and she is awed and cautious about his tears. Which is not to say there is not one man or one woman who can't make a marriage—i.e., home—run correctly and many even happily but it happens so infrequently. Or as a relative of mine in one of her profound moments said, "Marriage is give and take—you give and he takes." And I laughed because it was the kind of hip thing I was laughing about then. And even if that's true, so what? Somebody has to give and somebody has to take. But people set roles out, though the better you play them the more useless you are to that person. People move in conflicts. To me sex is an essence. . . . It's a basic of human relationships. And sex is conflict; it could be considered a miniwar between two people. Really. I think so. So i began to consider being a writer.[32]

We Black women are the single group in the West intact. And anybody can see we're pretty shaky. We are, however, (all praises), the only group that derives its identity from itself. I think its been rather unconscious but we measure ourselves by ourselves, and I think that's a practice we can ill afford to lose. For whatever combination of events that made us turn inward, we did. And we are watching the world trying to tear us apart. I don't think it will happen. I think the Lena Youngers will always survive and control in the happy sort of way they do. I don't really think it's bad to be used by someone you love. As Verta Mae pointed out, "What does it mean to walk five paces behind him?" If he needs it to know he's leading, then do it— or stop saying he isn't leading. Because it's clear that no one can outrun us. We Black Women have obviously underestimated our strength. I used to think why don't they just run ahead of us? But obviously we are moving pretty fast. The main thing we have to deal with is, What makes a woman? Once we decide that everything else will fall into plan. As perhaps everything has. Black men have to decide what makes a man.[33]

(6)

While Nikki Giovanni's poetry is urban social realism, Toni Morrison's work is earthy fantastic realism. Deeply rooted in history and mythology, her work resonates with mixtures of pleasure and pain, wonder and horror. There is something primal about her characters. They come at you with the force and beauty of gushing water, seemingly fantastic but as basic as the earth they stand on. While Paule Marshall carefully sculpts her characters, Toni Morrison lets hers erupt out of the wind, sometimes gently, often with force and horror. Her work is sensuality combined with an intrigue that only a piercing intellect could create.

She has written two novels: *The Bluest Eye* (1970) and *Sula* (1974). Her novels illustrate the growth of a theme as it goes through many transformations, in much the way a good jazz musician finds the hidden melodies within a phrase. Both novels chronicle the search for beauty amidst the restrictions of life, both from without and within. In both novels, the black woman, as girl then grown woman, is the turning character looking at the world outside as she peers inside herself. In both novels friendship between two women or girls serves as the periscope through which the overwhelming contradictions of life are measured. Her heroines are double-faced—looking outward and searching inward, trying to find some continuity between the seasons, the earth, other people, the cycles of life and themselves. Her novels are rich not only with characterizations, but also with signs, symbols, omens sent by nature. Wind and fire, robins in the spring, marigolds that won't grow are as much characterizations in her novels as the human beings who people them.

The Bluest Eye startles the reader with its straight-arrow aim as well as its experimentation, for Toni Morrison finds the language to describe the psychic trauma experienced by so many black girls growing up in a culture where blue eyes and blonde hair are the culmination of beauty. Because she takes risks with the language, she communicates a link between one's sense of one's physical self and the developing spiritual psyche. The beauty searched for in the book is not just the possession of blue eyes, but the harmony that they symbolize:

> It had occurred to Pecola sometime ago that if her eyes, those eyes that held the pictures, and knew the sights—if those eyes of hers were different, that is to say, beautiful, she herself would be different. Her teeth were good, and at least her nose was not big and flat like some of those who were thought so cute. If she looked different, beautiful, maybe Cholly would be different and Mrs. Breedlove, too. Maybe they'd say, "Why look at pretty-eyed Pecola. We musn't do bad things in front of those pretty eyes."
>
> Pretty eyes. Pretty blue eyes. Big blue pretty eyes. Run, Jip, run. Jip runs. Alice runs. . . . They run with their blue eyes. Four blue eyes. Four pretty blue eyes. Blue-jay eyes, blue-like Mrs. Forrest's blue blouse eyes. Morning-glory-blue eyes. Alice-and-Jerry-blue storybook eyes.
>
> Each night, without fail she prayed for blue eyes.[34]

Pecola's search for blue eyes ends in visible madness because she does not transfer the physical thing itself into a symbolic aim. Others also seek their version of the bluest eye, only within the accepted mores of the society:

> They go to land-grant colleges, normal schools and learn how to do the white man's work with refinement: home economics to prepare his food; teacher education to instruct black children in education; music to soothe the weary master and entertain his blunted soul. Here they learn the rest of the lesson; the careful development of thrift, patience, high morals and good manners. In short, how to get rid of the funkiness. The dreadful funkiness of passion, the funkiness of nature, the funkiness of the wide range of human emotions.
>
> Wherever it erupts, this Funk, they wipe it away; where it crusts they dissolve it, wherever it drips, flowers or clings they find it and fight it until it dies. They fight the battles all the way to the grave. The laugh that is a little too loud; the enunciation a little too round; the gesture a little too generous. They hold their behind in for fear of a sway too free; when they wear lipstick, they never cover the entire mouth for fear of lips too thick, and they worry, worry, worry, about the edges of their hair.[35]

Pecola and Sula, Toni Morrison's heroine in her next book, share many qualities in common. They are women who become scapegoats in their communities because they look at the truth of things and will not or cannot disguise it, becoming the dumping ground for those feelings of helplessness and horror people have about their own lives. Pecola's madness makes everyone feel sane. Sula's evilness highlights everyone's goodness.

In *Sula*, Toni Morrison takes us further down those dangerous paths her characters tread to find personal wholeness. In this book her setting becomes even more important than in *The Bluest Eye*, for the town emphasizes the restrictions of living that are the very nature of life itself. The Bottom had started as a nigger joke, a joke played on a nigger by a white man:

> A good white farmer promised freedom and a piece of bottom land to his slave if he would perform some very difficult chores. When the slave completed the work, he asked the farmer to keep his end of the bargain. Freedom was easy—the farmer had no objection to that but he didn't want to give up any land. So he told the slave that he was very sorry that he had to give him valley land. He had hoped to give him a piece of the Bottom. The slave blinked and said he thought the valley land was bottom land. The master said, "Oh no! See those hills? That's bottom land rich and fertile." "But it's high up in the hills," said the slave. "High up from us," said the master, "but when God looks down it's the bottom. That's why we call it so. It's the bottom of heaven—best land there is." So the slave pressed his master to try to get him some. He preferred it to the valley. And it was done. The nigger got the hilly land, where planting was backbreaking, where soil slid down and washed away the seeds, and where the wind lingered all through the winter.[36]

It is in this place that Sula is born and grows up. It is to this place that she returns after long years of searching for that wholeness she must have. And it is to her only friend Nel, with whom she shared adolescence, the accidental drowning of a young boy, and the intimacies of being female that she returns. But the two women are no longer one. Sula wants everything or nothing and therefore flies in the face of compromising traditions that keep this community intact. It is her honesty, her absolute resolve to face the meanness of life that binds her to Shadrack, the shell-shock soldier who started National Suicide Day. Nel, on the other hand, marries, has children, tries to suit her desires to the restrictions of life. In one of the crucial passages of the book, Sula sees Nel as "one of those spiders whose only thought was the next rung of the web, who dangled in dark dry places suspended by their own spittle, more terrified of the free fall than the snake's breath below."[37] Nel has become like those who are "Bent into grimy sickles of concern":

> The narrower their lives, the wider their hips. Those with husbands had folded themselves into starched coffins, their sides bursting with other people's skinned dreams and bony regrets. Those without men were like sour-tipped needles featuring one constant empty eye.[38]

In contrast, Sula Peace recalls the spiraling roads she has run:

> Nel was one of the reasons she had drifted back to Medallion, that and the boredom she found in Nashville, Detroit, New Orleans, New York, Philadelphia, Macon and San Diego. All these cities held the same people, working the same mouths, sweating the same sweat. The men who took her to one or another of those places had merged into one large personality: the same language of love, the same entertainments of love, the same cooling of love. Whenever she introduced her private thoughts into their rubbings or goings, they hooded their eyes. They taught her nothing but love tricks, shared nothing but worry, gave nothing but money. She had been looking for a friend, and it took her a while to discover that a lover was not a comrade and could never be—for a woman.[39]

Toni Morrison then brings this passage to a climax:

> Had she [Sula] paints, clay, or knew the discipline of the dance, or strings; had she anything to engage her tremendous curiosity and her gift for metaphor, she might have exchanged the restlessness and preoccupation with whim for an activity that provided her with all she yearned for. And like any artist with no art form, she became dangerous.[40]

Either way you lose. Nel loses her husband to Sula, begins to see that her children will grow old and leave her with nothing to fill in the spaces. Sula dies from boredom and spiritual malnutrition as much as from anything else. Their broken friendship is a measure of their broken lives, lives that are cramped from the very start. As counterpoints, all the other women in this book must either fit themselves into the place life has set for them or defy it with tragic circumstances proportionate to their degree of nonaccommodation.

Sula's grandmother, Eva, is as fine an example of the mama who is both sacrificer and sacrifice, as woman who learns to accommodate to life's meanness but only with a vengeance. She is forceful, conniving, intriguing. It is rumored that when she could no longer support her children she had a train run over her leg so that she could collect money for the rest of her life. When her only son Plum returns from the war and continues to cling to her—as she puts it, tries to climb back into her womb—she lovingly burns him to death. In simple justice, she sees her daughter Harriet (Sula's mother) burned to death beneath her window before she can prevent it. Eva is Sula's opponent from that day, for she sees her granddaughter watching her own mother burn with interest rather than horror. Eva knows Sula is much like her, and so enters into combat with her. Sula puts her grandmother in an old folk's home, but Eva outlives her and has the last word when many years later Nel visits her. Then she accuses Nel, and therefore Sula, of having drowned that little boy. If the warm, all-nourishing mama stereotype were alive and well, the creation of Eva has done away with it. Eva as mother both gives and takes life away. She is as complex a character because of and in spite of her motherhood as any I have read about. She is as mean as life, as energetic as the cold wind up in the Bottom, as unpredictable as warm weather in January.

Toni Morrison's characters illustrate how far we have moved from the stereotypes of the nineteenth century. How could one classify Eva, Sula, even Nel? Into what category could one put Nikki Giovanni as she projects herself in her poetry? What stereotypes would suit Paule Marshall's Selina or Silla? If there is one prevalent trend in this literature it is the movement away from stereotype, whatever the price. Stereotype can be comforting as well as denigrating, and to go beyond set images can be painful. There are so many fine black Afro-American women writers, including June Jordan, Mari Evans, Toni Cade, Alice Walker, Sonia Sanchez, Jane Cortez, not to mention the playwrights whom I have neglected in this analysis. Whether they be primarily political, cultural, historical, philosophical, or eclectic in their point of reference, whether they write about the city, country, or suburbs, whether they weave fantasies or tend toward social realism, whether they are experimental or traditional in style, they leave us with the diversity of the black woman's experience in America, what she has made of it and how she is tranforming it.

NOTES

1. Sterling Brown, *The Negro in American Fiction* (1937; Reprint, New York: Atheneum, 1969), pp. 1-89.
2. Ibid.
3. Gerda Lerner, ed., *Black Women in White America* (New York: Vintage Press, 1972), pp. 7-72.
4. John Mbiti, *African Religions & Philosophy* (New York: Doubleday Anchor, 1970).
5. Lerner, *Black Women*, pp. 7-72.
6. Howard Odum and Guy Johnson, *Negro Workaday Songs* (Chapel Hill: University of North Carolina Press, 1926), p. 145.
7. Ibid., pp. 142-143
8. Ibid., pp. 153-154
9. Ibid., p. 146
10. Zora Neale Hurston, *Dust Tracks on the Road* (Philadelphia: J. B. Lippincott Co., 1942), p. 61.
11. Florette Henri, *Black Migration, Movement North 1900-1920* (New York: Doubleday Anchor, 1975).
12. Zora Neale Hurston, *Their Eyes Were Watching God* (New York: J. B. Lippincott, 1937; Reprint, New York: Fawcett Publishers, 1965). p. 159.
13. Ibid.
14. Ibid.
15. Ibid., p. 16
16. Ibid.
17. Gwendolyn Brooks, *Selected Poems* (New York: Harper & Row, 1963), p. 4.
18. Gwendolyn Brooks, "Maud Martha" *The World of Gwendolyn Brooks* (New York: Harper & Row, 1971), pp. 228-289.
19. Paule Marshall, *Browngirl, Brownstones* (New York: Avon, 1959), p. 11.
20. Ibid.
21. Ibid.
22. Ibid., p. 60.
23. Ibid., pp. 143-144.
24. Ibid., p. 252.
25. Nikki Giovanni, "Scrapbooks," *My House* (New York: Morrow, 1972). p. 33.
26. Nikki Giovanni, "The True Importance of Present Dialogues, Black vs. Negro," *Black Feeling, Black Talk, Black Judgement* (New York: Morrow, 1970), p. 19.
27. Giovanni, *Black Feeling*, p. 38.
28. Ibid., p. 77.
29. Ibid., p. 78.
30. Giovanni, *My House*, pp. 6-7.
31. Ibid., p. 16.
32. Nikki Giovanni, *Gemini* (New York: Morrow, 1971), p. 37.
33. Ibid., p. 145.

34. Toni Morrison, *The Bluest Eye* (New York: Holt, Rinehart & Winston, 1970), p. 40.
35. Ibid., p. 68.
36. Toni Morrison, *Sula* (New York: Knopf, 1974). p. 5.
37. Ibid., p. 121.
38. Ibid., p. 122.
39. Ibid., p. 121.
40. Ibid.

2 The Contrary Women of Alice Walker: A Study of Female Protagonists in *In Love and Trouble** (1980)

In 1978, I taught a seminar on Alice Walker's works, at U. C. Berkeley, a course that had not been taught there before, or possibly anywhere else. For me, teaching a subject has always been a process of appreciation and learning—a space where an idea can reverberate through the minds and experiences of interested persons. I was inspired by the depth of Walker's body of work and was curious about its effect on an audience that was growing by leaps and bounds. I was not disappointed by student response. The course enrollment had to be limited, despite the fact that students had to commit themselves to a great deal of work.

To a large extent, this essay grew out of that experience. I had limited myself to Walker's novels in the book I was working on, but was fascinated by the effect In Love and Trouble *had on my students and by the craft Walker had exhibited in that most difficult form, the short story.*

My students' response to her only collection of short stories at that time illuminated for me one major tension in the work of Afro-American women writers—that of pain. To what extent does one expose the pain of being a black woman? Does such exposure cast us in the role of victim so emphatically that complaint and despair become the motifs of the writing? Can one ignore the pain—which is, in fact true—and focus only on "positive" experiences? How does one balance the pain with the development of consciousness, an important (though intangible) victory? Can one's audience listen, if one is really effective in portraying their pain?

"The Contrary Women of Alice Walker" was an attempt to approach these questions through an analysis of In Love and Trouble. *In hindsight, it is clear to me that Walker's second collection of short stories,* You Can't Keep a Good Woman Down, *which is more optimistic in tone, could not have been written*

*First published in *The Black Scholar* 12, no. 2 (March/April 1981).

*unless she had exposed the pain of this first collection. And it is
also important to note that although my students tended to focus
on the most violent of the stories, other stories which they
ignored in Walker's first collection like "The Welcome Table,"
and "The Revenge of Hannah Kemhuff" are triumphant in their
portraits of Afro-American women in confrontation with oppressive aspects of southern society.*

(1)

In Love and Trouble, Alice Walker's collection of short stories, is
introduced by two seemingly unrelated excerpts, one from *The Concubine* by the contemporary West African writer Elechi Amadi, the other
from *Letters to a Young Poet* by the early twentieth-century German
poet, Rainer Maria Rilke. In the first excerpts, Amadi describes the
emotional state of the young girl, Ahurole, who is about to be engaged.
She is contrary, boisterous at one time, sobbing violently at another. Her
parents conclude that she is "unduly influenced by *agwu*, her personal
spirit," a particularly troublesome one. Though the excerpt Walker chose
primarily describes Ahurole's *agwu*, it ends with this observation:
"Ahurole was engaged to Ekwueme when she was 8 days old."*

The excerpt from Rilke beautifully summarizes a view of *the living*,
setting up a dichotomy between the natural and the social order:

> People have (with the help of conventions) oriented all their solutions
> toward the easy and toward the easiest side of the easy; but it is clear that we
> must hold to what is difficult; everything in nature grows and defends itself
> in its own way, and is characteristically and spontaneously itself, seeks at all
> costs to be so against all opposition.

How are these two excerpts from strikingly different traditions related,
and why are they preludes, the tone-setters to a volume of short stories
about black women?

I am coordinating a seminar on the works of Alice Walker. We have
read and discussed *Once*, Walker's first volume of poetry, *The Third Life
of Grange Copeland*, her powerful first novel. The tension in the class
has steadily risen. Now we are approaching *In Love and Trouble*. There
is a moment of silence as class starts. Then one of the black women, as if
bursting from an inexplicable anger says: "Why is there so much pain in
these books, especially in this book?" I know this student; her life has
much pain in it. She is going to school against all odds, in opposition to
everything and everyone, it would seem. She is conscious of being black;

*All quotes in this essay are from Alice Walker, *In Love and Trouble, Stories of
Black Women* (New York: Harcourt Brace Jovanovich, 1973).

she is struggling, trying to figure out why her relationships as a woman are so confused, often painful. She repeats her question adding a comment—"What kind of images are these to expose to—(pause)?" To whom, she will not say. "I don't want to see this, know this." There is more anger, then silence. But she is riveted by the stories in this and other class sessions and insists on staying in this class. She seems, by all appearances, to be together, well-dressed, even stylish, a strong voice and body, an almost arrogant, usually composed face. But now she is angry, resistant, yet obsessed by these stories.

Who are the characters in these stories? What happens to them? More to the point, what do they do that should cause this young black woman, and many others like her, to be so affected? What have they or she to do with *agwu* or with Rilke's words?

(2)

In these eleven stories, Walker's protagonists share certain external characteristics that at first might seem primarily descriptive. All are female; all are black; most are southern; all are involved in some critical relationship—to lover, mother, father, daughter, husband, woman, tradition, God, nature—that causes them some discomfit. But the external characteristics, so easily discerned, are not emblems. They are far more complex and varied. The words, *southern black woman*, as if they were a sort of verbal enchantment, evoke clusters of contradictory myths, images, stories, meanings according to different points of view. Who is a southern black woman? To a white man, those words might connote a mammy, a good looking wench, or Dilsey, as it did to Faulkner. To a white woman it might connote a servant, a rival, or a wise indefatigable adviser, as it did to Lillian Hellman. To a black man, it might connote a charming, soft-spoken, perhaps backward woman, or a religious fanatic and a vale of suffering, as it did to Richard Wright. But what does *being* a southern black woman mean to her, or to the many who are like her?

Focal to Walker's presentation is the point of view of individual black southern girls or women who must act out their lives in the web of conventions that is the South—conventions that they may or may not believe in, may or may not feel at ease in, conventions that may or may not help them to grow. And because societal conventions in the South have much to do with the conduct of relationships—between man and woman, young and old, black and white—our female protagonists, by their very existence, must experience and assess them. So naturally, Walker's women are in love and trouble. However, unlike Toomer's women in *Cane*, who too are restricted by their race, sex, and origins, Walker's women are not silent. Her women are not presented through a perceptive male narrator, but through the private voices of *their* imaginations or through their dearly paid for words or acts.

The way in which Walker uses her point of view characters is not mere technique, but an indication of how free her protagonists are to be themselves within the constraints of convention. If they cannot act, they speak. If they cannot speak, they can at least imagine, their interiority being inviolate, a place where they can exercise autonomy, be who they are. Through act, word, or dream, they naturally seek to be "characteristically and spontaneously" themselves. In order to defend the selves they know they are, they must hold to what is difficult, often wishing, however, that they were not so compelled. Like all natural things, they must have themselves—even in conflict. So their *agwu*, their personal spirits, are troubled as they strain against their restraints. And their acts, words, dreams take on the appearance, if not of madness, of contrariness.

What specifically are some of the conventions that so restrict them, causing their spirits to be troubled even as they seek love? It is interesting to me that the stories from this volume my students found most disturbing take place within the imagination of the character, and that often that character sees herself as different from her external self. She sees a different self—a dangerous self, as if a reflection in a mirror.

Roselily is such a character. The form of her story, itself a marriage ceremony, is a replica of the convention, the easy solution to which she has been oriented. As a poor black woman with four illegitimate children, she is, it seems, beyond redemption. Thus, her wedding day, attended as it is by satin voile and lily of the valley, is from any number of viewpoints a day of triumph. But *she*, how does she see it? Walker does not use "I," the first person point of view, but the pronoun "she" throughout this marriage ceremony, as if Roselily is being seen from an external point of view. Yet what she does is dream: "She dreams; dragging herself across the world" (p. 3). It is as if even in Roselily's mind, the being who wonders about, questions this day of triumph, is both herself and yet not herself.

Troubled, though feeling she should not be troubled, Roselily's meditation on the words of the ceremony is intensely focused, almost fixated on images of entrapment. "She feels old. Yoked" (p. 6). "Something strained upward behind her eyes. She thinks of the something as a rat trapped, cornered, scurrying to and fro in her head peering through the window of her eyes" (p. 8). Even the flowers in her hand, flowers associated with the sweet South, seem "to choke off three and four and five years of breath" (p. 4). Yet because of her condition, she feels she should not feel this way. She should want: "Respect, a chance to build. Her children at last from underneath the detrimental wheel" (p. 4). What she feels is—trapped in her condition—trapped in her delivery from that condition.

As Roselily struggles with her *agwu*, as she resists the urge to rip off satin voile, to toss away lily of the valley, her dreaming also gives us insight into the complexity, the sheer weight of the conventions that have trapped her. Different sets of values are affecting her life. They are as different, as they are black, in the way they restrict her or allow her to grow. One set of values seems to be giving way to another, satin voile to black veil. Tradition is undergoing change, affecting the society's definition of her role as a woman, intensifying the conflict within herself.

She comes from a southern black community, poor, Christian, rural, its tradition held together by "cemeteries and the long sleep of grandparents mingling in the dirt"(p. 6). Here she can be "bare to the sun" (p. 6). But she must be poor; she must work in a sewing plant—work from which no growth will occur, work only for the purpose of survival. Here she must be a mother, preferably within the confines of marriage, where her sensuality will be legitimatized and curbed. But even without marriage she must be a mother. Tradition decrees it. Here the responsibility of her children's fathers is minimized, their condition as restricted as hers except they have mobility, can drive by "waving or not waving"(p. 7). Here the quality of suffering is legitimatized by Christianity, as rooted in sorrow as the graves of her grandparents. Here there is nothing new, as the cars on the highway whiz by, leaving behind a lifestyle as rooted in the past as the faces at this country wedding.

What is new comes from the North, challenging this traditional way of life. New gods arise, affecting the quality of Roselily's life. What freedoms do these new conventions afford her? The nameless New England father of her fourth child brings the god of social justice. Though he exalts common black people, he cannot "abide TV in the living room, 5 beds in 3 rooms, no Bach except from 4-6 on Sunday afternoons"(p. 5). He cannot abide the backward ways of the people who in the abstract he wants to save.

To the man she is marrying, God is Allah, the devil is the white man, and work is building a black nation. But he cannot abide the incorrect ways of Roselily's community, their faith in a white Christian God, and their tolerance of sensuality. Just as the old women in the church feel that he is "like one of their sons except that he had somehow got away from them"(p. 8-9), he feels that this community is black except that it has got away from its blackness. For him, a veiled black woman in his home is a sign of his righteousness, and in marrying Roselily he is redeeming her from her backward values. With him, she will have black babies to people the nation.

Whether southern or northern, traditional or modern, rural or urban, convention confines Roselily to a role, a specific manifestation of some dearly held principle. As a result, her *agwu*, though expressed only in her dreaming, is even more troubled by change. For even as she glimpses possibilities, she is left with the same vision of confinement. She can only dream that "she wants to live for once. But doesn't quite know what that means. Wonders if she has ever done it. If she ever will" (p. 8). Not even the "I do" that she must speak in order to accept the delivery from her condition is allowed, in this story, to interrupt the dreaming. She does not speak aloud. Her dreaming is as separate from her external behavior as this Mississippi country church is from her future home, cinder-filled Chicago. But at least she can, in her imagination, know her confinement to be troublesome and recognize in a part of herself that this change is not the attainment of *her* fulfillment.

(3)

As the first story in this volume, Roselily's meditation on her condition touches major themes that will be explored in most of the others. Distinctions between the forms of convention to which people are usually oriented and the marrow of a living, functional black tradition are examined in most of these stories in terms of the span and degree of freedom afforded the black woman. Like "Roselily," "Really, Doesn't Crime Pay?" focuses on the limited image of black femaleness within southern tradition. Only now the image is no longer a "peasant" one but a black, middle class one as modified by the sweet smelling idealizations of the southern lady.

Both Roselily's and Myrna's stores are couched in the images of sweet-smelling flowers. But while Roselily's name emphasizes the natural quality of her southern environment, Myrna buys her artificial scents from the shopping mall. Her creamed, perfumed body proclaims her a well-kept lady and evokes images of the delicate, decorative southern belle. But the South's mystique, as evoked through Roselily's name and Myrna's perfumes, chokes rather than pleases both these women. Natural or artificial, peasant or lady, they are trapped by myth.

To all appearances, for that is what counts, Myrna has succeeded in ways that Roselily has not. After all, Myrna is married to Reul (Rule), an ambitious southern black man, who wants her to have babies that he will support and insists on keeping her expensively dressed and scented. But, although Reul and Roselily's new husband are worlds apart, they agree on basic tenets: that the appearance and behavior of their wives mirror the male's values and that their women stay at home and have babies. Both women must, in their physical make-up, be the part. Roselily must be clearly black; Myrna must look nonblack, like a Frenchwoman or an Oriental. Both must wear appropriate uniforms: Roselily's black veil, Myrna's frilly dresses. Both must withdraw from the impure outer world, providing a refuge for their husbands and children. But while Roselily does not know what she *wants* to do, when she is "rested," Myrna knows that she wants to write, must write.

As in "Roselily," "Really, Doesn't Crime Pay?" takes place within the imagination of the character. But while Roselily dreams during her wedding, Myrna's imagination is presented through her entries in her writing notebook. Unlike Roselily, whose critical musings never move beyond her interior, Myrna's break for freedom lies in trying to express herself in words. However, like Roselily, when Myrna confronts the conventions she is expected to adhere to, she also experiences discomfit within her *agwu*.

As is often true with Walker's stories, the first few sentences succinctly embody the whole:

> September 1961
> page 118
> I sit here by the window in a house with a 30 year mortgage looking down at my Helena Rubenstein hands. . . . And why not? Since I am not a serious writer, my nails need not be bitten off. My cuticles need not have jagged edges. (p. 10)

These first lines not only tell us that Myrna's story will be told through her entries in her writing notebook, but that she knows her value is perceived to be in her appearance and social position, not in her creativity. And because she has no external acknowledgement of her value as a writer, she, with some irony, doubts her own ability. Her husband's words to her, written as an entry, clearly summarize society's view:

> Everytime he tells me how peculiar I am for wanting to write stories, he brings up having a baby or going shopping, as if these things are the same. Just something to occupy my time. (p. 15)

As a result of her own doubts, constantly reinforced by her husband, magazines, billboards, other women, doctors, Myrna is open, both sexually and artistically, to Mordecai, an artiste. He rips her off on both counts, precipitating the mental breakdown and her aborted murder of her husband that we see developing in her entries.

The presentation of entries, which begin with September 1961, go back in time, and finally move beyond that date, is crucial to Myrna's story. For when we meet her, she has already tried to write and has been rebuffed by her husband. She has been ripped off by Mordecai, has attempted murder, has been confined to a mental institution, and has eventually been returned to her husband. Like Charlotte Perkin's *The Yellow Wallpaper*, the entries that make up the substance of this story express the anger and rage, in madly logical terms, which drive the house-prisoned woman writer crazy. But the story goes beyond that impotent rage. Having tried the madness of murder and failed, Myrna concocts a far more subtle way, contrariness rather than madness, to secure her freedom. Now she says "yes" to everything—the smiles, the clothes, sex, the house—until she has yessed her husband to fatigue. She triumphantly tells us that "the women of the community feel sorry for him to be married to such a fluff of nothing"(p. 22). She confides that "he knows now that I intend to do nothing but say *yes* until he is completely exhausted" (p. 23). Cunningly, she secretly takes the Pill, insuring her eventual triumph over him. But it is her discovery of the magnificence of the manipulation of words that brings her to a possible resolution of her troubled *agwu*. Like Ralph Ellison's nameless narrator's grandfather in *Invisible Man*, she yesses them to death, though in a peculiarly female way.

In saying *yes* to mean *no*, Myrna uses the manipulative power of the word and secures some small victory. But it is a victory achieved from the position of weakness, for she has no alternative. Like countless southern belles, she has found that directness based on self-autonomy is ineffectual and that successful strategies must be covert. Such strategies demand patience, self-abnegation, falsehood. Thus, at the end of this story, Myrna has yet to act: "When I am quite, quite tired of the sweet, sweet smell of my body, and the softness of these Helena Rubenstein hands, I will leave him and this house" (p. 23).

What happens when a black woman goes against convention, transgresses a deeply felt taboo, and says *no* directly and aloud? In perhaps the most powerful, certainly the most violent story of this volume, the woman in "The Child Who Favored Daughter" speaks practically one word in the entire story, *no* (p. 44). By saying *no* with such firmness she resists convention, insisting on the inviolability of her *agwu*.

This story is as important in the light that it sheds on the black men in other stories, Reul and Roselily's Muslim husband, as it is in its own right. Moving back and forth between the imaginations of the woman and her father, it presents in almost cinematic rhythm, a black male and female point of view. In committing the most damnable act for a black woman, falling in love with a white man, the Child Who Favored Daughter sorely touches the vulnerability of the black man who has felt the whips of racism. To a compelling degree, Reul's desire that Myrna be feminine and Roselily's husband's insistence that she be pure and sheltered are related to these men's need to be on par with the white man. To have a wife who is a visual representation of one's financial achievement, or to protect and keep pure the black woman, despite the white man's often successful attempts to drag down the race, are goals essential to their view of themselves as men. Racism has the effect not only of physically and economically restricting these men, but also of reinforcing their need to imitate the oppressor's conventions in order to match his worth.

But "The Child Who Favored Daughter," though encompassing the sexist results of racism, goes beyond them, for it is based on an apparently universal ambivalence men have toward the sexuality of their female kin, especially their daughters. Thus, it begins with an epigraph, the equivalent of which is found in every culture:

That my daughter should
fancy herself in love
with *any* man
How can this be?— Anonymous (p. 35)

And only a few words later, Walker underlines the result of such a sentiment. Succinctly defining *patriarch*, while exposing its absurdity, she introduces the father in this story in conceptual terms: *"Father, judge, giver of life"* (p. 35).

Walker juxtaposes points of view of the Child and her Father by using the parts of this definition, *judge, giver of life*, as pivotal areas of contrast. As Father, the man judges his daughter based on one piece of evidence, a letter she has written to her white lover. As in "Really, Doesn't Crime Pay?," the written word takes on immense significance as proof of the woman's autonomy outside the realm of the man's kingdom. In an indelible way, the Child's written words are proof not only of her crime against her father and societal conventions, but also of her consciousness in committing it. Thus, we are introduced to her: "She knows he has read the letter" (p. 35), as she prepares herself for his inevitably harsh judgment. Her father, too, is mesmerized by the letter itself, for it is both a proclamation of her separateness from him and, ironically, a judgment on his life. The words he selects to remember from the letter heighten our sense of his vulnerability: "'Jealousy is being nervous about something that has never, and probably won't ever, belong to you'" (p. 42).

Again, as in "Roselily," although we are inside the characters' psyche, Walker uses the third person "she" and "he" rather than the first person "I." But here, this usage has a different effect; unlike Roselily, neither the child nor her father are presenting a different self to the world. Rather the "she" and "he" used in the absence of personalized names give the characters an archetypal quality, as if the Child stands not only for this individual black woman, but for all daughters who have transgressed against their father's law; and the Father stands not only for this bitter black man, but for all fathers who have been sinned against by their daughters.

That particular interpretation of the Child's act is organic to the story, since the Father, not the Child, defines himself as a patriarch. The Child does not see him as Father but as *her* father. There are other men who exist besides him; other laws that also govern. Her act proclaims this.

Her words in the letter make it clear that she cannot be owned. It is precisely this difference in their interpretation of their roles that causes his *agwu* to be so agonized that it inflicts trouble on hers. To the man in this story, he is Father, she is Daughter, a possessive relationship that admits no knowledge of any individual histories or desires. It is true that he clings to an individual history, his sense of his first betrayal by a woman who he loves. But that apparently individual story leads us back to the archtypal, for this woman is his sister, is called "Daughter," the original Daughter, rather than a particular name. Her image blots out all individualized details in other women, until all women, especially those who are "fragmented bits of himself" (p. 38) are destined to betray him. Sister, Daughter, he perceives them and their actions as a judgement of his own worth and capacity to be loved. From his perspective, because they have such power over him, they cannot exist apart from him. They must exist for him, because of him. Thus he must control them: "If he cannot frighten her into chastity with his voice he will threaten her with the gun" (p. 37). That he feels is his right as Father, as *"judge."*

The authority vested in him as Father implies not only that he has the power to enforce obedience, but that he has a right to this power precisely because he is the *"giver of life."* Walker intensifies the archetypal tone of this tale by repeating two sets of poetic motifs in a relationship of tension between nature and time. One motif, "Lure of flower smells/The sun" (p. 36), emphasizes the sensuality of nature. The other, "Memories of Once/Like a mirror reflecting" (p. 40), transforms the temporal into an eternal moment, obliterating the possiblity of redemption. The father's perception of himself as the *"giver of life"* is juxtaposed in the story to the keen awareness of his sister and daughter's sexuality, vital and beyond his control. He is affected by their sensual bodies, naturally capable of giving life, his daughter's "slight, roundly curved body" (p. 41), his sister's, "honey, tawny, wild and sweet" (p. 38). His ambivalence toward that part of them that he can never have, that part of them that will naturally take them away from him, intensifies the physical feeling of betrayal he imagines has been dealt him by women.

"Father, judge, giver of life," yet he cannot control it. Has he created it? Walker uses, throughout this story, images of Nature that overwhelm his senses: "the lure of flower smells," the busy wasps building their paper houses, the flower body of the Child. All around the Father life escapes his control, in much the same way that his daughter's body and her will overpower him. Like Nature, his sister and daughter are "flowers who pledge no allegiance to banners of any man" (p. 45). As he will burn the wasps' paper houses down "singeing the wings of the young wasps before they get a chance to fly or to sting him" (p. 37), he must protect himself

from "the agony of unnameable desire" (p. 45) caused by his sensuous, wayward daughter.

If he cannot control the life he has given, then he must take it back. The violence the father inflicts on his daughter, for he literally cuts off her sexual organs in biblical fashion ("If their right hand offend thee, cut it off"), confirms his own sexual desire for her. It also underscores his fear of her proclaimed autonomy, her independence from him, which is based on her sexuality. In destroying her sexually, he is destroying that unknowable part of himself that he feels is slipping out of his control:

he draws the girl away from him *as one pulling off his own arm* and with quick slashes of his knife leaves two bleeding craters the size of grapefruit on her bronze chest [emphasis mine]. (p. 45)

This father kills *his* daughter, not with the phallic gun, but with a knife, the instrument used in sacrificial blood ritual. He sacrifices her to his definition of himself—what he and therefore she should be. And the brutality of his act also suggests that he must doubly kill her since he cannot attack the other object of his rage, her white lover. He kills in one blow, his desire for her and his long-frustrated rage at the white man. No longer can the white man despoil his sister or his daughter, for they no longer exist; no longer must he love what he cannot control. Now he is left with "the perfection of an ancient dream, his nightmare" (p. 45) and the gun, the child he now cradles, which he can completely control.

The father's troubled *agwu* stands in contrast to the child's throughout this ballad of a tale. Her *agwu* is threatened from without, but it is not troubled within. Like Nature, she must be herself, grow and defend herself in her own way, not as defined by her father or society.

She must have herself, even though she has learned that "it is the fallen flower most earnestly hated, most easily bruised" (p. 43) and that she has been that fallen flower the moment her father presumed to give her life. She cannot "abandon her simple way of looking at simple flowers" (p. 43), so she accepts her father's beating, rising from it strong-willed and resolved, but she cannot, will not, deny that she loves whom she loves. It is her composure, paradoxically her contrariness, and her lack of torment that echoes for the father the original daughter's preference for the Other—worse, her complete indifference to his pained love. Thus, her ability to be so surely herself results in her destruction. Her inner spirit and her outer actions are as one; she is a woman. But to her father, she must act and speak as a Child, though she may think as a woman, for then her sexuality will not be a danger to him.

"The Child Who Favors Daughter" lyrically analyzes two constraints of convention that, when fused, are uniquely opposed to the growth of black women. It merges the impact of racism not only on society but on the person, with the threat woman's sexuality represents to patriarchal man. One feeds the other, resulting in dire consequences for the black woman who insists on her own autonomy, and for whom love, the giver of life, knows "nothing of master and slave" (p. 39). Such a woman strikes at the heart of hierarchy, which is central to racism and sexism, two variants of the patriarchal view of life.

(4)

The young protagonists of "Roselily," "Really, Doesn't Crime Pay?" and "The Child Who Favored Daughter" develop from one story to the next in their awareness of the conventions imposed upon them and in their insistence on growing and defending themselves in their own way. Associated with the flowers of the South, their relationship to sweet-smelling nature mirrors their consciousness. Thus, Walker presents Roselily as one who clutches lily of the valley, the symbol of her new condition, even as she questions her deliverance, though only in one part of her mind. Myrna does more than dream. Although she douses herself with gardenia perfume, the symbol of her comfortable prison, she writes of her intention of freeing herself and has learned the difficult strategy of saying *yes* to mean *no*. The Child Who Favors Daughter goes even one step further. She will not give up "her simple way of looking at simple flowers," and her spoken word, "No," is a declaration of her internal freedom of mind. She is destroyed by her father and by convention, however, precisely because she tries to grow in her own way.

She is very much like most of Walker's elder protagonists in that their *agwus* are not as much troubled from within as they are from without. A major difference between the Child and these elders— Hannah Kemhoff, Mama in "Everday Use," and the old woman in "The Welcome Table"— is that they have survived. Perhaps they had also walked the paths of a Roselily or Myrna until they came to the realization that there is nothing more precious than being characteristically and spontaneously themselves. Too, they have become the repositories of a living tradition, which they know not only in conventional forms but more importantly in its spirit.

The old woman in "The Welcome Table" exemplifies the *agwu* that, though troubled from without, is aware of what is necessary for its fullness and tranquility. Her story is about her relationship to God, which for her is above and beyond any conventions to which people have oriented their solutions. In contrast to the young flower heroines of this volume, she is described in nature imagery that expresses endurance rather than sensuality: "She was angular and lean as the color of poor gray Georgia earth, beaten by king cotton and the extreme weather" (p. 82). Rather than smelling of flowers, she smells of "decay and musk— the fermenting scent of onionskins and rotting greens" (p. 84).

Again, Walker uses the third person, "she" and "they," rather than the first person "I." This time she uses it so that we can hear both the old woman's mind and those opposed to her *agwu*, so that we can experience the contrast in spirit—for what she must do is prepare herself to be welcomed into the arms of her Jesus. For that overwhelming reason, she goes to the big white church without any regard for the breach of southern convention she is committing. All that she is concerned with is the "singing in her head" (p. 84). In contrast the whites see her act as contrariness. For *they* see *her* as black and old, doubly terrifying to them because one condition awaits them all and the other frightens them. So they are able to throw her out of *their* church even as they beseech their God, according to convention, for protection and love.

Walker contrasts the two points of view in "The Welcome Table" in much the same way as she does the Child and the Father in "The Child Who Favors Daughter." Neither the old black woman nor the white congregation have names or specific identifying characteristics, except that each exists in Georgia. This absence of personalized detail gives the characters a quality that is both archetypal and southern, while emphasizing the contrast in the way the old woman and the white congregation relate to southern convention.

On one hand the white congregation does not see the old woman as worthy enough to enter their church, precisely because she is black and old, yet they relate to her in familial terms for exactly the same reasons. Their confusion about how they are to react to her unconventional act is expressed in their uncertainty about whether they should address her in the traditional familiar terms—"Auntie," or "Grandma." Their emphasis on this point is characteristic of the contradictions inherent in the white South's relation to its black folk. The old woman, on the other hand, is clear about her actions. She ignores them, then is clearly *bothered* by these people who claim familial ties with her, yet know her or care about her not at all. In ignoring the conventions, she exposes the tradition of black and white familial ties as nothing more than form. All the sacred words of this tradition are brought into question by her simple act: "God, mother, country, earth, church. . . . It involved all that and well they knew it" (p. 84).

It is also significant that the white men, all of whom seem younger than the old black woman, are the ones who express this confusion. It is the white women who are clear about their true relationship to this old black woman, for they do not idealize it. From their point of view, in coming to their church, this old black woman challenges the very thing that gives them privilege. Both they and she are women—but they are white, their only claim to the pedestal on which they so uneasily stand. They know they can only hold their position if that pedestal is identified with the very essence of southern convention, that this old woman, and others like her, are literally and symbolically the bodies upon which that pedestal rests. Just as sexism is reinforced by racism in "The Child Who Favored Daughter," so in "The Welcome Table" racism distorts the natural relationship that should exist between woman and woman and mutes the respect, according to convention and nature, that the young should have for the old.

According to white southern thought, Christianity is the system upon which its culture and definition of woman and man is based. At the center of that system is the image of a white Jesus. Ironically, Jesus' picture, which she has stolen from a white woman she worked for, is the old black woman's source of solace. But Walker does not present the old woman's white Jesus as an affront to her blackness; rather through the dynamics of her imagination and her culture, the old woman transforms this image into her own. For instead of being the meek and mild Jesus, her image of him is one of righteousness and justice. The words of the old spiritual, the epigraph of this story, embodies this old black woman's relationship to *her* Jesus:

I'm going to sit at the welcome table
shout my troubles over
Walk and talk with Jesus
Tell God how you treat me
One of these days—Spiritual (p. 81)

One stereotypical image of the southern black woman is that of the fanatically religious old mammy so in love with a white Jesus that she becomes the white man's pawn. "The Welcome Table" obliterates that image as it probes the depth of black southern tradition. This old woman cracks the conventional shell of white southern Christianity and penetrates the whiteness of Jesus' face to "the candle . . . glowing behind it" (p. 85), for she insists on the validity of her own faith and tradition and on the integrity of her relationship with her God. Walker further reinforces the integrity of a black Christian tradition, of which southern black women were the heralds, by dedicating her composition of her spiritual in prose form to Clara Ward, the great black gospel singer. Like the slaves in their spirituals, the old black woman in "The Welcome Table" makes Christianity her own, going beyond its European images to its truth as it applies to her. It is her spirit that "walked without stopping" (p. 86).

This old woman's act and the acts, words, even dreams of so many of Walker's protagonists in this volume, appear to others, sometimes even to themselves, as manifestations of the innate contrariness of black women. The term *contrary* is used more often and with greater emphasis in Afro-American culture than it is in white culture. In fact, blacks often use it as if they all suffer from it. Yet behind their use of the word is a grudging respect for, sometimes even a gleeful identification with, a resistance to authority.

However, Walker's analysis of the contrariness of her main characters goes beyond the concept of unfocused rebellion. Her women behave as if they are contrary, even mad, in response to a specific convention that restricts them, and they pay a price for their insistence on retaining their integrity. Even when they triumph, then, their stories are rooted in the pain caused by the trouble they must bear. And Walker insists on probing *both* the white society and the black community's definition of black women. For in both worlds, words such as *contrariness* or a troublesome *agwu* are used to explain away many seemingly irrational acts of women, without having to understand them as appropriate responses. Her protagonists often discover that because they are black they are perceived by whites as "the other," or because they are women they are perceived by men as "the other." In either world they are not the norm. Their deviant behavior, then, is expected and therefore need not be understood.

That is why the excerpt from Amadi's *The Concubine* sets the tone so precisely for this volume, for Ahurole's contrariness, even in a black culture not yet affected by racism, is explained away as natural. Her life as an African woman is planned for her, regardless of her personality, desires, or development. And such a plan is so rooted in tradition, that Ahurole is allowed in her society to have this one outlet, which will neither change her situation or cause others to question it.

Yet Ahurole's story is not the story of Roselily, Myrna, The Child, or the Old Woman. For these black women must not only bear the traditional definitions of women in their culture, but they must confront as well the sexist myths of another race that oppresses them. The conventions that they are expected to hold to are not even the conventions of their own communities, but ones imposed on them. It is no wonder then that these women seem mad whenever they insist on being "spontaneously and characteristically" themselves.

The stories in *In Love and Trouble* provoke readers, especially black women, the audience to which they are clearly addressed, not only because of the pain or violence in them, but because Walker subversively admits to the contrariness of her black female protagonists. It is as if she says we do think as they suspect we do; we do speak and act as they say we do. What she does is to interpret that contrariness as healthy, as an attempt to be whole rather than a defect of nature or as nonexistent. And in exposing the contrariness, in demonstrating its appropriateness, she assesses the false paths of escape from psychic violence that so many of us are wont to believe in or follow—those easy conventions that we would like to see as solutions. These stories act out Rilke's words, for they show that there is no possibility for any living being to be whole unless she can be who she is. More disturbing, they show that no matter how she might want to appear, no matter what conventions are imposed on her, no matter how much she resists herself, she will oppose those who inflict trouble on her. In the final analysis, these stories are about the most natural law of all, that all living beings must love themselves, must try to be free—that spirit will eventually triumph over convention, no matter what the cost.

3 Community and Nature:
The Novels of Toni Morrison* (1980)

Between my completion of Black Women Novelists and its publication, Toni Morrison published a third novel, Song of Solomon. While her theme of the relationship between Nature and Community is certainly one important element in my previous analysis of The Bluest Eye and Sula, it seemed to me that Song of Solomon further refined this concern of hers. And since Black Women Novelists focused on the development of black women characters in the novels, I did not have the space to delve as much as I wanted into Morrison's philosophical orientation. "Community and Nature" focuses on this orientation while including an analysis of Morrison's most recent novel.

During the last eight years, Toni Morrison has created a world of her own in three critcally acclaimed novels. Though different in emphasis, *The Bluest Eye* (1970), *Sula* (1974), and *Song of Solomon* (1977) present communities whose particular view of Nature transforms the air they breathe, the earth they walk. In few contemporary American novelists is the meaning of Nature so important as it is in the novels of this black woman writer. The interpretation of Nature is not only central to her characters' attempts to understand themselves, but to the fables Morrison weaves, the way she tells her tales.

This particular theme of Morrison's, the relationship between her characters' belief system and their view of Nature, is basic to her works and is one of the principal reasons why her novels emanate a feeling of timelessness even as they are so pointedly concerned with the specificity of her characters' communities. The relationship between Nature and a particular human community is the kernel of the contemporary fable as Morrison has wrought it.

At first glance, each of her novels may seem to be primarily about one character: Pecola in *The Bluest Eye,* Sula in *Sula,* and Milkman Dead in *Song of Solomon.* But as we read the novels, what impresses us is not only these characters, but their blood relations. The people from whom the major characters derive their sense of themselves are as memorable, as finely drawn, as the focal characters. Who can read *Sula* without being struck by Eva, Sula's grandmother? As much time is spent in *The Bluest*

*First published in *The Journal of Ethnic Studies* 7, no. 4 (February 1980).

Eye on Pauline Breedlove as on Pecola. And what would *Song of Solomon* be like without Pilate, Milkman's marvelous aunt? In fact, because Morrison penetrates the essence of her focal characters, we discover that a necessary aspect of their central conflict in the novel is their relationship to their natal communities, the people who gave them life. Like many oral storytellers, Morrison spins tales about how the characters' conduct of their lives is connected to their community's value system. Her novels present worlds that are very much like villages in which kinship ties are woven into the dreams, legends, the subconscious of the inhabitants.

That is why we are first introduced in these novels to the place that the characters inhabit, the land of the community. Like the ancestral African tradition, place is as important as the human actors, for the land is a participant in the maintenance of the folk tradition. It is one of the necessary constants through which the folk dramatize the meaning of life, as it is passed on from one generation to the next. Setting, then, is organic to the characters' view of themselves. And a change in place drastically alters the traditional values that give their life coherence.

Migration from the rural South to a more or less urban North has had great impact on the lives of Afro-Americans. And in the movement north, blacks not only migrated to large cities, as so much of Afro-American literature indicates, but to many small towns as well. The effect of such a migration on the characters of the novel is a major thematic consideration in *The Bluest Eye*. Morrison emphasizes the importance of this change by first introducing Lorain, Ohio as a land that would allow neither the marigolds nor Pecola to grow, even before we know the significance of the shriveled marigold seeds or who Pecola is. The characters we will focus on are recent arrivals to this town, whose connection to another place, the South, had been intense and life sustaining if only because they'd had to forge a tradition of survival against great odds. As new inhabitants, and as black people, they are looked down upon by the more established white community of Lorain, Ohio. The black migrants must therefore learn how to survive in this land that is at present a sterile one for them, even as they try to evolve a tradition that is functional in this place. Until they do, their lives will lack coherence.

Pauline, Pecola Breedlove's mother, is representative of the loss of a center with which these migrants are infected. Separated from the rural South, which allowed her privacy and freedom of imagination, and cut off from the tradition of her maternal ancestors, she falls prey to the destructive ideas of physical beauty and romantic love as measures of self-worth. Her life in urban Lorain, Ohio removes her from her customary avenues for expressing herself and for wresting some meaning out of her life. As a result, she lays the blame for her misfortunes on her incapacity as a black woman to be beautiful and therefore worthy of a good life. The difference between Pauline's adopted value system, derived from loneliness and the images of the movies, and the value system of southern black women, like her husband's Aunt Jimmy, is heightened in the novel. Lacking coherence in her own life, Pauline is unable to understand the effects of displacement on her husband and children. Women like Aunt Jimmy, however, had taken the limits of their existence and had transformed them by recreating them in their own image and in the image of their community. Both Pauline and Aunt Jimmy suffer, but their different perceptions of their self-worth are indications of the impact that a lack of functional traditions, as embodied in the land, has on a community.

Yet, even as we experience the tragedy of Pauline's daughter, Pecola, as a result of her feelings of total unworthiness that her family and her community have given her, we also begin to sense the stirrings of a viable tradition in this new land. For in spite of their obsession with Shirley Temple dolls and other golden symbols of the outer society's values, Mrs. McTeer and her circle of friends maintain their strong woman ties as well as an equally strong sense of family. As they absorb the different cycle of seasons that they now experience, they begin to see the town as their town. As a result, one of their daughters, Claudia, is able to tell us the story of Pecola Breedlove's tragedy and is able to wrest understanding rather than waste out of this new land.

In Morrison's second novel, *Sula*, she extends her introduction of the land beyond that of *The Bluest Eye*, for she tells us the story of the Bottom's beginnings. This tale is as much myth as it may be fact, for its core is the community's perceived sense of reality, its intuitive rendering of its precarious position in the hostile world. In presenting the Bottom's origins as a "nigger joke" and by juxtaposing its birth to its death, the author signals to the reader that her story will be concerned with the community's philosophy of survival. This philosophy, in Morrison's narrative, is very much related to the land—for the Bottom is actually topland where survival is precarious. But because a slavemaster, the previous owner of the land, had not wanted to pay his slave the good land he had promised him, he called this hilly land "the bottom of heaven." This black community is born, then, as a result of a white man's inversion of the truth, and it is destroyed years later when whites again alter the truth, the worth of the land, to suit their own desires.

Thus, a tradition evolves during the life span of the Bottom that is inextricably connected to its beginning, a tradition that is rooted in the nature of the land as the bottom on the top. Beset as it is by the hostile elements of heat and cold, wind and rain, the Bottom holds to the tenet that the only way one can defeat evil is by outlasting it. This view of resistance will be crucial to the story of Sula Peace; since she does not conform to the Bottom's view of woman, she is perceived by her community as a manifestation of the evil side of Nature. Rather than focusing its attentions on the pervasive evils of racism and poverty that continually threaten it, the community expends its energy on outlasting the evil Sula. Finally, the community's concept of resistance, which has its basis in its history and the vulnerability of the land, proves too weak in the face of the outside world to ensure the community's survival.

In addition to its vulnerability, the insularity of the land is a contributing factor to its distinctiveness. Like *The Bluest Eye*, a change in place is crucial to the community, though for a different reason. The Bottom is so tucked away from the rest of the world that few of its women ever leave it. And when they do, they come back with a new perspective. Morrison emphasizes the impact of the exposure of these women to the outer world, as well as the infrequency of such occasions, by having Nel Wright leave her community but once. It is at this time that she learns she is an individual:

> "I'm me. I'm not their daughter. I'm not Nel. I'm me. Me." Each time she said the word *me* there was a gathering in her like power, like joy, like fear. (p. 24-25).

Such an appreciation of selfhood is contrary to the Bottom's definition of woman, as we discover when, years later, the marked woman Sula returns to the community after being absent for ten years. As *The Bluest Eye* focuses on the effect of a change in place on the community, particularly its women, so *Sula* emphasizes the effect of insularity on the women of the Bottom. As its conservative element, the women help the community retain its distinctive traditions. But because they are so insulated, the traditions of the community are seldom challenged and revitalized and are in danger of becoming obsolete. Thus, the nature of the land, its vulnerability, its insularity, its distinctiveness, will have untold effects on the black community in this novel and on the way major characters are perceived by that community.

Though distinctly different from her first two novels, Morrison's third novel is also characterized by her emphasis on the relationship between the nature of the land and the traditions of the community. Like *The Bluest Eye*, there are two black communities presented in *Song of Solomon*, one in the South and one in the North, which are contrasted though closely related. *Song of Solomon*, like Morrison's first two novels, begins with our introduction to one of these communities. Significantly, the land that this community occupies is inseparable from that of the white community. Yet the newly arrived blacks retain some of their old traditions and transform the land through the process of naming, a process that keeps alive their own memories, their history as it develops. The importance of naming, of creating significance through the word, is a central theme in this novel. The black inhabitants of this town may not have any official power in the government of the town, but they hold their own as a community because they will not accept the names that others give to things that affect them. Thus, Mercy Hospital, is named by the black community No Mercy, because they were not allowed there. By giving the hospital its correct name, they demonstrate the inversion of the truth that is operative in this land.

But, of course, the process of naming is also a tentative one. Because the community is controlled by others in areas critical to its survival, its names can also be changed. Like *Sula*, at the center of this novel's action is a "nigger joke" that has to do with naming. Just as the top is called the Bottom because of a white man's greed, so the Dead Family are erroneously named because of a white man's mistake. Nonetheless, this black family retains their dreaded name, for it paradoxically embodies their vitality as well as their oppression. And they perfect it by starting their own tradition of naming by randomly selecting the first names of their children out of the Bible.

Though many in the North would try to retain their collective memories through the process of naming the land, others would change their view of the land. In attempting to fulfill the promise that the North represents to them, these few would see it as an object for their use, for profit, rather than a living entity, an embodiment of their past. In their pursuit of money, they endanger the community by renting its fabric, by creating a hierarchy based on those who own things. The story of Milkman Dead is radically affected by the change in values from his southern grandfather's defense of his land with his life, to his northern father, who almost destroys his entire family in the pursuit of more and more property. And Milkman's search for gold, the profit from the land of his origins, which ironically he wants in order to free himself from his family, underscores the difference between the old traditions and the new. But the land reaffirms itself, for in his search for the gold, Milkman discovers a greater treasure, his real name and his roots in the land, which enable him to fly beyond it to a greater truth.

The land, then, on which the community dwells is not merely a place; it is one of the significant bases of its value system. And because Morrison sees human beings as part of the land, rather than apart from it, the community's view of Nature is crucial to the substance of her works. In all three novels, different societies' interpretations of Nature—as a physical or spiritual force, one that can or cannot be affected by human forces—are filtered through their definition of woman. The conflict between these different interpretations often results in the establishment of certain ideas of Truth by the dominant group—ideas that may, in fact, be an inversion of truth for other groups. Morrison's novels, thematically and structurally, are characterized by the use of inversion, sometimes in the form of humor, sometimes as tragedy, but always as a rendering of how complex any truth is. Like the blues, which fuses laughter and tears, her use of inversion portrays her villages as marvelously themselves even as they are infected by a different, usually hostile, world. Like Nature, her villages are both wonderful and terrible.

In *The Bluest Eye*, the central theme is the effect of the standardized western ideas of physical beauty and romantic love not only on the black women of Lorain, Ohio, but also on the black community's perception of its worth. All of the adults in the book, in varying degrees, are affected by their acceptance of the society's inversion of the natural order. For in internalizing the West's standards of beauty, the black community automatically disqualifies itself as the possessor of its own cultural standards. But beyond the statement of cultural mutilation that Pecola's desire for the bluest eye illustrates, Morrison challenges the unnatural-ness of a belief system in which physical beauty is associated with virtue, and love is romance. Such a system creates a hierarchy in which only a few can be worthy of love and happiness, while the rest are condemned to yearn hopelessly for self-fulfillment. The thwarting of the natural urge for love distorts the process of growth and rebirth of the land itself. Thus, the rape of Pecola by her own father in the spring, a dramatic instance of inversion, is related to the inability of the marigolds to sprout in the unyielding earth of the land: "The seeds shriveled and died; her baby too" (p. 3).

The community's view of Nature as a disorderly process is also related to its acceptance of the paramount importance of physical beauty and romantic love. The struggle between the natural order, which involves funk and passion, and the desire for uncomplicated sweetness and light is embodied by the array of houses that Morrison presents. From the ugly storefront of the Breedloves to the standardized house of the Dick and Jane primer, the houses in this novel reflect the worth of their inhabitants according to the norms of the society and emphasize the destructiveness of a hierarchical order. Like the concept of physical beauty, the appearances of the houses, as measured by their inhabitants' ability or inability to erase the funk of nature, is an indication of their worth in the society. So that outward appearance rather than inner qualities becomes the measuring stick, and there must, by nature of a hierarchy, always be someone above and below each person who threatens her self-worth. As people come to believe that they *are* their appearance, they behave more and more as society expects them to. So the Breedloves fight and destroy each other in their ugly storefront because they come to believe in their own ugliness, their intrinsic unworthiness. The natural relationship they share as a family is distorted until the mother denies her own daughter for the white girl-doll who is her employer, the father finally rapes his own daughter in his search for godliness, and the daughter negates her own existence by pursuing and eventually obtaining the bluest eyes.

While the characters of *The Bluest Eye* are assaulted by the value system of another culture that has power over them, the characters in *Sula* are presented as having a world of their own. But though they may appear to be autonomous and separate, their continued survival is also gravely affected by the control of the outer society. In contrast to *The Bluest Eye*, the emphasis in *Sula* seems to be on the one quality the Bottom community shares with the world—their definition of woman, her span and space. In actuality, the impact of racism on their interpretation of Nature further reinforces this view.

The people of the Bottom do not believe that "Nature [is] ever askew—only inconvenient" (p. 78). Unlike the newly arrived inhabitants of Lorain, Ohio, they incorporate the funk and the sweetness, the evil and the good into their definition of Nature. But because Nature is so all encompassing, they use their feeling of human smallness as a bulwark against action and experiments. They relate their dictum, that Nature should be allowed to run its course, to the world of human events as well and therefore make no effort to alter them. But though the folk identify Nature and Evil as forces to be outlasted, they also believe that these phenomena express themselves through signs. Thus, the plague of robins or the mark over Sula's eye can be read if one has the wisdom to understand them. Not that this understanding can be used to alter the course of events, for these forces are perceived as indifferent ones that are slightly affected by human behavior. Rain falls alike on the good and the bad. And "the only way to avoid the hand of God is to get in it" (p. 56). As a result, the folk's only defense against evil is endurance. And in order to endure, they must hold tautly in place the commandment that woman must "make others." Their view of survival and of Nature exists only on the physical plane and is rooted in the fear of dying rather than in the desire to live. Convinced that they can only outlast the evils that are caused by humans, they do not pursue any other means of resistance.

Because of women's essential role in their struggle to survive, at least physically, the people of the Bottom might seem to be as slack in their toleration of female behavior as they are accepting in their attitude toward Nature. In the novel, they are willing to absorb the domineering style of Eva Peace, even unto her ritual killing of her only son in order to save his manhood; they avert their eyes from the free sexual behavior of Eva's daughter, Hannah; and they tolerate the hypocritical, high-toned behavior of the lady, Helen Wright. But in reality, they conform to a rigid bottom line—that the bearing of children or the relationship to males be central in a woman's life. That is why the friendship between Nel Wright and Sula Peace develops within these girls' recognition that because "they were neither white nor male, all freedom and triumph was forbidden to them" (p. 44). While Nel Wright eventually assumes her natural position according to the norm of the Bottom, Sula Peace insists on making herself.

Sula is similar to heroes, mostly male, in other American novels—the nameless narrator in *Invisible Man*, Damon Cross in Wright's *The Outsider*—in that she seeks her own individuality as a means to self-fulfillment. But as woman, her desire to make herself rather than others goes against the most basic principle of the community's struggle to survive. Since she does not fit the image of mother, the loose woman, or the lady-wife as Eva, Hannah, and Helene do, the community relegates her to their other category for woman, that of the witch, the evil conjure woman who is a part of the evil forces of Nature. In spite of their attitude toward Sula, the community does not expel her. Rather it uses her, in spite of herself, for its own sake, as a pariah, as a means of reaffirming their oneness as a community. But in doing so, they block the creativity that is also a part of Nature—leaving it to seek destructive channels. Ironically, they achieve the opposite of what they intend, for they do not take from Sula what she has to offer them—the leap into living, the insistence on knowing oneself, the urge to experiment and thus move forward. In allowing her to run her course, as they allow Nature to run its course, they surrender to death and destruction in the path of evil forces.

Morrison resists the idea that either individual pursuit or community conservatism is enough for fulfillment. Left without a context, the self has "no speck from which to grow" (p. 103), and deprived of creative spirits, the community succumbs to death and destruction. This important though complicated idea is expressed in the novel through the author's exploration of the community's view that Sula is a selfish, unnatural woman and through the relationship of the community's well-being and eventual destruction of the River Road. Through much of the book, the men of the Bottom are excluded from helping to build this road because they are black. After Sula's death and a hard fall and a stingy Thanksgiving, many folk of the Bottom are drowned and suffocated when the tunnel for the road collapses. Exhausted from allowing Nature to run its course, exhausted from "hoping" that racism could be outlasted, the Bottom strikes an appropriate and tragic blow against the River Road they are not allowed to build and are physically destroyed. As Sula dies from self-absorption, so they die from their too-long insistence on mere survival. Later, after the road is built, the river subdued, white folks take over the now desirable land of the Bottom as it becomes what it was first called "the bottom of heaven."

Macon Dead, in *Song of Solomon*, would not have erred, as the characters in *Sula* did, on the side of letting Nature run its course. For his main goal in life is the acquisition of property as a means of securing more and more wealth. His view of Nature, representative of a rising middle class, is to own it, rather than to live within it. The importance of possession applies not only to Nature, but to his family as well. He possesses them and displays his wife and children as signs of his wealth. The result of this philosophical view of Nature and therefore of his family and his community is a movement away from life. In transforming the land into an object, into a thing that is not alive, he threatens to destroy the basis of his continuity, which is by nature, a part of Nature.

Just as Macon represents the ideology of a rising northern middle class, whose experience of racism in the South breeds in them an insatiable need for security, so Pilate, his sister, represents the tradition that identifies with Nature; it has no desire for material things. Pilate is presented in the novel as the healer of the spirit, the guide to essences beyond outward appearance or material things. Born without a navel, she learns how important, though misleading, appearances are to people. Thus, she learns to rely on inner qualities rather than outer manifestations. Yet paradoxically, her understanding of the spiritual is based on her appreciation of the land of her origins. Just as Macon's legacy is the land and the houses he owns, Pilate's "inheritance" is the bag of her father's bones. In some ways, this conjure woman without a navel who holds to no societal norms is very much like the marked Sula. But Pilate is able to do what Sula could not. She embodies the tradition of her family, of the southern community in which she originated, even as she makes herself.

The contrast in values between the Dead brother and sister is the axis of this third novel of Morrison's. The conflict between the Deads will attempt to resolve itself in the character Milkman Dead, Macon's son and Pilate's nephew. In a most significant way, Milkman is even more Pilate's child than he is Macon's, for without her conjuring, he would not have been conceived or born. Milkman must travel through the territory of his father's, the deadening effects of Macon's drive for money and security on his mother, his sisters and himself, as well as the geography of Pilate's, its magic and its limitations. Milkman's quest for gold is propelled by his father's belief that Pilate's inheritance is gold rather than a bag of bones. And in the son's pursuit of the father's goal, he finds his grandfather's bones, the essence of the truth of his ancestors.

Milkman's process of discovering that truth is as complicated and as related to his community's view of Nature as the lesson that Nel Wright learns in acknowledging the relationship between Sula's life and death, and the life and death of the Bottom. For he finds that neither Macon nor Pilate's way holds the entire truth. One cannot fulfill one's self through the pursuit of wealth and security; nor can one live completely in the past.

In living apart from the world that now surrounds her, Pilate is not able to sustain Hagar, her granddaughter. "Not as strong as Pilate, not as simple as her mother Reba, Hagar could not make up her life as they had. She needed a chorus of women relations to give her "the strength life demanded of her—and the humor with which to live it" (p. 307). Unable to cope with the values of the world as it is, she succumbs to its terrors. The particular one that destroys her is interestingly enough linked to the major theme of *The Bluest Eye* and to the role that the community in *Sula* ascribes to woman. For in basing the whole reason for her existence on Milkman's love for her, Hagar comes to believe that he rejects her because she does not possess "silky hair," "lemon-colored skin," and "gray-blue eyes" (p. 316). Even the all-encompassing attention and love that she receives from her mother and grandmother cannot stop the poison of worthlessness that finally kills her.

Macon's way also results in death, as illustrated by the choked lives that his wife and daughters must endure. Seen primarily as symbols of his wealth and accomplishments, these women are condemned to a life of ladyhood in which all passion is erased. As the daughter of the town's only black doctor, Ruth was bred to this narrow existence so thoroughly that all her passion is directed first to the father who gave her life, and then to the son whom she unnaturally nurses until late in childhood because she needs some physical contact, some connection with Nature. Her only outlets are the flowers that she grows and the watermark on the big table that connects her with the past. Ruth is symbolic of the terror that awaits those women who become the emblem of a man's wealth. Her son, Milkman, who also becomes an extension of his father's business, finds that at 35 he has no reason for being. It is only his inadvertent discovery of his grandfather's land and his great-grandfather's name that allows him to understand the reasons for both his father's and Pilate's point of view. And in understanding this ancestry, Milkman finds meaning in life, that he can fly beyond the preoccupation with earthy things.

The relationship between the community and its interpretation of Nature is not only a significant theme that runs throughout *The Bluest Eye, Sula,* and *Song of Solomon,* it is also one of the major structural elements of their composition. Based as they are on the interaction between her communities and Nature, Morrison's patterns are not just arbitrary, nor are they only a means of reinforcing her thematic emphasis. More importantly, her structural use of Nature is central to her rendering of her tales as fables, as stories that teach a lesson about life.

As in the fables of old, an interpretation of Nature is critical to the moral code of a particular human community. And implicit in the lesson is the awareness that although a particular interpretation of Nature might be assessed in a specific time, it refers to all time. In Morrison's novels, Time is a unified entity, rather than a chronology that is divided up into discrete fractions of past, present, and future, for it is the impact of significant events on the lives of the folk. In dramatizing the traditions of her community, Morrison's novels resemble the oral techniques of the storyteller, who tells her story in a particular time and in relation to a particular place, but whose treatment of Time and Nature endows the tale with those unbreakable connections between the folk of her community and the rest of the natural and human world.

In *The Bluest Eye*, the seasons, Nature's timing, are the major structural technique that Morrison uses to dramatize the unnatural inversion of truth contained in the ideas of physical beauty and romantic love. The book is divided into four sections, each named for the season in which an event is presented that has an overwhelming impact on Pecola as she enters womanhood. And we are prepared for their use in the structure of this novel by Claudia's introduction to the story: "Quiet as it's kept, there were no marigolds in the fall of 1941." Just as the mimicking Dick and Jane words that head each section remind us of the flat, standardized norms of the society, so the seasons reiterate the wonder and terror of Nature which is beyond standardization. As Nature's timing, the seasons also defy man-made systems of reckoning in which all is predictable, manageable, in which all funk is wiped away.

The language of the novel is based on this conflict between the natural order and the inversions of that order in human society. According to Nature, birds should fly and young things should grow, but they cannot, if their instinctive need for love and freedom is denied them. Morrison not only characterizes this conflict, she juxtaposes it to the perennial process through which human beings learn that in order to experience the preciousness of Nature and of life, they must also experience its meanness. This view of Nature is especially emphasized in the Winter section when the meanness of this season is disrupted by a false spring in the figure of Maureen Peal, the high-yellow dream child, whose physical appearance enchants everyone, but whose temperament is based on her knowledge that "she is cute," while the black girls like Pecola "are ugly, blackamoors." As trapped by her appearance as they are, she may not move beyond that assessment of her own worth. And though she is seen as the possessor of beauty, that most valued gift, she seeks knowledge about sex from Pecola with whom she identifies such things. Like Pecola, Maureen is assigned to an unnatural place in the order of human society. Her appearance, characterized as a false spring, is as much an inversion as is Pecola's name, associated as it is with the mulatta who hates her black mother in the movie *Imitation of Life*.

Throughout the novel, Nature, both constant and forever changing, is the basic metaphor through which Morrison's use of the inversion of the truth is sifted, so that the seasonal flow of birth, death, and rebirth is inverted in the human society. Pecola will not experience rebirth in the spring; rather she will be raped in the season of love by her father and will descend into madness in the sterile summer. Pecola will spend:

> her tendril, sap-green days, walking up and down, up and down, her head jerking to the beat of a drummer so distant only she could hear. Elbows bent, head on shoulders, she flailed her arms like a bird in an eternally grotesque futile effort to fly. (p. 162).

The use of Nature and Time as primary structural elements is perhaps even more pronounced in *Sula*. As in *The Bluest Eye*, the seasons naturally exert much influence on Morrison's community. But in *Sula*, the primal elements, rather than the seasons, are the aspect of Nature that is emphasized. And time is used in this novel more in terms of the folk's interpretation of it than as a part of Nature.

Sula is divided into a prologue, two parts, and an epilogue. The prologue introduces us to the Bottom, its birth and death, as based on the vulnerability and insularity of the land. Part I begins with another introduction, this time to Shadrack, the shell-shocked soldier who initiates National Suicide Day, a ritual that would get the fear of dying out of the way so "that the rest of the year would be safe and free" (p. 12). From this point on in the novel, we are shown those safe and free years, years that focus on Sula's and Nel's childhood, and then their experience as grown women in the Bottom. Finally, there is the epilogue called "1965," a year of understanding for Nel Wright, and a eulogy to the Bottom, a now extinct community.

What is initially striking about *Sula*'s parts is that they are, in spite of Shadrack's ritual, permeated by death and are headed by the names of years. It appears that time is expressed in a chronological numerical fashion, but in actuality, it is not, for each year-chapter does not tell us what happened during that year, so much as it uses a privotal event, usually a death that occurred in that year, as a point of focus for fusing the past, present, and future. Thus the chapter, "1921," focuses on Eva's ritualistic burning to death of her son Plum in order to save his manhood. But most of the events related in this chapter do not occur in the year 1921; rather we learn about Eva's life and her personal qualities, qualities that will have considerable impact on her granddaughter Sula. Eva's sacrifices for her children, her domineering manner as well as her love of maleness are juxtaposed with her murder of her son and are absolutely necessary to an understanding of this most unnatural of acts. Time, in *Sula*, is not chronology but significant action.

This view of time is interwoven with fire, water, air, and earth in Morrison's dramatization of the relationship of the folk to Nature. The elements are the basic metaphor through which the chapter-years are presented. As a result, we come to see death as the most drastic consequence of the elements' interaction with human beings, often because of an inversion of the truth. Part I, for example, begins with chapter 20, Nel's journey to the funeral of the grandmother. That death is followed by Eva's ritual burning of Plum in the chapter "1921," which is connected to Hannah's accidental burning in the chapter "1923," both of which are separated by the accidental burning of Chicken Little by Sula and Nel in the chapter "1922."

The images of fire and water are particularly dominant in Part I. As both creative and destructive forces, fire and water have always been associated in the human mind with powerful spiritual forces and are symbolic of the inherent complexity of the natural order in which life and death are inextricably connected. These images, which are so prevalent in Part I, are fused in the chapter "1927," the last chapter of that section, when Nel marries Jude. This dream of a wedding, in effect, destroys Nel's sense of the individuality she had glimpsed in her one trip outside the Bottom and that had flourished in her friendship with Sula Peace. And we have been prepared for the symbolic reverberations of this wedding, which is Nel's initiation as a grown woman into the community. For as Eva, the dream expert, has told us in her analysis of Hannah's premonition of her own death, the dream of a wedding is death. This interpretation of a human ritual is consistent with the effects of the elements, for the wedding is seen as both death and birth. It is the end of Nel's enjoyment of her own individuality, the price she pays in order to take on the roles of mother and wife without which the community cannot survive.

The characters of this novel are also associated with particular elements. Eva and Hannah are associated with fire; Nel, Sula's best friend, is as consistent as the earth; Ajax, her lover, wants to fly. Sula, whose marked eyes are "as steady and clean as rain," (p. 45) is identified with water, that primal force which has power of fluidity but must be creatively contained within a form, or it will become destructive. It is the overflowing release of Sula's hurt emotions caused by her mother's words that she may love her but she does not like her that results in her accidental drowning of Chicken Little. And it is her fluidity, her need to explore and experiment that causes the community to turn her into a pariah. Because she has no context, however, her fluidity becomes destructive. Without a friend, she has "only her own mood and whim," and "Like any artist with no art form, she becomes dangerous" (p. 105).

The community, too, is associated with the elements. The people are "mightily preoccupied with earthly things," and the women are characterized as "bronze dusted with ash," their spirits rigidly contained within their bodies. Just as Sula crosses over into "a sleep of water always," the folk are destroyed by the excesses of the elements, as the earth turns cold then hot, and they are drowned or suffocated in the tunnel they were not allowed to build.

In *Sula*, the elements, particularly fire and water, are metaphors for the struggle that takes place between Sula and her community. In *Song of Solomon*, all of the elements are again used as structural points of reference, but this time the emphasis is very much on flying, on riding the air. Morrison uses the contrast between the artificial and natural to dramatize the two value systems represented by the Dead brother and sister. But beyond that conflict, Morrison uses the folk myth of the blacks in America who flew back to Africa, a myth that is found wherever Africans were enslaved, as the foundation of this work. In incorporating this myth into the story of Milkman's quest for gold, Morrison suggests that in order to be free, one must surrender to the most dangerous yet necessary of the elements—air. Air is the breath of life, and by learning to work with it, rather than trying to conquer it, one may learn to fly without even leaving the ground.

The first scene of the novel announces the centrality of this idea to the book, as well as the conflict between different value systems with which the black community in this midwestern town is confronted:

> The North Carolina Mutual Life Insurance agent promised to fly from Mercy to the other side of Lake Superior at 3:00. (p. 3)

In this introduction to the story of Milkman Dead, the mercenary philosophy of men like his father as well as the folk's connection with the still-living past, the artificiality of ladyhood as well as the naturalness of the desire to soar are all compressed into a scene much resembling a form of worship. Amid Mr. Smith's attempted flight in his blue silk wings, the artificial red velvet roses flying out of Ruth Dead's basket, and the singing of "O Sugarman done fly," Milkman begins his struggle down his mother's womb to be born. But as he enters the earth and grows older, he learns that "only birds and airplane could fly." . . . "To have to live without that single gift saddened him and left his imagination so bereft that he appeared dull even to the women who did not hate his mother" (p. 9). The rest of this novel is concerned with Milkman's recapture of this desire and his final attainment of that gift.

While Milkman is associated with flying, Guitar Bains, his best friend, is identified with the earth. A natural hunter, he misses the smells and sounds of the woods he had known in the South. He has the clarity of the earth. But like the earth, which is turned soggy by the blood of racism, he is maimed. He uses his natural capacity as a hunter to try to change the situation in which he and his people are caught, and his involvement with The Seven Days is his way of balancing the generations of blacks killed by whites. But in so doing, he must also snuff out his other natural instincts until he becomes totally absorbed with earthly solutions to the evils that surround him.

Song of Solomon is structurally based on the conflict between this preoccupation with earthly matters and the need to fly, that is by nature a part of each of us. The novel is divided into two parts. Part I emphasizes the tension between these two poles within Milkman's natal community in the North, while Part II traces the resolution of this tension as a result of Milkman's quest in his southern community. But in every section of this novel, these two thrusts are woven together, for there is continual interplay between the community of the North and the South, the past and the present, and Macon and Pilate's respective points of view. In developing the relationship of Milkman to these two communities, Morrison uses the elements as her structural guides.

Bereft of Nature's nourishment, Ruth Dead has but a few things that assure her that "the world was still there . . . that she was alive somewhere" (p. 11). One is the large watermark on her fine mahogany table, which connects her past to her present and "behaved as though it were itself a plant and flourished into a huge suede-gray flower that throbbed like fever and sighed like the shift of sand dunes" (p. 13). Another, for a time, is the nursing of her son beyond a reasonable age in the room that smells of damp greenness. This act is as much soaring as she is allowed and is the basis for her son's love-name. As Milkman's mother attempts to satisfy her need for nature in odd ways, his father staves off the fear, which he had acquired in his youth, of being a lonely, landless wanderer. By fondling the magic keys that declare him the owner of property he becomes landlocked. Pilate, on the other hand, is as landless as the birds. Though she would not set foot on an airplane, she is Milkman's pilot to another view of life. "A tall black tree," she is rooted in the earth even as she points to the sky.

In Part II, Milkman follows the trail Pilate had made in her youth. But instead of finding gold, that precious metal of the earth, Pilate's geography leads him to another community that is unknown to him, though a part of him. Again the elements are touchstones in his quest, for in Shalimar, the earth is not owned but lived with. The people are so much a part of it that they know the language that was before language, the language of the animals, of the earth itself. Milkman learns, through the music of the earth, the rivers, and the folk, the name of his ancestor, the one his father had glimpsed in his imagination years before:

> Surely, he thought, he and his sister had some ancestor, some lithe young man with onyx skin and legs as straight as cane stalks who had a name that was real. (p. 17)

Not only does Milkman find the onyx, the cane stalks, and the name, he discovers that this ancestor could fly. The knowledge of this legacy frees him and may help to free his family from the dead end that they are fast approaching, for one important ingredient in being able to fly is to know who you are.

But though Milkman now knows that the air can be a hospitable element, he must still suffer the consequences of his former quest for gold. The final scene of the novel is a climax of Morrison's use of the elements as structural basis. As Milkman and Pilate bury the bag of bones that is their inheritance, Pilate is shot by Guitar, Milkman's best friend, who believes that he has been cheated of the gold. And as Pilate dies, Milkman sings to her a song about their origins. Her death is followed, as if on the air of the song, by the appearance of a bird, which flies off with the earring box that contains her name. And from Soloman's Leap, the land from which his ancestor flew, Milkman leaps into Guitar's arms, as he is transformed by the language of the rocks and the hills into a lodestar. In order to fly, he learns that he must surrender his life to the air rather than own it: "You want my life? You need it? Here" (p. 337).

The novel *Song of Solomon* is Toni Morrison's most recent exploration of the way in which the past myths of the folk and the significant events of their present merge to create still another variation in Nature's relationship to the human community. There is a consistency of vision in her three novels, for they all focus on the seemingly contradictory urges of human beings to be a part of Nature, yet distinct from it. Her characters instinctively yearn to be as fruitful as the earth, as fluid as water, as vivid as fire, as free as air. Yet they also live in human societies that are based on distinctions among their members. Morrison's dramatization of human societies emphasizes the tension between the natural order and the unnatural points of discrimination—race, sex, money, class—employed by human societies.

As a result, there is an admonition in these fables, which inevitably leads us back to the inherent desire for growth in each being, an admonition that this desire will manifest itself either in natural terms or in derangement. And because Nature is a part of each human being, it is too complex to be categorized or wiped away. Thus society's perennial attempts to ignore the relationship between human beings and Nature result in waste, pain, and often death.

Yet, as is true of most fables, Morrison's novels also remind us of the marvelous resiliency of Nature and therefore of human society—that though the marigolds may not sprout in the fall of 1941, they may in another year, if we understand the nature of the soil in which they shriveled; that water may be creative as well as destructive if it is allowed to discover a form that suits it; and that one may ride the air, if one is willing to surrender to it.

NOTES

1. Toni Morrison, *The Bluest Eye*, Holt, Rinehart & Winston, New York, 1970.
2. Toni Morrison, *Sula*, Bantam Books, New York, 1973.
3. Toni Morrison, *Song of Solomon*, Alfred A. Knopf, New York, 1977.

4 Testing the Strength of the Black Cultural Bond: Review of Toni Morrison's *Tar Baby* * (1981)

Book reviews are an immediate, succinct response to a writer's work, quite different, it seems to me, from essays in which one has the time and space to analyze their craft and ideas. They are necessary to the creating of a wider, more knowledgable audience for the writer's work—an important responsibility of the critic. Often, however, book reviews of works by Afro-Americans are written as if the reviewer is not aware that an Afro-American intellectual tradition exists, that certain ideas may, at the time, be under critical discussion, or as if the writer had not written anything else.

This review is an example of my testing of an initial response. Because Morrison's work has been an abiding concern of mine, I, of course, responded to Tar Baby *in the context of her previous work. Because of the need to state succinctly my point of view on the novel, writing the review helped me to further refine my sense of Morrison's development and led to a longer paper on the concept of class in her work.*

In Toni Morrison's *Tar Baby*, the urbane Jadine screams at Son, her unambitious black lover:

> I was learning how to make it in *this* world. The one we live in, not the one in your head. Not that dump Eloe, *this* world. And the truth is I could not have done that without the help and care of some poor old white dude who thought I had brains enough to learn something (p. 264).

Son retorts:

> You can do exactly what you bitches have always done: take care of white folks children. . . . You turn little black babies into little white ones; you turn your black brothers into white brothers; you turn your men into white men . . . (p. 270).

*First published in *In These Times*, July 14, 1981, (Chicago: Institute for Public Affairs).

He punctuates his accusation by reciting to Jadine the black folk tale *Tar Baby*. Morrison's fourth novel turns on this folk tale, a story that very simply embodies the continuing dilemma of Afro-Americans.

In the folk tale, a farmer tries to catch a rabbit, whom he sees as a thief, by making a tar baby, visually attractive, sticky, and placing it in the middle of his cabbage patch. In Morrison's version, the folk tale is extended to a contemporary fable as she analyzes the complexities of class, race, and sex and how they affect Afro-Americans still held captive in the present-day West.

In her version, the farmer is Valerian Street, the owner of a candy empire, products as attractive and sticky as tar. The aging candy emperor retires to a Caribbean island, Isle de le Chevalier, whose people had produced the sugar and cocoa from which the candy was made, and who are left with neither cocoa, sugar, nor money. Here Valerian's only concern is his greenhouse, which he built on this tropical land of uncontrolled and overwhelming growth as "a place of controlled, ever-flowering life to greet death in" (p. 53). Named after a Roman emperor, Valerian, in turn, bestows his name on a red and white candy, which is neither profitable nor tasty. He brings with him his much younger wife, Margaret, whose red hair and white skin closely resemble Valerian's candy, but who is a child of ethnic lower class parents. Locked in by his wealth and the tradition of his family, her claims to worth, as far as the world is concerned, are her beauty, now fading, and Michael, the ever-absent son she has borne the majestic candy king. As his concern is his greenhouse, hers is the preservation of her beauty and her relationship with her son.

Valerian also brings with him his two trustworthy black servants of many years, Sydney and Ondine. Their entire lives are spent ministering to his and Margaret's needs in exchange for which they have steady jobs, a relatively unhassled existence, and the opportunity through him to educate and spoil their orphaned niece, Jadine. Because of their industriousness, they label themselves Philadelphia Negroes and see themselves as a cut above their slovenly brethen; in actuality, they are cut off from any community in order to keep their jobs. They, in turn, are ministered to by two black natives of the island, Gideon (Yardman) and Therese, whose humanity Ondine and Sydney do not even acknowledge so much as to ask their names. As we meet the house servants, they seem to be in control of Valerian and his house, though finally they are controlled by his whims.

Their niece, Jadine, who is spending a few months on the Isle, is drawn by Morrison to resemble an Afro-American princess. Beautiful, bright, educated, ambitious, she lives with her patrons, the Streets, discussing perfumes with Margaret, exchanging witticisms and eating meals with

Valerian, while her aunt and uncle serve dinner and make the beds. Assisted by Valerian, she has completed a degree in Art History at the Sorbonne, has been a successful model in Paris, and is being wooed by a wealthy Parisian who has proposed marriage. Her major concern is "making it," being comfortable and happy. Having been accepted by those in control, she is lulled into dream until she is awakened one day in Paris by the sight of an authentically beautiful African woman with skin like tar against a canary yellow dress, who invalidates the marvelously successful Jadine by spitting at her. Though seemingly unimportant, the woman haunts Jadine, making her feel "lonely and inauthentic." She flees Paris to recuperate in the bosom of her relatives.

Into this clean, cool, and civilized cabbage patch comes Son, the rabbit, the thief, the swamp nigger. A man with many different names and social security numbers, he belongs to that company of men identified by their "refusal to equate work with life and an inability to stay anywhere for long" (p. 166). Born and raised in Eloe, a black village in Florida, he treasures fraternity above profit, living alone, making it. On the run for the accidental but enraged killing of his unfaithful wife, he has roamed, starved, and thought about life. When he steals into Valerian's house like a refugee, he is at first driven by hunger, thirst, and fatigue, then attracted to the cool, civilized house by the sound of a piano. Later he lives a nighttime existence, unknown to anyone in the house, as he falls in love with the sleeping Jadine, "his appetite for her so gargantuan, it lost focus and spread to his eyes, the curtains, the moonlight" (p. 138).

In keeping with Morrison's other three novels, *The Bluest Eye, Sula*, and *Song of Solomon*, nature is as complex and important a character as the human beings who live in it. Much of the novel takes place in Isle de la Chavelier, the sight of which 300 years before struck slaves blind. According to the natives of Dominique, some of these blind ones were carried by the "water-lady" current to the Isle where they rode their horses and screwed the swamp ladies. Their descendants do not see with their eyes but with the eye of the mind and therefore cannot be trusted. The Isle de Chavelier is a land that human beings have tried to control, evicting the river from where it had lived, forcing the champion daisy trees to alter their growth. Here the emperor butterflies talk, and the swamp whispers in the voices of women. Nature is both lush and menacing, resisting the candy king's greenhouse by sending troops of soldier ants to invade it, pulling the slick Jadine into quicksand after a picnic on the beach, straining with all its might against stringent measures of human control.

When Son emerges from the water-lady, as if reborn on the island, the native Therese thinks he is one of the mythical horsemen who has come to take the lovely but errant Jadine away. And when Jadine first sees him alone, she responds to him as one who cannot be trusted. Like a field slave who invades the Big House, Son's presence exposes the illusions of relationships that Valerian, Margaret, Sydney, Ondine, and especially Jadine have woven. His appearance of wild blackness exposes Sydney and Ondine's short-sighted, classist hypocrisy, for they jump to protect their master Valerian from one of their own. Son's resistance to Valerian's authority by insisting on the bond he believes must exist between Gideon and Therese and Sydney and Ondine finally leads to Ondine's exposure of Margaret's secret—that in hatred for her husband she habitually abused her son Michael when he was a baby. This revelation in turn exposes Valerian's great crime that only those in power can afford. He is guilty of innocence; he had not known that secret or the havoc he had wreaked because "he had not taken the trouble to know" (p. 242). At first it is Son's fullblown virility that confronts Jadine, sexual fears that recall her haunting childhood memory of a bitch in heat humped by every male dog in the neighborhood then cracked in the head for it. "She decided at the age of 12, never to be broken at the hands of any man . . ." (p. 124). She wanted to always be in control.

The most critical conflict in the novel, however, is between the values of the individualistic, materialistic Jadine and the roots-bound Son. These two respond to something deep inside each other; as Therese the myth-teller has said, Son had come for Jadine. But Jadine goes for herself, even if it means using what whites give her, which finally binds her even more to their ways. They escape to New York, which she sees as a black woman's town where the manifesto is "Talk Shit, Take None" (p. 222). Son sees it as a place where "the black girls were crying" (p. 215) and where "the street was choked with beautiful males who had found the whole business of being black and men at the same time too difficult and so they dumped it" (p. 216). He loves Eloe, his black village, where there is hardly electricity but much fraternity. But Eloe restricts Jadine as a person and a woman. Her dreams there become nightmares filled with women—her mother, Ondine, the African woman in yellow—who upbraid her and make her feel obscene. For her, in Eloe, "there was maybe a past but definitely no future" (p. 259). What Jadine wants Son to do is to get a job, use his talents, make some money. These things Son will not do, for he feels that the world excludes him as himself: "The conflict between knowing his power and the world's opinion of it secluded him, made him unilateral. He wanted another way" (p. 166).

But just as Jadine knows her way only too well, Son knows no other way but one that is built on alienation and running. The critical questions that Morrison asks in this novel are whether there is a functional black culture in the present-day West, a contemporary black community that is held together by bonds that work. Are blacks essentially upwardly mobile? Is color merely a camouflage? Is race in America operating as a communal bond or is it merely an indication of a past history once functional but no longer perceived by contemporary blacks as operative in their responses to each other?

Jadine and Son finally do not mesh. She flees back to the Isle where she refuses to cherish even her aunt and uncle, and finally takes off for Paris, her makeup intact, her conclusion being "she *was* the safety she longed for" (p. 290). Too late, Son follows her back to the Isle after deciding that his opinion of Eloe was incorrect—that the place was miserable. But Therese, the myth-teller, will not let him succumb to the tar baby. She takes him to the back of the island where the horsemen still hide, blind and seeing.

As he steps gingerly into those mists of myth, we are still left with the dilemma of *Tar Baby*, for Son moves to another world that has little impact on this one, and Jadine cops out to a world of values that eventually must be a dead end, if not for her, most decidedly for her own. Finally, both their solutions are individual, not at all applicable to the concrete realities that their brethren must face everyday. At no point does either Son or Jadine act with others to resolve this group dilemma.

Besides the artificial facileness of the novel, what is disturbing about it is Morrison's insistence that stereotypes that were not true 100 years ago have now become reality. The myth that house slaves traditionally separated themselves from field slaves is not supported by historical evidence. What emerges about slavery is that both groups usually saw themselves as bound to each other by their race, culture, and oppression. Morrison also uses another aspect of the old stereotypes by characterizing the house slave as female and the field slave as male, an assertion that is also negated by history. Yet, if Morrison's perceptions are correct, the devastating effects of American values on blacks in this century may mean that we are worse off then we were 100 years ago.

5   The Concept of Class in the Novels of Toni Morrison* (1981)

This piece was presented as a paper for the PAPC conference in 1981. That organization was just beginning to include panels on Afro-American women writers as well as feminist perspectives on literature. "The Concept of Class in the Novels of Toni Morrison" is not only an essay that attempts to revise and expand the thesis that I had worked on in Black Women Novelists, *but I also took the occasion of the panel to look more closely at* Tar Baby, *about which I had recently written a review. Such occasions were priceless, in that I rarely had the opportunity to talk about Afro-American women writers with the few scholars who then saw their work as significant, as well as to investigate assumptions about what areas literary criticism ought to include.*

In this essay I intend to look at the novels of Toni Morrison in relation to the concept of class. Before I can focus on that issue with any meaning, I have found that the concept of class in this contemporary novelist's work is so rooted in history that it is necessary to outline past literary images of black women in relation to class. The first part of this paper, then, will briefly describe that history and serve as an introduction to my main topic.

Clearly, sexism and racism are systems of societal and psychological restrictions that have critically affected the lives of Afro-American women. Since sex and race have been so interrelated in the history of America, it is not surprising that when black women published novels, they necessarily reflected on that relationship, whether they intended to or not. From Frances Harper's *Iola Leroy*, published in 1892, to Toni Morrison's *Tar Baby*, published in 1981, the tradition of Afro-American women novelists as an entirety is a stunning expression of various configurations of societal definitions that have been inflicted on the black woman. One of the stories that this tradition relates is the attempt to insidiously control a race of people by attacking their definition of what it means to be male or female. This story, extending over 80 years of American literary history is what I tried to illuminate in my book, *Black Women Novelists, the Development of a Tradition*.

*A portion of this essay was published in *Black Working Women, Debunking the Myths: A Multidisciplinary Approach*, a monograph published by the Center for the Study, Education and Advancement of Women, University of California, Berkeley.

Given the impact of racism and sexism, it is not surprising that the works of black women have been studied by literary critics in terms of their history and expression, as black and female. However, as I wrote my book, and as I read it myself, another story also began to unfold, one that runs alongside the story of the relationship in America between race and gender. That story, which has meaning, I believe, for all American women, has to do with the concept of class as a major factor upon which the societal norm of what a woman is supposed to be is based. Just as blacks as a group were relegated to an underclass in America by virtue of their race, so women were relegated to a separate caste by virtue of their sex. But within that separate caste, a standard of woman was designed in terms of a class definition.

Let me explain a bit more concretely what I mean. The ideal southern lady image of eighteenth-century America is one with which we are still familiar, an ideal that has been one of the dominant factors in America's conception of woman. She was expected to be beautiful in an ornamental way, chaste, pious, married, and eventually, a mother. She was, obviously, white; a respectable woman, she did not work. She was a lady who provided a haven of comfort and security for her husband, who by nature of his superior character and mastery was expected to control the outer world in which *he* moved. Clearly, the ideal southern lady is, in essence, an upper middle-class image that could hardly be entertained if there were not lower-class servants to do the work necessary to keep her home functioning and to preserve her beauty. Nor could she retreat so far from the world if her husband were not financially well-off. I am not saying that American women existed as ideal southern ladies in large numbers. But though the ideal was not real, it was, and probably still is, seen as the standard toward which a woman should aspire. For centuries, then, the American standard of woman has been gravely affected by this upper middle-class image of the ideal southern lady.

The respectable lady, the desired concept of woman in the society, then, is not only sexist and racist, it is also classist. And because black women were, by nature of their race, conceived of as lower class, they could hardly approximate the norm. They had to work; most could not be ornamental or withdrawn from the world; and, according to the aesthetics of this country, they were not beautiful. But neither were they men. Any aggressiveness or intelligence on their part, qualities necessary for participation in the work world, were construed as unwomanly and tasteless. On one hand, they could not achieve the standard of womanhood; on the other hand, they were biologically females, with all the societal restrictions associated with that state.

The novels of black women from 1892 to the present have had to react to the element of class as one of the factors upon which the societal definition of the black women is based. In *Iola Leroy*, Frances Harper tried to present a socially acceptable image of the black woman. And that did not only mean presenting her as a mulatta, and therefore beautiful, it also meant presenting her as upper middle class—as having breeding, economic status, and "high" moral standards. Because of her feminist leanings and her racial background, Harper extends that definition to mean a lady with a good education and social conscience. Nonetheless, Harper took on the class values of the American standard of womanhood in attempting to present a positive image of the black woman, which had little to do with the conditions that prevailed. To a large extent, the same is true of Fauset's and Larsen's heroines who try to overcome race restrictions with class values. Their novels are sure indications that these authors understood the class basis of society's definition of the ideal woman.

Zora Neale Hurston and Ann Petry also responded to the element of class that affected the definition of woman. In *Their Eyes Were Watching God* (1936), Hurston presents Janie Stark as a mulatta who refuses to accept the righteousness of the position, "Queen of the Porch," and who sees the limitations of being a middle-class lady to the extent to which she has access to it. For being Queen of the Porch means being cut off from her community and from the world. It finally means being controlled by convention. Ann Petry does another variation on this same theme by portraying Lutie Johnson of *The Street* (1945) as a working-class woman who is nonetheless beautiful like the mulatta and has the "high" moral values of the upper middle-class image. Both Hurston and Petry challenge the class aspects of the definition of the ideal woman, as well as delineating the image's sexist and racist elements. Petry's novel is particularly interesting from the vantage point of class definitions, for on one hand she gives us a character who is working class, and on the other hand has that character aspire to the values of the ideal upper middle-class lady. *The Street* is a story that emphasizes the tragedy that can result from such a contradiction.

In the contemporary period, black women novelists have continued to analyze the relationship between class, race, and gender. One of our finest novelists, Toni Morrison, has illuminated in her four novels, *The Bluest Eye, Sula, Song of Solomon,* and *Tar Baby,* the definition of woman in relation to race and class assumptions.

The Bluest Eye is about a black girl's desire for the bluest eyes, the symbol for her of what it means to be beautiful and therefore worthy in our society. At the center of the novel is Pecola Breedlove, who comes from a family that is poor and virtually cut off from the normal life of a community. The Breedloves despise themselves because they believe in their own unworthiness, which is translated into ugliness for the women of that family. Associated with their condition is funk, violence, ugliness, and poverty, symbolized by their storefront house. In contrast, Pecola's mother, Pauline, works as a domestic in a beautiful house that is a reflection of the ideal woman. She is, in effect, a black mammy to the wealthy blonde girl-doll who lives in the beautiful house. In a pivotal section of the novel, Pauline expels her "ugly," "poor," daughter Pecola from this house because she drops a hot pan of blueberry pie and dirties the floor. Instead of comforting her daughter, who has been burnt, Pauline rushes to console the girl-doll who is upset by the accident. This scene is beautifully constructed to contrast the extremes of class positions in terms of what is desirable. For Pauline hates the ugliness of her house, her daughter, her family, herself and blames her sense of unworthiness on being black and poor. Instead, she aspires to the polished copper and sheen of the kitchen she works in where everyone is clean, well-behaved, and pretty. For her, any violation of that paradise by anyone, even her daughter, is paramount to a crime. The mother's own internalization of the desirable woman as beautiful, well-taken-care-of, cuddled, results in her rejection of her own daughter, who by virtue of her blackness and her poverty cannot possibly obtain such a standard.

Between the bottom, Pecola and her storefront house, and the top, the little girl-doll in her perfect home, Morrison presents us women situated on different points along the scale. Their positions are generally symbolized by the order of their homes and their shade of skin color. Just below the girl-doll is Maureen Peal, the light-skinned dream girl with green eyes who lives in a fine house, wears immaculate clothes, and is seen by everyone around her as a princess. Geraldine is slightly darker than Maureen. Because she is precariously on the edge of bright skin, she hates any element of funk, which she associates with blackness, and she rigidly maintains her prissy home. She also expels Pecola from her house, for this black girl with her nappy hair represents to Geraldine both racial and class deterioration. In the novel, both Maureen and Geraldine are also associated with a fear of sex. Maureen is clearly interested in learning about "it." But since that would violate the status of her position, she tries to learn about "it" from Pecola, who, because she is black, must know about such nastiness. Geraldine is so afraid of funk creeping into her pseudo-white middle-class life that she is frigid in much the same way southern ladies were supposed to be.

Freida and Claudia McTeer's mother is just one level above the Breedloves, at least economically. Somehow she has managed to hold onto her self-respect, despite her love of Shirley Temple dolls, "good hair," and bright skin. Her home is not a storefront, though stuffed newspapers in the cracks are necessary to keep out the cold. Instead, there is a hard, firm love that permeates her home. She and her women friends form their own community as they waver precariously on the edge, between Mrs. Breedlove's total alienation from any community and their desire not to work and to own a neat home like Geraldine.

Morrison comments on these various positions throughout the novel by using a device that underlines the pervasiveness of normative class distinctions. The words from the Dick and Jane primer are juxtaposed to appropriate sections in the novel. The primer tells us what the society says the ideal family should be like and is based on a middle-class ideal where the father works, the mother stays home, the children are happy, clean, and well-behaved, and even the dog and cat are well-groomed, friendly, socialized. There are no messy emotions, no unsatisfied needs, no funk.

The Bluest Eye, at core, is about the contradiction fostered by racism, sexism, and class distinctions that assails the black girls of this book. These contradictions are too intense for Pecola to sustain her sense of worth. As a result, she descends into madness. The other girls, Claudia and Frieda, barely manage to survive. Claudia, the narrator of this story, summarizes Pecola's tragedy in this way:

> All of our waste which we dumped on her and which she absorbed. And all of our beauty, which was hers first and which she gave to us. All of us—all who knew her—felt so wholesome after we cleaned ourselves on her. We were so beautiful when we stood astride her ugliness. Her simplicity decorated us, her guilt sanctified us, her pain made us glow with health, her awkwardness made us think we had a sense of humor. Her inarticulateness made us believe we were eloquent. Her poverty kept us generous. Even her waking dreams we used—to silence our own nightmares. And she let us, and thereby deserved our contempt. We honed our egos on her, padded our characters with her frailty, and yawned in the fantasy of our strength.[1]

At the crux of the novel is society's need for a pariah, the need of its members to have someone to look down upon and therefore enhance one's constantly threatened sense of worth. Beyond the economic basis, one of the major psychological effects of class distinction is a need for a sense of superiority. Morrison's first novel succinctly expresses the vulnerability of poor black girls and how easily they can become the pariahs, which the structure of our society must have.

Morrison's second novel, *Sula*, pushes the idea of the black woman as pariah even further. Although she constructs the hierarchy of class relations in *Sula* quite differently from *The Bluest Eye*, the concept of class and its relation to sex and race is still very much a part of the novel. On an obvious level, Nel's mother, Helen Wright, could be called the image of the lady in the novel. She is presented in the hypocritical contours of this image. What is more interesting to me, however, is the complex way in which Morrison shows us how woman as helpmate, mother, and housekeeper is connected to the sense of failure black men often feel in a world that denies them status. Jude marries Nel in the novel because of his sense of this failure, his need to feel himself a man after being denied a job building the River Road:

> The more he thought about marriage, the more attractive it became. Whatever his fortune, whatever the cut of his garment, there would always be the hem—the tuck and fold that hid his raveling edges; a someone sweet, industrious and loyal to shore him up. And in return he would shelter her, love her, grow old with her. Without that someone he was a waiter hanging around a kitchen like a woman. With her he was head of a household pinned to an unsatisfactory job out of necessity. The two of them together would make one Jude.[2]

The standard of womanhood that Nel represents in the novel, at least during her marriage to Jude, is not the pure image of the ideal southern lady. Rather it is the variant that is based on the status of black men, on the status, in fact, of working-class men in the society. This role is seen by Nel's community as *good*, while Sula is seen as *evil*. For Sula not only refuses that role, she steps outside the caste of woman, beyond any class definition within that caste, when she insists on making herself. She does not work, but neither is she taken care of; she is freely sexual, but is not really that interested in men as men; she is interested neither in being beautiful nor becoming a mother. She defines herself outside of the sex, class, race definitions of the society. That she becomes a pariah in her community has much to do with her resistance to any clearly recognizable definition of a woman that the Bottom can tolerate.

In *Sula*, Morrison captures most profoundly the way concepts of good and evil are related to societal definitions of woman. For the Bottom, that definition has much to do with the status of black people within the larger society, which ironically is the basis for the adventure and rebellion that Sula represents. As important, the Bottom characterizes all its women as a class, though not in terms of dependent beautiful ornaments. Because of this black community's vulnerability, the distinguishing characteristics of the class of woman is that she make others, that she insure the continuity of the community by bearing children and by supporting the beleaguered men either sexually, emotionally, or financially. Such a position can result in the strength of an Eva, the rebellion of a Sula, or the stolid endurance of a Nel. But in the end none of these positions, it seems to me, results in self-fulfillment.

Morrison's third novel, *Song of Solomon*, does not primarily focus on the concept of woman, for its protagonists are men. Yet class in relation to race becomes even more focal in this novel than in her first two. For though Milkman's quest for his identity is the dominant thread of the novel, the major obstacle he must overcome is the deadening effects of his father's need to own as much property as possible in order to protect himself against racism. And Milkman is accidentally propelled on his search for himself as a result of his desire for gold. That journey leads him back through his personal past to a racial history that had been vehemently opposed to materialism and greed. It is a history that was created from the suffering imposed upon his people by the greed of others.

Although Morrison does not focus primarily on the relationship of gender to class in *Song of Solomon*, she does integrate that concern into her major theme. There are two important women in Milkman's life: his mother, Ruth, and his aunt, Pilate. As the daughter of the only black doctor in town, Ruth is bred to an upper middle-class existence. She is presented in the novel as the underside of the ideal southern lady image. She is totally cut off from life—benevolently imprisoned by her father who tries to make her into his girl-doll, spitefully contained by her husband who marries her because of her class position, then despised by him for her inherent weakness. Ruth's life is one of uneventful waste, interrupted only by the birth of her son, who she tries to keep a baby as long as possible. After he is grown, the only sign of life in her world is the watermark on her impressive dining room table, for her sole achievement had been the elaborate centerpieces she arranges for it. Ruth is symbolic of the terror that awaits those women who become the emblem of a man's wealth and class position.

While Ruth is the quintessence of the ideal southern lady image carried to a grotesque extreme, Pilate is the woman without a navel, the woman completely outside societal structures. She is the guide in the novel to essences beyond outward appearance or material things. As Ruth is a society lady, so Pilate is totally outside society as symbolized by her house outside the town, which is not even wired for electricity. Yet Pilate is also the embodiment of the tradition of her family and is the pilot for Milkman in his necessary journey to the past. Morrison compares and contrasts these two women in this marvelous passage:

> They were so different, these two women. One black, the other lemony. One corseted, the other buck naked under her dress. One well read but ill traveled. The other had read only a geography book, but had been from one end of the country to another. One wholly dependent on money for life, the other indifferent to it. But those were the meaningless things. Their similarities were profound. Both were vitally interested in Macon Dead's son, and both had close and supportive posthumous communication with their fathers.[3]

They come together in this novel, the upper middle-class lady and the conjure woman, to save Milkman, in a sense the symbol of their continuity. That both these women are nurturers is, I believe, important, especially when one juxtaposes them with Sula. In *Song of Solomon* and in her latest novel, *Tar Baby*, Morrison seems to modify the image of Sula as an ideal. Sula was so powerful a character that she ignited the imagination of many readers, who reversed the Bottom's judgement, transforming her from the evil witch into a totally positive ideal. But though Sula is a product of her community, she has no concern for it. And Morrison has her die for lack, it seems, of a community. The distinction that Morrison makes in *Song of Solomon* between class and community and between autonomy and self-absorption is represented, I think, by the towering figure of Pilate, who is totally beyond class distinctions and yet is the embodiment of the spirit of her community. In having Ruth and Pilate come together, Morrison may be suggesting that the effect of class distinctions, the fragmentation of community, may be able to be overcome by women in their overriding concern for the living.

Pilate, however, is rooted in the past. Although she is still effective in the present, she leaves us no future. One cannot pretend that electricity does not exist and that the world is a village. Missing from Pilate's character is a sense of contemporary life. Cut off from men, her daughter Reba becomes obsessed with them and her granddaughter Hagar is finally killed by her insatiable desire for Milkman. Ironically, her community, made up solely of women, becomes psychically dependent on men, because it does not know them. Pilate, then, is so apart from the everyday world that her way cannot be the basis for transforming it. As heroic as she is, Pilate belongs to another time.

In *Tar Baby*, Morrison adds the quality of contemporaneity to her characterization of an independent black woman. And in the love story of Jadine and Son, she develops her most compelling relationship between a man and a woman. But Jadine is presented in the novel as essentially classbound. Her desire to "make it" in the world binds her not just to whites, but to upper-class whites. Her values are not so much that of the ideal southern lady as they are of the white male world. She does not wish to be the lady dependent on the husband's wealth and status. She wants parity, but it must be parity in a world of material gain. In no way is she a nurturer, not even to her aunt and uncle, who made her access to wealth possible by becoming life-long servants to the rich Valerian.

To Jadine, independence for a woman means looking out for herself— she is not concerned with any community or with justice for anyone. In developing a Jadine, who uses her belief in herself as a woman as a rationale for "making it," Morrison may be suggesting not only that class concerns are now more critical than racial bonds, but that women, in their search for autonomy, may be taking on patriarchal values. Jadine is a feminist in appearance without any of the concern for social justice that the concept should embody.

In contrast to Jadine, Son, her lover, is a man totally outside of society, a runaway criminal. Like Pilate, he resists the materialism of the society. Like Pilate, he has no future, for he really lives in Eloe, a country of the past. More importantly, he refuses to contend with the social forces that deprive him of fulfillment. His solution is to retreat, run, opt out. Although he feels an intense racial identity, he does not join with others to change anything. He is not so much beyond class as much as he is perceived as part of an under class—totally alienated from the world he moves in. He finally moves into the realm of myth.

Both Jadine and Son are at a dead end. In going to Paris, Jadine will probably marry a wealthy Parisian, repeating the pattern of some of her foremothers, except that they were *forced* by circumstances to enter the more dominant race and class through their use of their sexuality. As independent as she might seem, then, her need for material well-being makes her dependent on the class of the wealthy and powerful. Son, on the other hand, simply leaves this world for another, affecting nothing for anyone.

Whatever the flaws of *Tar Baby*, it is Morrison's most recent example of how she consistently creates a world of characters, each of whom represents a specific social value. In all her books, the particular concept that is foremost in her mind is divided into different aspects that her characters embody. In *The Bluest Eye*, the idea of physical beauty is looked at in terms of its impact on black girls and women along class lines and skin shade. In *Sula*, the idea of woman is represented by the many female archetypes that the world has invented, from the domineering Eva through the handmaiden Nel to the witch Sula. In *Song of Solomon*, she investigates the meaning of black racial identity, how that common history is responsible for people as diverse as the rebellious Guitar, the materialistic Macon, and the spiritual Pilate. And in *Tar Baby*, where the relationship between class and race is pivotal, Morrison introduces white characters, the wealthy Valerian and his wife, as well as non-American blacks, Gideon and Therese, who are practically serfs in their Caribbean home. As Morrison creates a body of work, her analysis of our society through the creation of these diverse characters asks basic questions about whether sex, race, or class are separate entities, at least in America. Or whether, like the images of a kaleidoscope, these elements are so organically connected that one must understand their interrelationship in spite of their ever-shifting appearance.

NOTES

1. Toni Morrison, *The Bluest Eye* (New York: Holt, Rinehart & Winston, 1970), p. 163.
2. Toni Morrison, *Sula* (New York: Knopf, 1974), p. 82.
3. Toni Morrison, *Song of Solomon* (New York: Knopf, 1977), p. 139.

6 Alice Walker: The Black Woman Artist as Wayward* (1981)

By 1981, some writers and scholars were becoming aware of the literary explosion of Afro-American women writers that had occurred during the 1970s. In no other decade in American history had so many Afro-American women been published. Mari Evans, herself a poet and teacher, began a project to include in one volume a critical evaluation of some portion of these contemporary writers.

This essay was written for that volume, which became Black Women Writers: A Critical Evaluation, 1950-1980. *The volume is unique in that it gives two critics the opportunity to respond to each writer's entire work. Rather than a piecemeal approach, scholars could respond to the entire opus of the writers. Afro-American women writers were finally being seen as serious writers, as working writers.*

Evans' project gave me a chance to look at all of Alice Walker's works, her poetry, short stories, essays, and novels, in the context of the time they were written, as part of the Afro-American women's intellectual tradition. Writing this essay was one of my most enjoyable experiences. The essay was amended in 1983 to include You Can't Keep a Good Woman Down *and* The Color Purple, *works Walker has published since 1981.*

I find my own
small person
a standing self
against the world
an quality of wills
I finally understand[1]

Alice Walker has produced a significant body of work since 1968, when *Once*, her first volume of poetry, was published. Prolific, albeit a young writer, she is already acclaimed by many to be one of America's finest novelists, having received both the American Book Award and the coveted Pulitzer in 1983.

*First published in Mari Evans, ed., *Black Women Writers: A Critical Evaluation, 1950-1980*, Doubleday Anchor, 1984.

Her substantial body of writing, though it varies, is characterized by specific recurrent motifs. Most obvious is Walker's attention to the black woman as creator, and to how her attempt to be whole relates to the health of her community. This theme is certainly focal to Walker's two collections of short stories, *In Love and Trouble* and *You Can't Keep a Good Woman Down*, to her classic essay, "In Search of Our Mothers' Gardens," and to *Meridian* and *The Color Purple*, her second and third novels. It also reverberates in her personal efforts to help rescue the works of Zora Neale Hurston from a threatening oblivion. Increasingly, as indicated by her last collection of poems, *Good Night Willie Lee*, Walker's work is black women-centered.

Another recurrent motif in Walker's work is her insistence on probing the relationship between struggle and change, a probing that encompasses the pain of black people's lives, against which the writer protests but which she will not ignore. Paradoxically, such pain sometimes results in growth, precisely because of the nature of the struggle that must be borne, if there is to be change. Presented primarily through three generations of one family in Walker's first novel, *The Third Life of Grange Copeland*, the struggle to change takes on overt societal dimensions in *Meridian*, her second novel. Characteristically this theme is presented in her poetry, fiction, and essays as a spiritual legacy of black people in the South.

One might also characterize Walker's work as organically spare rather than elaborate, ascetic rather than lush, a process of stripping off layers, honing down to the core. This pattern, impressionistic in *Once*, is refined in her subsequent volumes of poetry and clearly marks the structure of her fiction and essays. There is a concentrated distillation of language, which, ironically, allows her to expand rather than constrict. Few contemporary American writers have examined so many facets of sex and race, love and societal changes, as has Walker, without abandoning the personal grace that distinguishes her voice.

These elements—the focus on the struggle of black people, especially black women, to claim their own lives, and the contention that this struggle emanates from a deepening of self-knowledge and love—are characteristics of Walker's work. Yet it seems they are not really the essential quality that distinguishes her work, for these characteristics might be said to apply to any number of contemporary black women writers such as Toni Morrison, Paule Marshall, June Jordan. Walker's peculiar sound, the specific mode through which her deepening of self-knowledge and self-love comes, seems to have much to do with her contrariness, her willingness at all turns to challenge the fashionable belief of the day, to reexamine it in the light of her own experiences and of dearly won principles that she has previously challenged and absorbed. There is a sense in which the "forbidden" in the society is consistently approached by Walker as a possible route to truth. At the core of this contrariness is an unwavering honesty about what she sees. Thus in *Once*, her first volume of poems, the then twenty-three-year-old Walker wrote, during the heyday of Afro-Americans' romanticizing of their motherland, about her stay in Africa, in images that were not always complimentary. In her poem "Karamojans" Walker demystified Africa:

A tall man
Without clothes
Beautiful
Like a statue
Up close
His eyes
Are running
Sores[2]

Such a perception was, at that time, practically blasphemy among a progressive element of black thinkers and activists. Yet, seemingly impervious to the risk of rebuke, the young Walker challenged the idealistic view of Africa as an image, a beautiful artifact to be used by Afro-Americans in their pursuit of racial pride. The poet does not flinch from what she sees—does not romanticize or inflate it ("His eyes/Are running/Sores"). Yet her words acknowledge that she knows the ideal African image as others project it: "Beautiful/Like a statue." It is the "Up close" that sets up the tension in the lines between appearance and reality, mystification and the real, and provides Walker's peculiar sound, her insistence on honesty as if there were no other way to be. The lines, then, do not scream at the reader or harp on the distinction between the image and the man she sees. The lines *are* that distinction. They embody the tension, stripping its dimensions down to the essentials. "Karamojans" ends:

The Karamojans
Never civilized
A proud people
I think there
Are
A hundred left.[3]

So much for the concept of pride without question.

At the cutting edge of much of Walker's early work is an intense examination of those ideas advocated by the most visible of recent Afro-American spokespersons. In 1970, at the height of cultural nationalism, the substance of most black literary activity was focused on the rebellious urban black in confrontation with white society. In that year Walker's first novel, *The Third Life of Grange Copeland*, was published. By tracing the history of the Copeland family through three generations, Walker demonstrated the relationship between the racist sharecropping system and the violence that the men, women, and children of that family inflict on each other. The novel is most emphatically located in the rural South, rather than the northern urban ghetto; its characters are southern peasants rather than northern lumpen, reminding us that much of the Afro-American population is still under the yoke of a feudal sharecropping system. And the novel is written more from the angle of the tentative survival of a black family than from an overt confrontation between black and white.

Walker's first novel, like Marshall's *The Chosen Place, the Timeless People* (1969) and Morrison's *The Bluest Eye* (1970), also seemed out of step with the end-of-the-decade work of such writers as Imamu Baraka or Ishmael Reed—black writers on opposing sides of the spectrum—in that the struggle her major characters wage against racism is located in, sometimes veiled by, a network of family and community. The impact of racism is felt primarily through the characters' mistaken definitions of themselves as men and women. Grange Copeland first hates himself because he is powerless, as opposed to powerful, the definition of maleness for him. His reaction is to prove his power by inflicting violence on the women around him. His brief sojourn in the North where he feels invisible, a step below powerlessness, causes him to hate whites as his oppressors. That, however, for Walker, does not precipitate meaningful struggle. It is only when he learns to love himself, through his commitment to his granddaughter Ruth that Grange Copeland is able to confront the white racist system. And in so doing, he must also destroy his son, the fruit of his initial self-hatred.

The Third Life of Grange Copeland, then, is based on the principle that societal change is invariably linked to personal change, that the struggle must be inner as well as outer directed. Walker's insistence on locating the motivation for struggle within the self led her to examine the definition of *nigger*, that oft-used word in the literature of the late sixties. Her definition, however is not generalized but precise: a nigger is a black person who believes he or she is incapable of being responsible for his or her actions, who claims that the white folks are to blame for everything, including his or her behavior. As Grange says to his son Brownfield in their one meaningful exchange in the novel: "'. . . when they get you thinking they're to blame for everything they have you thinking they're some kind of gods. . . . Shit, nobody's as powerful as we make them out to be. We got our own souls, don't we?'"[4]

The question lingering at the end of this novel—whether the psychological impact of oppression is so great that it precludes one's overcoming it—is also a major undercurrent of the literature of this period. There is a tension in the militant literature of the late sixties between a need to *assert* the love of black people for black people and an anger that black people have somehow allowed themselves to be oppressed. The ambivalence caused by a desire for self-love and an expression of shame is seldom clearly articulated in the literature but implied in the militant black writers' exhortations to their people to stop being niggers and start becoming black men and women. What Walker did, in her first novel, was to give voice to this tension and to graph the development of one man in his journey toward its resolution.

Grange Copeland's journey toward this resolution is not, however, an idea that Walker imposes on the novel. A characteristic of hers is an attempt to use the essence of a complex dilemma organically in the composing of her work. So the structure of *The Third Life of Grange Copeland* is based on the dramatic tension between the pervasive racism of the society and the need for her characters to accept responsibility for their own lives if they are to hold on to self-love. The novel is divided into two parts, the first analyzing the degeneration of Grange's and then his son Brownfield's respective families, the second focusing on the regeneration of the Copelands, as Grange, against all odds, takes responsibility for Brownfield's daughter Ruth. Within these two larger pieces, Walker created a quilt of recurring motifs that are arranged, examined, and rearranged so that the reader might understand the complex nature of the tension between the power of oppressive societal forces and the possibility for change. Walker's use of recurring economical patterns, much like a quilting process, gives the novel much of its force and uniqueness. Her insistence on critically examining the ideas of the time led her not only to analysis, but also to a synthesis that increasingly marks her work.

Walker is drawn to the integral and economical process of quilt making as a model for her own craft, for through it, one can create out of seemingly disparate, everyday materials patterns of clarity, imagination, and beauty. Two of her works especially emphasize the idea of this process: her classic essay "In Search of Our Mothers' Gardens" and her short story "Everyday Use." Each piece complements the other and articulates the precise meaning of the quilt as idea and process for this writer.

In "In Search of Our Mothers' Gardens", Walker directly asks the question that every writer must: From whence do I, as a writer, come? What is my tradition? In pursuing the question she focuses most intensely on her female heritage, in itself a point of departure from the route most writers have taken. Walker traces the images of black women in the literature as well as those few who were able to be writers. However, as significant as the tracing of that literary history is, Walker's major insight in the essay is her illumination of the creative legacy of "ordinary" black women of the South, a focus that complements but finally transcends literary history. In her insistence on honesty, on examining the roots of *her own* creativity, she invokes not so much the literature of black women, which was probably unknown to her as a budding child writer, but the creativity of her mother, her grandmother, the women around her.

What did some slave women or black women of this century do with the creativity that might have, in a less restrictive society, expressed itself in paint, words, clay? Walker reflects on a truth so obvious it is seldom acknowledged: They used the few media left them by a society that labeled them lowly, menial. Some, like Walker's mother, expressed it in the growing of magnificent gardens; some in cooking; others in quilts of imagination and passion like the one Walker saw at the Smithsonian Institution. Walker's description of that quilt's impact on her brings together essential elements of her more recent work: the theme of the black woman's creativity, her transformation, despite opposition, of the bits and pieces allowed her by society into a work of functional beauty.

But Walker does not merely acknowledge quilts (or the art black women created out of "low" media) as high art, a tendency now fostered by many women who have discovered the works of their maternal ancestors. She is also impressed by their *functional* beauty and by the process that produced them. Her short story "Everyday Use" is in some ways a conclusion in fiction to her essay. Just as she juxtaposed the history of black women writers with the creative legacy of ordinary black women, so she complemented her own essay, a search for the roots of her own creativity, with a story that embodies the idea itself.

In "Everyday Use," Walker again scrutinized a popular premise of the times. The story, which is dedicated to "your grandmama," is about the use and misuse of the concept of heritage. The mother of two daughters, one selfish and stylish, the other scarred and caring, passes on to us its true definition. Dee, the sister who has always despised the backward ways of her southern rural family, comes back to visit her old home. She has returned to her black roots because now they are fashionable. So she glibly delights in the artifacts of her heritage: the rough benches her father made, the handmade butter churn that she intends to use for a decorative centerpiece, the quilts made by her grandma Dee after whom she was named—the *things* that have been passed on. Ironically, in keeping with the times, Dee has changed her name to Wangero, denying the existence of her namesake, even as she covets the quilts she made.

On the other hand, her sister Maggie is not aware of the word *heritage*. But she loves her grandma and cherishes her memory in the quilts she made. Maggie has accepted the *spirit* that was passed on to her. The contrast between the two sisters is aptly summarized in Dee's focal line in the story: "'Maggie can't appreciate these quilts!' she said. 'She'd probably be backward enough to put them to everyday use.'"[5] Which her mother counters with: " She can always make some more. Maggie knows how to quilt. "[6]

The mother affirms the functional nature of their heritage and insists that it must continually be renewed rather than fixed in the past. The mother's succinct phrasing of the meaning of *heritage* is underscored by Dee's lack of knowledge about the bits and pieces that make up these quilts, the process of quilting that Maggie knows. For Maggie appreciates the people who made them, while Dee can only possess the "priceless" products. Dee's final words, ironically, exemplify her misuse of the concept of heritage, of what is passed on:

"What don't I understand?" I wanted to know.
"Your heritage," she said. And then she turned to Maggie, kissed her and said. "You ought to try to make something of yourself, too, Maggie. It's a new day for us. But from the way you and mama still live you'd never know it."[7]

In critically analyzing the uses of the concept of heritage, Walker arrived at important distinctions. As an abstraction rather than a living idea, its misuse can subordinate people to artifact, can elevate culture above the community. And because she used, as the artifact, quilts that were made by southern black women, she focused attention on those supposedly backward folk who never heard the word heritage but fashioned a functional tradition out of little matter and much spirit.

In "Everyday Use," the mother, seemingly in a fit of contrariness, snatches the beautiful quilts out of the hands of the "black" Wangero and gives them to the "backward" Maggie. This story is one of eleven in Walker's first collection of short stories, *In Love and Trouble*. Though written over a period of some five years, the volume is unified by two of Walker's most persistent characteristics: her use of a southern black woman character as the protagonist, and that character's insistence on challenging convention, on being herself, sometimes in spite of herself.

Walker sets the tone for this volume by introducing the stories with two excerpts, one from *The Concubine*, a novel by the contemporary West African writer Elechi Amadi, the other from *Letters to a Young Poet* by the early twentieth-century German poet Rainer Maria Rilke. The first excerpt emphasizes the rigidity of West African convention in relation to women. Such convention results in a young girl's contrariness, which her society explains away by saying she is unduly influenced by *agwu,* her personal spirit. The second excerpt from Rilke summarizes a philosophy of life that permeates the work of Alice Walker:

People have (with the help of conventions) oriented all their solutions toward the easy and toward the easiest of the easy; but it is clear that we must hold to what is difficult; everything in nature grows and defines itself in its own way, and is characteristically and spontaneously itself, seeks at all costs to be so against all opposition.[8]

The protagonists in this volume embody this philosophy. They seek at all costs to be characteristically and spontaneously themselves. But because the conventions that gravely affect relationships between male and female, black and white, young and old, are so rigid, the heroines of *In Love and Trouble* seem backward, contrary, mad. Depending on their degree of freedom within the society, they express their *agwu* in dream, word, or act.

Roselily, the poor mother of illegitimate children, can express her *agwu* only through dreaming, during her wedding to a northern black Muslim. Though her marriage is seen by most as a triumphant delivery from her poor backward condition, she sees that as a woman, whether single or married, Christian or Muslim, she is confined. She can only dream that "She wants to live for once. But doesn't quite know what that means. Wonders if she ever has done it. If she ever will."[9]

In contrast to Roselily, Myrna, the protagonist of "Really, Doesn't Crime Pay?" is the wife of a middle-class southern black man. Still, she is also trapped by her husband and society's view of woman, though her confinement is not within a black veil but in the decorative mythology of the southern lady. However, unlike Roselily, Myrna does more than dream, she writes. In a series of journal entries, she tells us how the restrictions imposed upon her creativity lead her to attempt to noisily murder her husband, an act certainly perceived by her society as madness.

Most of the young heroines in this volume struggle through dream or word against age-old as well as new manifestations of societal conventions imposed upon them. In contrast, the older women act. Like the mother in "Everyday Use," the old woman in "The Welcome Table" totally ignores convention when she enters the white church from which she is barred. The contrary act of this backward woman challenges all the conventions—"God, mother, country, earth, church. It involved all that and well they knew it."[10]

Again, through juxtaposing the restrictions imposed on her protagonists with their subsequest responses, Walker illuminates the tension as she did in *The Third Life of Grange Copeland* between convention and the struggle to be whole. Only this time, the focus is very much on the unique vortex of restrictions imposed on black women by their community and white society. Her protagonists' dreams, words, acts, often explained away by society as the expressions of a contrary nature, a troubled *agwu*, are the price all beings, against opposition, would pay to be spontaneously and characteristically themselves. In *In Love and Trouble*, Walker emphasized the impact of sexism as well as racism on black communities. Her insistence on honesty, on the validity of her own experience as well as the experience of other southern black women, ran counter to the popular notion of the early seventies that racism was the only evil that affected black women. Her first collection of short stories specifically demonstrated the interconnectedness of American sexism and racism, for they are both based on the notion of dominance and on unnatural hierarchical distinctions.

Walker does not choose southern black women to be her major protagonists only because she is one, but also, I believe, because she has discovered in the tradition and history they collectively experience an understanding of oppression that has elicited from them a willingness to reject convention and to hold to what is difficult. Meridian, her most developed character, is a person who allows "an idea—no matter where it came from—to penetrate her life." The idea that penetrates Meridian's life, the idea of nonviolent resistance, is really rooted in a question: When is it necessary, when is it right, to kill? And the intensity with which Meridian pursues that question is due to her view of herself as a mother, a creator rather than a destroyer of life. The source where she goes for the answer to that question is her people, especially the heritage that has been passed on to her by her maternal ancestors. She is thrilled by the fact that black women were "always imitating Harriet Tubman escaping to become something unheard of. Outrageous." And that "even in more conventional things black women struck out for the unknown."[11] Like Walker in "In Search of Our Mothers' Gardens", Meridian seeks her identity through the legacy passed on to her by southern black women.

Yet Walker did not rest easy even with this idea, an idea that glorifies the black woman. For in *Meridian* she scrutinized that tradition that is based on the monumental myth of black motherhood, a myth based on the true stories of sacrifice black mothers performed for their children. But the myth is also restrictive, for it imposes a stereotype of black women, a stereotype of strength that denies them choice and hardly admits the many who were destroyed. In her characterization of Margaret and Mem Copeland in *The Third Life of Grange Copeland*, Walker acknowledged the abused black women who, unlike Faulkner's Dilsey, did not endure. She went a step further in *Meridian*. Meridian's quest for wholeness and her involvement in the Civil Rights Movement is initiated by her feelings of inadequacy in living up to the standards of black motherhood. Meridian gives up her son because she believes she will poison his growth with the thorns of guilt, and she has her tubes tied after a painful abortion. In this novel, then, Walker probed the idea of black motherhood, as she developed a character who so elevates it that she at first believes she can not properly fulfill it. Again, Walker approaches the forbidden as a possible route to another truth.

Not only did Walker challenge the monument of black motherhood in *Meridian*, she also entered the fray about the efficacy of motherhood in which American feminists were then, as they are now, engaged. As many radical feminists blamed motherhood for the waste in women's lives and saw it as a dead end for a woman, Walker insisted on a deeper analysis: She did not present motherhood in itself as restrictive. It is so because of the little value society places on children, especially black children, on mothers, especially black mothers, on life itself. In the novel, Walker acknowledged that a mother in this society is often "buried alive, walled away from her own life, brick by brick."[12] Yet the novel is based on Meridian's insistence on the sacredness of life. Throughout her quest she is surrounded by children whose lives she tries to preserve. In seeking the children she can no longer have, she takes responsibility for the lives of all the people. Her aborted motherhood yields to her a perspective on life—that of "expanding her mind with action." In keeping with this principle, Walker tells us in her essay "One Child of One's Own":

> It is not my child who has purged my face from history and herstory and left mystory just that, a mystery; my child loves my face and would have it on every page, if she could, as I have loved my own parents' faces above all others, and refused to let them be denied, or myself to let them go.[13]

In fact, *Meridian* is based on this idea, the sacredness and continuity of life—and on another, that it might be necessary to take life in order to preserve it and make it possible for future generations. Perhaps the most difficult paradox that Walker has examined to date is the relationship between violence and revolution, a relationship that so many take for granted that such scrutiny seems outlandish. Like her heroine, Meridian, who holds on to the idea of nonviolent resistance after it has been discarded as a viable means to change, Walker persists in struggling with this age-old dilemma—that of death giving life. What the novel *Meridian* suggests is that unless such a struggle is taken on by those who would change society, their revolution will not be integral, for they may destroy that which they abhor only to resurrect it in themselves. Meridian discovers only through personal struggle in conjunction with her involvement with the everyday lives of her people that the respect she owed her life was to continue, against whatever obstacles, to live it, and not to give up any particle of it without a fight to the death, preferably not her own. And that this existence extended beyond herself to those around her because, in fact, the years in America had created them One Life.[14]

But though the concept of One Life motivates Meridian in her quest toward physical and spiritual health, the societal evils that subordinate one class to another, one race to another, one sex to another, fragment and ultimately threaten life. The novel *Meridian*, like *The Third Life of Grange Copeland*, is built on the tension between the African concept of animism, "that spirit inhabits all life," and the societal forces that inhibit the growth of the living toward their natural state of freedom.

Because of her analysis of sexism in the novel as well as in *In Love and Trouble*, Walker is often labeled a feminist writer. Yet she also challenges this definition as it is formulated by most white American feminists. In "One Child of One's Own" (1978), Walker insisted on the twin "afflictions" of her life: that white feminists as well as some black people deny the black woman her womanhood—that they define issues in terms of blacks on one hand or women (meaning white women) on the other. They miss the obvious fact—that black people come in both sexes. Walker put it strongly:

> It occurred to me that perhaps white women feminists, no less than white women generally, cannot imagine that black women have vaginas. Or if they can, where imagination leads them is too far to go.
>
> Perhaps it is the black woman's children, whom the white woman—having more to offer her own children, and certainly not having to offer them slavery or a slave heritage or poverty or hatred, generally speaking: segregated schools, slum neighborhoods, the worst of everything—resents. For they must always make her feel guilty. She fears knowing that black women want the best for their children just as she does. But she also knows black children are to have less in this world so that her children, white children, will have more. (In some countries all.)
>
> Better than to deny that the black woman has a vagina. Is capable of motherhood. Is a woman.[15]

And Walker *also* writes of the unwillingness of many black women to acknowledge or address the problems of sexism that affect them because they feel they must protect black men. She asserts that if black women turn away from the women's movement, they turn away from women moving all over the world, not just in America. They betray their own tradition, which includes women such as Sojourner Truth and Ida B. Wells, and abandon their responsibility to their own people as well as to women everywhere.

In refusing to elevate sex above race, by insisting on the black woman's responsibility to herself and to other women of color, Walker aligns herself neither with prevailing white feminist groups nor with blacks who

,e to acknowledge male dominance in the world. Because her analysis ٍs not yield to easy generalizations and nicely packaged clichés, she continues to resist the trends of the times without discarding the truths upon which they are based.

Walker's second collection of short stories, *You Can't Keep a Good Woman Down* (1981), delves even more emphatically into the "twin afflictions" of black women's lives. Like *In Love and Trouble*, this book probes the extent to which black women have the freedom to pursue their selfhood within the confines of a sexist and racist society. However, these two collections, published eight years apart, demonstrate a clear progression of theme. While the protagonists of *In Love and Trouble* wage their struggle in spite of themselves, the heroines of *You Can't Keep a Good Woman Down* consciously insist upon their right to challenge any societal chains that bind them. The titles of the two collections succinctly indicate the shift in tone, the first emphasizing trouble, the second the self-assertiveness of the black woman so bodaciously celebrated in the blues tradition. The name of a famous blues song, "You Can't Keep a Good Woman Down," is dedicated to those who "*insist* on the value and beauty of the authentic."[16] Walker's intention in this volume is clearly a celebration of the black woman's insistence on living. From whence does this insistence come, Walker asks. How does it fare in these contemporary times.

The stories in this collection are blatantly topical in their subject matter, as Walker focuses on societal attitudes and mores that women have challenged in the last decade—pornography and male sexual fantasies in "Porn," and "Coming Apart," abortion in "The Abortion," sadomasochism in "A Letter of the Times," interracial rape in "Advancing Luna—and Ida B. Wells." And the forms Walker invents to illuminate these issues are as unconventional as her subject matter. Many of the stories are process rather than product. Feminist thinkers of the seventies asserted a link between process (the unraveling of thought and feeling) and the way women have perceived the world. In keeping with this theory, Walker often gives us the story as it comes into being, rather than delivering the product, classic and clean. In doing so, Walker not only breaks the rules by writing about "womanist" issues (Walker defines a womanist as a "black feminist"), she also employs a womanist process. For many of these stories reflect the present, when the process of confusion, resistance to the established order, and the discovery of a freeing order is, especially for women, a prerequisite for growth.

Such a story is "Advancing Luna—and Ida B. Wells," in which a young southern black woman's development is reflected through her growing understanding of the complexity of interracial rape. At the beginning of the story, practically everything she tells us is tinged with an air of taking things for granted. She lightly assumes that black people are superior. This generalization, however, is tested when Luna, a white friend of hers, tells her that during the "movement" she was raped by a black man they both know. Our narrator naturally is opposed to rape; yet she had not believed black men actually raped white women. And she knows what happens if a black man is even accused of such an act. Her earlier sense of clarity is shattered. Doubts, questions, push her to unravel her own feelings: "Who knows what the black woman thinks of rape? Who has asked her? Who *cares?*"[17]

Again Walker writes about a forbidden topic, and again she resists an easy solution. For although she speaks from the point of view of sisterhood with all women, she also insists, as she did in "One Child of One's Own," that all women must understand that sexism and racism in America are critically related. Like all her previous fiction, this blatantly contemporary story is rooted in and illuminated by history, in this instance the work of the great antilynching crusader Ida B. Wells. The dialogue between our narrator and this nineteenth-century black womanist focuses on the convoluted connection between rape and lynchings, sex and race, that continues to this day. As a result, "Advancing Luna" cannot end conclusively. There are two endings, Afterthoughts, Discarded Notes, and a Postscript as the narrator and writer mesh. Walker shows us her writing process, which cannot be neatly resolved, since the questions she posed cannot be satisfactorily answered. The many endings prod the reader, insisting on the complexity of the issue and the characters.

> Dear God,
> Me and Sophie work on the quilt. Got it frame up on the porch. Shug Avery donate her old yellow dress for scrap, and I work in a piece every chance I get. It's a nice pattern call Sister's Choice.[18]

The form of *The Color Purple* (1982), Walker's most recent novel, is a further development in the womanist process she is evolving. The entire novel is written in a series of letters. Along with diaries, letters were the dominant mode of expression allowed women in the West. Feminist historians find letters to be a principal source of information and facts about the everyday lives of women and their own perceptions about their lives, a source of both "objective" and "subjective" information. In using the epistolary style, Walker is able to have her major character, Celie, express the impact of oppression on her spirit as well as her growing internal strength and final victory.

Like Walker's other two novels, this work spans generations of one poor rural southern black family, interweaving the personal with the flow of history. Like her essays and fiction, the image of quilting is central to its concept and form. But in *The Color Purple*, the emphases are on the oppression black women experience in their relationships with black men (father, brother, husbands, lovers) and the sisterhood they must share with each other in order to liberate themselves. As an image for these themes, two sisters, Celie and Nettie, are the novel's focal characters. Their letters, Celie's to God, Nettie's to Celie, and finally Celie's to Nettie, are the novel's form.

Again, Walker approaches the forbidden in content as well as form. Just as the novel's form is radical, so are its themes, for she focuses on incest in a black family and portrays a black lesbian relationship as natural and freeing. The novel begins with Celie, a fourteen-year-old who is sexually abused by her presumed father and who manages to save her sister Nettie from the same fate. Celie is so cut off from everyone and her experience is so horrifying, even to herself, that she can only write it in letters to God. Her letters take us through her awful pregnancies, her children being taken away from her, and the abuses of a loveless marriage. She liberates herself—that is, she comes to value herself—through the sensuous love bond she shares with Shug, her husband's mistress, her appreciation of her sister-in-law Sophie's resistant spirit, and the letters from her sister Nettie, which her husband had hidden from her for many years. We feel Celie's transformation intensely, since she tells her story in her own rural idiomatic language, a discrete black speech. Few writers since Zora Neale Hurston have so successfully expressed the essence of the folk's speech as Walker does in *The Color Purple*.

In contrast to Celie's letters, Nettie's letters to Celie from Africa, where she is a missionary, are written in standard English. These letters not only provide a contrast in style, they expand the novel's scope. The comparison-contrast between male-female relationships in Africa and the black South suggest that sexism for black women in America does not derive from racism, though it is qualitatively affected by it. And Nettie's community of missionaries graphically demonstrates Afro-Americans' knowledge of their ancestral link to Africa, which, contrary to American myth, predates the Black Power Movement of the 1960s.

Though different in form and language, *The Color Purple* is inextricably linked to Walker's previous works. In *In Search of Our Mothers' Gardens*, Walker speaks about three types of black women: the physically and psychologically abused black women (Mem and Margaret Copeland in *The Third Life of Grange Copeland*), the black women who is torn by contrary instincts (Meridian in her youth and college years), and the new black woman, who recreates herself out of the creative legacy of her maternal ancestors. Meridian begins that journey of transformation. But it is Celie, even more than her predecessor, who completes Walker's cycle. For Celie is a "Mem" who survives and liberates herself through her sisters' strength and wisdom, qualities that like the color purple, are derived from nature. To be free is the natural state of the living. And Celie's attainment of freedom affects not only her sisters, but her brothers as well.

Both Walker's prose and her poetry probe the continuum between the inner self and the outer world. Her volumes of poetry, like her fiction and essays, focus on the self as part of a community of changers, whether it is the Civil Rights Movement in *Once*, the struggle toward liberation in *Revolutionary Petunias*, or the community of women who would be free in *Good Night Willie Lee*. Yet her poems are distinguished from her prose in that they are a graph of the self that is specifically Alice Walker. Perhaps even more than her prose, they are rooted in her desire to resist the easiest of the easy. In her poetry, Walker, the wayward child, challenges not only the world but herself. And in exposing herself, she challenges us to accept her as she is. Perhaps it is the stripping of bark from herself that enables us to feel that sound of the genuine in her scrutiny of easy positions advocated by progressive blacks or women.

Her first volume, *Once*, includes a section, "Mornings/ of an Impossible Love," in which Walker scrutinizes herself not through her reflections on the outer world, as she does in the other sections, but through self-exposure. In the poem "Johann," Walker expresses feelings forbidden by the world of the 1960s.[19]

In "So We've Come at Last to Freud," she arrogantly insists on the validity of her own emotions as opposed to prescriptives:

Don't label my love with slogans;
My father can't be blamed
                    for my affection

Or lack of it.
Ask him
He won't understand you.[20]

She resists her own attempt at self-pity in "Suicide":

Thirdly if it is the thought
of rest that
fascinates
laziness should be admitted
in the clearest terms[21]

Yet in "The Ballad of the Brown Girl," she acknowledges the pain of loss, the anguish of a forbidden love.[22]

As these excerpts show, Walker refuses to embellish or camouflage her emotions with erudite metaphor or phrase. Instead she communicates them through her emphasis on single-word lines, her selection of the essential word, not only for content but for cadence. The result is a graceful directness that is not easily arrived at.

The overriding theme of *Once*, its feel of unwavering honesty in evoking the forbidden, either in political stances or in love, persists in *Revolutionary Petunias*. Walker, however, expands from the almost quixotic texture of her first volume to philosophical though intensely personal probings in her second. *Revolutionary Petunias* examines the relationship between the nature of love and that of revolution. In these poems she celebrates the openness to the genuine in people, an essential quality, for her, in those who would be revolutionaries. And she castigates the false conventions constructed by many so-called revolutionaries. As a result, those who are committed to more life rather than less are often outcasts and seem to walk forbidden paths.

The volume is arranged in five sections, each one evoking a particular stage in the movement forward. In the first section, "In These Dissenting Times," Walker asserts that while many label their ancestors as backward, true revolutionaries understand that the common folk who precede them are the source of their strength. She reminds us that we "are not the first to suffer, rebel, fight, love and die. The grace with which we embrace life, in spite of the pain, the sorrows, is always a measure of what has gone before."[23]

The second section, "Revolutionary Petunias, The Living Through," is about those who know that the need for beauty is essential to a desire for revolution, that the most rebellious of folk are those who feel so intensely the potential beauty of life that they would struggle to that end without ceasing. Yet because the narrow-minded scream that "poems of/ love and flowers are/ a luxury the Revolution/ cannot afford," those so human as to be committed to beauty and love are often seen as "incorrect." Walker warns that in living through the contradictions of revolutionary struggle one must "Expect nothing/ Live frugally on surprise . . . wish for nothing larger/ than your own small heart/ Or greater than a star."[24] And in words that reverberate throughout her works, she exposes herself as one who must question, feel, pursue the mysteries of life. The title of the poem "Reassurance" affirms for us her need to sustain herself in her persistent questionings.

I must love the questions
themselves
as Rilke said
like locked rooms
full of treasure
to which my blind
and groping key
does not yet fit.[25]

Flowing out of the second section, the third, "Crucifixion," further underscores the sufferings of those who would see the urge to revolution as emanating from a love for people rather than empty proscriptive forms. In it the ideologues drive out the lovers, "forcing . . . the very sun/to mangled perfection/for your cause."[26] And many, like the "girl who would not lie; and was not born 'correct,'" or those who "wove a life/of stunning contradiction" are driven mad or die.[27]

Yet some endured. The fourth section, "Mysteries . . . the Living Beyond," affirms the eventual triumph of those who would change the world because:

. . . the purpose of being
here, wherever we are, is to increase
the durability and the occasions of
love among and between peoples.[28]
                                    June Jordan

Love poems dominate this section, though always there is Walker's resistance to preordained form:

In me there is a rage to defy
the order of the stars
despite their pretty patterns[29]

And in "New Face," Walker combines the philosophical urge to penetrate the mysteries of life with the personal renewal which for her is love. From this renewal comes her energy to dig deeper, push further.[30]

A single poem, "The Nature of This Flower Is to Bloom," is the last movement in this five-part collection, as Walker combines through capitalized short phrases ("Rebellious. Living/Against the Elemental crush")[31] the major elements of *Revolutionary Petunias*. In choosing a flower as the symbol for revolution, she suggests that beauty, love, and revolution exist in a necessary relationship. And in selecting the petunia as the specific flower, she emphasizes the qualities of color, exuberance, and commonness rather than blandness, rigidity, or delicacy.

In completing the volume with this succinct and graceful poem, Walker also reiterates her own stylistic tendencies. Most of her poems are so cohesive they can hardly be divided into parts. I have found it almost impossible to separate out a few lines from any of her poems without quoting them fully, so seamless are they in construction. This quality is even more pronounced in her most recent volume of poetry, *Good Night Willie Lee, I'll See You in the Morning*. As in Walker's collections, though there are a few long poems, most are compact. In general, the voice in her poem is so finely distilled that each line, each word is so necessary it cannot be omitted, replaced, or separated out.

Like *Revolutionary Petunias, Good Night Willie Lee* is concerned with the relationship between love and change, only now the emphasis is even more on personal change, on change in the nature of relationships between women and men. This volume is very much about the demystification of love itself; yet it is also about the past, especially the pain left over from the "Crucifixion" of *Revolutionary Petunias.*

Good Night Willie Lee is a five-part journey from night into morning, the name of each movement being an indication of the route this writer takes in her urge to understand love, without its illusions or veils. In the first movement, "Confession," Walker focuses on a love that declines into suffering. In letting go of it, she must go through the process of "stripping bark from herself" and must go deeper to an understanding of her past in "Early Losses, a Requiem." Having finally let the past rest in peace, she can then move to "Facing the Way," and finally to a "Forgiveness" that frees her.

The first poem of "Confession" is entitled "Did This Happen to Your Mother? Did Your Sister Throw Up a Lot?," while the last poem of this section ends "Other/ women have already done this/ sort of suffering for you/ or so I thought."[32] Between these two points, Walker confesses that "I Love a man who is not worth/ my love" and that "Love has made me sick."[33] She sees that her lover is afraid "he may fail me . . . it is this fear/ that now devours/ desire."[34] She is astute enough to understand that this fear of love caused him to hold "his soul/ so tightly/ it shrank/ to fit his hand."[35] In tracing the decline of love she understands the pull of pain: "At first I did not fight it/ I *loved* the suffering/ It was being alive!" "I savored my grief like chilled wine."[36]

From this immersion in self-pity, she is saved by a woman, a friend who reminds her that other women have already done this for her and brings her back to herself. The steps of this first movement are particularly instructive for the rest of this volume, since Walker does not pretend, as so much feminist poetry does, that she is above passion or the need or the desire for sharing love with a man. What she does is to communicate the peaks and pitfalls of such an experience, pointing always to the absolute necessity for self-love. Only through self-love can the self who can love be preserved. And for Walker, self-love comes from "Stripping Bark from Myself." In one of the finest poems of this volume, Walker chants her song of independence. Her wayward lines are a response to a worldwide challenge:

> because women are expected to keep silent
> about their close escapes I will not keep silent
>
>   . . .
>
> No I am finished with living
> for what my mother believes
> for what my brother and father defend

for what my lover elevates
for what my sister, blushing, denies or rushes
to embrace

for she has discovered some part of her self:

Besides
my struggle was always against
an inner darkness: I carry within myself
the only known keys
to my death . . . .

So she is

. . . happy to fight
all outside murderers
as I see I must[37]

Such stripping of bark from herself enables her to face the way, to ask questions about her own commitment to revolution, whether she can give up the comforts of life especially "the art that transcends time," "whose sale would patch a roof/ heat the cold rooms of children, replace an eye/ feed a life."[38] And it is the stripping of bark from herself that helps her to understand that:

the healing
of all our wounds
is forgiveness
that permits a promise
of our return
at the end.[39]

It is telling, I believe, that Walker's discovery of the healing power of forgiveness comes from her mother's last greeting to her father at his burial. In this volume so permeated by the relationship of woman to man, her mother heads the list of a long line of women—some writers, like Zora Neale Hurston, others personal friends of Alice Walker—who pass unto her the knowledge they have garnered on the essence of love. Such knowledge helps Walker to demystify love and enables her to write about the tension between the giving of herself and the desire to remain herself.

In her dedication to the volume she edited of Zora Neale Hurston's work, Walker says of her literary ancestor: "Implicit in Hurston's determination to 'make it' in a career was her need to express 'the folk' and herself. Someone who knew her has said: 'Zora would have been Zora even if she'd been an Eskimo.' That is what it means to be yourself; it is surely what it means to be an artist."[40] These words, it seems to me, apply as well to Alice Walker.

NOTES

1. Alice Walker, "On Stripping Bark from Myself," *Good Night Willie Lee, I'll See You in the Morning* (New York: Dial, 1979), p. 23.
2. Alice Walker, "Karamojans," *Once* (New York: Harcourt Brace Jovanovich, 1978), p. 20.
3. Ibid., p. 22.
4. Alice Walker, *The Third Life of Grange Copeland* (New York: Harcourt Brace Jovanovich, 1970), p. 207.
5. Alice Walker, "Everyday Use," *In Love and Trouble* (New York: Harcourt Brace Jovanovich, 1973), p. 57.
6. Ibid., p. 58.
7. Ibid., p. 59.
8. Walker, *In Love and Trouble*, epigraph.
9. Walker, "Roselily," *In Love and Trouble*, p. 8.
10. Walker, "The Welcome Table," *In Love and Trouble*, p. 84.
11. Alice Walker, *Meridian* (New York: Harcourt Brace Jovanovich, 1976), pp. 105-6.
12. Ibid., p. 41.
13. Alice Walker, "One Child of One's Own: A Meaningful Digression Within the Work(s)," *The Writer on Her Work*, ed., Janet Sternburg (New York: W. W. Norton, 1980), p. 139.
14. Walker, *Meridian*, p. 204.
15. Walker, "One Child of One's Own," pp. 131-32.
16. Alice Walker, *You Can't Keep a Good Woman Down* (New York: Harcourt Brace Jovanovich, 1981), dedication.
17. Ibid., p. 71.
18. Alice Walker, *The Color Purple* (New York: Harcourt Brace Jovanovich, 1982), p. 53.
19. Walker, *Once*, p. 65.
20. Ibid., p. 61.
21. Ibid., p. 74.
22. Ibid., p. 73.
23. Alice Walker, "Fundamental Difference," *Revolutionary Petunias* (New York: Harcourt Brace Jovanovich, 1973), p. 1.
24. Walker, "Expect Nothing," *Revolutionary Petunias*, p. 30.
25. Walker, "Reassurance," *Revolutionary Petunias*, p. 33.
26. Walker, "Lonely Particular," *Revolutionary Petunias*, p. 40.
27. Walker, "The Girl Who Died #2," *Revolutionary Petunias*, pp. 45-46.
28. Walker, "Mysteries" (June Jordan), *Revolutionary Petunias*, p. 51.
29. Walker, "Rage," *Revolutionary Petunias*, p. 61.
30. Walker, "New Face," *Revolutionary Petunias*, p. 66.
31. Walker, "The Nature of This Flower Is to Bloom," *Revolutionary Petunias*, p. 70.
32. Walker, "At First," *Good Night Willie Lee, I'll See You in the Morning*, p. 15.

33. Walker, "Did This Happen to Your Mother? Did Your Sister Throw Up a Lot?" *Good Night Willie Lee, I'll See You in the Morning,* p. 2.

34. Walker, "Threatened," *Good Night Willie Lee, I'll See You in the Morning,* p. 8.

35. Walker, "Gift," *Good Night Willie Lee, I'll See You in the Morning,* p. 5.

36. Walker, "At First," *Good Night Willie Lee, I'll See You in the Morning,* p. 15.

37. Walker, "On Stripping Bark from Myself," *Good Night Willie Lee, I'll See You in the Morning,* pp. 23-24.

38. Walker, "Facing the Way," *Good Night Willie Lee, I'll See You in the Morning,* pp. 44-45.

39. Walker, "Good Night Willie Lee, I'll See You in the Morning," *Good Night Willie Lee, I'll See You in the Morning,* p. 53.

40. Alice Walker, ed., *I Love Myself: A Zora Neale Hurston Reader.* . . ., Old Westbury, NY: Feminist Press, 1979, p. 3.

7 Paule Marshall: A Literary Biography* (1982)

I wrote an extensive analysis of Paule Marshall's first two novels in Black Women Novelists, *for her work ushered in a new period of female characters in Afro-American Literature. At that time there was little information that I could find about either her life or her works.* Trudier Harris's *and* Thadius Davis's *Dictionary of Literary Biography, for which this essay was written, goes a long way toward providing information and analysis to scholars and readers about major Afro-American writers of the twentieth century.*

The writing of this essay gave me insight as to how some knowledge of a writer's life can help us understand her work. According to some literary scholars the "text" is a sacred enclosed entity; to others, the author is dead. Frankly, I take help from wherever I can find it. Those of us who study Afro-American writers have scarcely had the chance to dilute or mar our literature by using the writer's life as a guide, or even to overestimate the importance of the writer as an individual in relation to society. Few of our writers have had book-length biographies devoted to them.

In building a literary tradition, we learn much, not only about the individual writer, but about the creative process itself by having a sense of how a writer comes to be the writer she is. Also, by seeing how the writer's life and work are related, one can see her entire opus as a developing piece rather than seeing each book as a separate achievement. In this essay, I was able to look at Marshall's novella and her short stories, as well as her novels, as a part of a whole.

Paule Marshall's first novel, *Browngirl, Brownstones,* established her as a relentless analyst of character within the context of a specific culture. Published in 1959, it issued in a new period of female characters in Afro-American literature, for it merged together qualities of earlier black women's fiction with major elements of black women's novels that were to emerge in the 1970s. *Browngirl, Brownstones* focuses on the

*An amended version of this essay was published in Thadius Davis, Trudier Harris, eds., *Dictionary of Literary Biography*, University of North Carolina Press, 1984.

development of an intelligent. complex Afro-American woman, as does Zora Neale Hurston's lyrical novel *Their Eyes Were Watching God* (1936) and Gwendolyn Brooks's exquisite novella, *Maud Martha* (1953). These three works present a black woman's search for personhood within the context of a specific black community rather than in reaction to a hostile white society. As such, they acknowledge the existence of a rich black culture. In search of themselves, their heroines both affirm and challenge their communities' definition of woman. Paule Marshall, however, extends the analysis of black female characters that Hurston and Brooks had begun by portraying the development of her heroine, Selina Boyce, in terms of the relationship between her mother, Silla, and her father, Deighton, as it is affected by the definitions of male and female of their Barbadian-American immigrant culture, which in turn is influenced by the hostile materialistic world of white America. Character and culture are so interrelated in Marshall that her literary work approaches that of sculpture, as space and form, lines of collective history and the individual person, are continually intersecting.

Marshall's *Browngirl, Brownstones* is also similar to Hurston's *Their Eyes* and Brooks's *Maud Martha* in that these three novels seem to be literary anomalies, not at all in tune with the published works of their respective periods. As a result, they might seem to be brilliant personal *tour de forces*, but they are scarcely indications of the reality of their times. Yet when one looks at the entire tradition of black women's novels, these three novels, especially, indicate points at which a leap was made, points at which the personhood of the black woman somehow surfaced despite the deeply etched stereotypes that were maintained by a racist society. *Browngirl, Brownstones* was published when the works of James Baldwin and Ralph Ellison (which focused primarily on the black man's search for his own manhood in the hostile world of a white America) were predominant, and just as that emphasis was giving way to the blatantly socio-political literature of the 1960s in which psychological penetration of character was subordinated to attacks on the white establishment. Marshall's first novel seemed to bear little relationship to the black literature that immediately preceded and followed it. Yet, it shared certain elements of Baldwin's psychological probings of the 1950s and LeRoi Jones's early political poetry of the 1960s, since Marshall dramatized the idea that racism is insidious not only in its impact on a person's definition of self as black or white, but also as male and female. And in paying such close attention to the portrayal of black female and male characters within the context of their own culture, Marshall attacked head on sexual/racial stereotypes, from the mammies and Uncle Tom's of the early twentieth century, the Amos n' Andies and Sapphires of the 1940s, to Moynihan's black matriarchs and weak black boys of the 1950s. Because of the novel's insistence on the relationship of woman as self and as part of a community, it prefigured the major themes of black women's fiction in the 1970s: the black woman's potential as a full person and necessarily a major actor on the social, cultural, and political issues of our times.

Who is Paule Marshall? How is it that she wrote such a singular novel in 1959, a novel that clearly prefigures black female literature of the 1970s? Certainly *her* context might help to answer that finally unanswerable question. A first generation Barbadian-American, she grew up in the context of a culture with firm roots in the Caribbean, which was trying in the 1930s to adjust to a new American setting. The people of her natal community knew they had a culture, precisely because it was foreign to the one in which they found themselves. Barbadian culture still held sway even as the newly arrived immigrants experienced a materialistic and racist America. Precisely because of the interaction between Barbadian and American culture in her community, Marshall developed, at an impressionable age, a sense of ritual, of shapes and forms of culture. Within that interaction, along with other elements of the culture, the definitions of male and female were affected.

A conspicuous element of Caribbean culture is its emphasis on the art of the verbal. In Marshall's essay, "Shaping the World of My Art," as well as Alexis de Veaux's interview with her in *Essence*, she talks about how she was influenced by the Barbadian women she knew as a child. Though not educated in a formal way, they were "talking women," who used language as an art and for whom that art was an integral part of life. Like Silla and her friends in *Browngirl, Brownstones*, these women gathered ritualistically around the kitchen table invoking images, creating character, dissecting life with words. Marshall comments on their impact on her:

> I was always so intimidated as a little girl by the awesome verbal powers of these women. That might be one of the reasons I started writing. To see if, on paper, I couldn't have some of that power.[1]

Browngirl, Brownstones abounds with such verbal power, as when Silla succinctly characterizes her husband, Deighton, as "one man [who] don know his own mind. He's always looking for something big and praying hard not to find it."[2]

Because of their desire to improve themselves, the main reason they left Barbados, most of these "talking women" worked outside their homes, often "cleaning house" in order to "buy house." Marshall recalls that they "transformed humiliating experiences into creative ones." Their dual experience of a feudal existence in Barbados coupled with the racism they found in America made politics central to their lives, a motif that is an undercurrent in *Browngirl, Brownstones*. Their lives as they knew it ran counter to the norm of woman upheld in America, for these Barbadian-American women could neither be passive nor cuddled creatures. But neither were they powerful matriarchs, since their community was assaulted by the forces of racism, discrimination against "aliens," and poverty. And to a large extent they desired the norm even as they had little access to it. What Marshall so deftly sculpts in *Browngirl, Brownstones* is the complexity of the kind of women she knew in her childhood. In the finely drawn character Silla Boyce, she portrays the relationship between these women's sense of their own power and their vulnerability, striking an unforgettable blow at the stereotype of the black matriarch by creating a unique human being as she moves within the space of her own context.

In her first novel, Marshall not only cracks the stereotype of the black matriarch, through her portrayal of Deighton Boyce she also penetrates the worn image of the ne'er-do-well black man. In showing the conflict between the concept of power, as it is defined for males in America, and Deighton's imaginative personality, she questions the values of the immigrant Barbadian-American community, so afraid of poverty that it takes on exclusively the material values of America. For Deighton, life is more than acquiring things; he would have to sacrifice so much of himself to succeed in America that he would no longer exist. Yet he also desires the norm of manhood that America upholds, for there is no other accepted definition of manhood even within his own community. He is caught, as Silla is, by the definitions of male and female that the dominant society insists upon. As recently arrived "Americans," with a black culture that is hardly acknowledged, neither of them is able to be themselves or fulfill themselves for each other.

But the novel is not Silla's or Deighton's. It is primarily about their daughter Selina, who, in sorting out the complexity of her mother and father takes an essential step toward understanding herself in terms of her culture as well as the wider society with which she must contend. However, although this novel is very much about the development of a brown girl into a woman, Marshall insists that at the core of every culture is the relationship between woman and man, and that societal definitions of what is male and female help to create or destroy the self as it situates itself in the world.

Paule Marshall completed *Browngirl, Brownstones* at the age of 30 after she finished college at Hunter College, married her first husband, and while she was working at a small black magazine called *Our World*. Her difficulty in finding work on a magazine staff was indicative of the times, when educated black women were expected to be either teachers or social workers, and when even black magazines were not hiring women. She was the only woman on the staff of *Our World* and felt, she later said, as if "the men were waiting for her to fall."[3] Though she worked on *Browngirl, Brownstones* after a day's work, she initially had no intention of becoming a writer. Worn out by the superficiality of magazine writing, she poured out *Browngirl, Brownstones* in what she calls her most exhilarating writing experience. Yet her account of her movement into fiction writing gives us insight as to why more black women novelists did not emerge in the 1950s. Typecast as social workers or teachers if they were educated, domestics and black matriarchs if they were not, it is not surprising that they seldom thought of themselves as writers, regardless of their inclinations or talents.

Despite fine reviews, *Browngirl, Brownstones* was a commercial failure—a commentary, as well, on the times. Marshall's subject matter, the development of a brown girl into a woman within the rituals and mores of a black cultural context, had yet to be seen as important. When I first encountered *Browngirl, Brownstones*, it was being used as a book for juveniles, just as Toni Morrison's *The Bluest Eye* later would be, despite their complex language and psychology. Many books for juveniles, are, of course, finely crafted. But the misrepresentation of both these books seemed to do with an inability on the part of publishing houses, journals, the literary establishment, to see the *Bildungsroman* of a black woman as having as much human and literary value as, say, D.H. Lawrence's *Sons and Lovers* or James Joyce's *Portrait of the Artist as a Young Man.*

The publication of *Browngirl, Brownstones* was important not only to the tradition of black women novels, it was also Paule Marshall's initiation into writing as a vocation. It is important, then, as the first published work of a significant Afro-American novelist. Writing it changed Marshall's life, for after its publication, she saw herself as *having to be* a writer of fiction, whether or not she was commercially successful. And as she has often commented, in writing *Browngirl, Brownstones*, she was learning how to write, was figuring out for herself her own personal mode of expression. The creation of character within the space of a physical and cultural context, a technique that relates individual personal development to a collective history, was the distinguishing characteristic of *Browngirl, Brownstones*, a technique Marshall explores even further in her next work, *Soul, Clap Hands and Sing* (1961).

This work is not a novel *per se*, but a collection of novellas, entitled "Barbados," "Brooklyn," "British Guiana," and "Brazil." The titles of the individual pieces immediately indicate how critical physical, cultural, and historical context is to Marshall. As significant is Marshall's juxtaposition of these various contexts, suggesting a relationship among them which she is exploring and shaping into a greater whole. In this collection, she emphasizes the African presence in the "New World," from the urban North and rural South of the U.S. through rural Barbados in the Caribbean to the British Colony of Guiana on the mainland of South America and finally to Rio de Janeiro, an urban center in South America. Though the historical and cultural context of these different places are dissimilar, black people are focal. And though they mix and mingle with other peoples—the British, American Jews, Chinese, Portuguese, Germans—and produce new cultural amalgams, their past and present are finally rooted in the culture of Africa and their common experience of enslavement and colonization. *Soul, Clap Hands and Sing* moves from the primarily American environment of *Browngirl, Brownstones* to a more Caribbean and simultaneously a more international perspective. From this point in her work, the Caribbean would increasingly become for Marshall the landscape she would explore as a more manageable yet a more inclusive context than North America.

Yet even as Marshall explores distinguishing characteristics of specific cultural contexts in *Soul, Clap Hands and Sing*, she reiterates the commonality between all of them. This collection of four novellas is focused on a common theme, as its title suggests. Taken from Yeats's famous poem, "Sailing to Byzantium," Marshall's title is a signal to the reader that her collection of novellas, like Yeats's poem, is based on the eternal intrinsic quality of spiritual values, as opposed to transient material ones, an idea that becomes increasingly compelling when the beauty of flesh falls away and "an aged man is but a paltry thing/a tattered coat upon a stick unless/soul clap hands and sing."

At the core of all four novellas is the theme of the aged man who finally understands the dire results of having refused to affirm some lasting values. Instead, Marshall's old men have based their lives on wealth or fame, cynicism or indifference. As always in her work, however, she demonstrates how personal choices are inextricably linked to the social order within which each individual character moves. What she specifically explores in this collection is how the personal past of each of her old men is gravely influenced by the history of oppression their people experienced. In the novella "Barbados," the old man Watford had spent his entire life making money in the U.S. so that he could come back to Barbados and live like the British colonials who once oppressed him. The memory of his early life conditioned all his perceptions:

> But because of their whiteness and wealth he had not dared to hate them. Instead his rancor, like a boomerang had rebounded, glancing past him to strike all the dark ones like himself . . .[4]

Desperately afraid of becoming like those dark ones, which in fact is who he is, Mr. Watford "had permitted nothing to sight which could have affected him."[5] But confronted by a young girl whom he desires and whom he finds dancing in abandon with a young man in his coconut grove, Watford learns that he is a "nasty pissy old man," and for the first time "gazed mutely upon the waste and pretense which had spanned his years."[6]

In contrast, in the story "British Guiana," the old mulatto, Gerald Motley, knows he has missed his opportunity to live. As a young man, he had shown much talent, had moved away from his upper middle-class roots and attempted to organize a strike among Guyanese workers. In order to set him back on the right path he is offered a job that would return him to his proper class, a class that based its existence on its imitation of a dying British order. Appropriately, the moment at which Motley could have believed in himself takes place within a jungle interior as characteristic of Guiana as the coconut groves are in Barbados. Motley is prevented from further penetrating the jungle and himself by his Negro-Chinese girl friend, Sybil. And it is his consciousness of his betrayal of himself, and Sybil's role in it, that shapes his life. For, from then on, he bases his life on a cynicism that shuts out any possibilty of growth.

Although these novellas are focused on men, all four protagonists discover the waste in their lives through their relationship with a woman. In two of the stories, "British Guiana" and "Brazil," this character is a part of their pasts, in many ways a mirror reflection of their own distorted values. In the other two stories, "Barbados" and "Brooklyn," she is a young woman whom they meet in their old age, whose fresh eyes penetrate their facade of wealth or stature. In *Soul, Clap Hands and Sing* as in *Browngirl, Brownstones*, the relationship between woman and man is central to the understanding of both the major character and the social order.

In one of the few essays she has published about her art, Marshall distinguishes *Soul, Clap Hands and Sing* from *Browngirl, Brownstones* by stating that in her second book she was consciously reaching for a political theme, while in her first novel she portrayed a rejection of American values in individual terms. *Soul, Clap Hands and Sing*, though not as well known as *Browngirl, Brownstones*, is a significant turning point for this author, not only because it is the first time she uses a New World framework as opposed to a primarily North American context, but also because she identifies political themes as central to her fiction.

Soul, Clap Hands and Sing was written after Paule Marshall had just had a baby. She tells us that despite her husband's objections, she got help to stay with her son and went off to a friend's apartment everyday to work on her new book. Even today, the woman writer who is a mother must often write against the backdrop of continuous interruption. In the last ten years, books such as Tillie Olsen's *Silences* and Alice Walker's "In Search of Our Mothers' Gardens" propelled into the public forum discussion about the relationship between woman's artistic creativity and the creativity of her womb. But in 1960 such discussion was hardly occurring, and the individual woman writer had to rely on the strength of her own belief that her need to express herself was as important as the society's demands on mothers. Writing *Soul, Clap Hands and Sing* was also a test of Marshall's determination to be a writer despite the society's belief that women did not need any other form of creativity than motherhood.

Eight years elapsed between the publication of *Soul, Clap Hands and Sing* and Marshall's second novel *The Chosen Place, The Timeless People* (1969), originally entitled "Ceremonies of the Guest House" in manuscript form. While she was working on this monumental novel, Marshall was divorced, raised her son, and published three short stories: "Reena" (1962), "To Da-duh, In Memorium" (1964) and "Some Get Wasted" (1968). Each of these stories represents a strand of Marshall's work as she attempted to refine the depth of character analysis in her first novel while enlarging the scope of social analysis that would be the distinguishing characteristic of her second.

"Reena" is the work of Marshall's that is most often anthologized, probably because it is a short piece that uses many of the distinctive characteristics of her best known work, *Browngirl, Brownstones*. Like that novel, "Reena" portrays the development of a West Indian-American woman. But, while *Browngirl, Brownstones* is primarily about Selina Boyce's journey through adolescence, "Reena" is told from the point of view of the middle-aged woman who Selina might have become. It is one of the first pieces of Afro-American literature to delve into the complex choices confronting the contemporary educated black woman. Through the character of Reena, the narrator in the story gives us a feeling for the peculiar contradictions such a woman encounters: the illusory freedom of college, the immersion into left wing politics that both helps to shape her yet finally does not deal with her problems, the frustrations of an interracial relationship, the restrictions of a black middle-class marriage. As is characteristic of Marshall, Reena's story is told to us during a distinctive ritual of her culture, a wake for her Aunt Vi. And Reena's assessment of her life is juxtaposed with and conditioned by her maternal history as represented by women like her aunt. Thus, Reena's sense of herself as a displaced person and her desire to take her children to see Africa are measured against the lives of women like Aunt Vi who "cleaned house" to "buy house" but never got to enjoy the bed of roses they could finally afford. The character Reena is also a foreshadowing of Merle Kimbona, the central character of *The Chosen*

Place, The Timeless People: Both are middle-aged black women who feel fragmented by their experience as oppressed people in the West and yet retain some measure of their own vitality.

Just as Reena could be an older Selina Boyce, the 9-year-old girl in "To Da-duh in Memorium" could be her younger sister. The story depicts a young Barbadian-American girl's visit to Barbados to see her grandmother, her da-duh, and uses the New World framework of *Soul, Clap Hands and Sing*. Like that collection, the focus in this story is on the collapsing of the past and the present into a moment of recognition. In "To Da-duh, in Memorium," however, that past and present are represented by the land of Barbados and the technology of America, linking this story to the old country versus New York conflict of *Browngirl, Brownstones*. The child and the grandmother of this story develop a strong bond based on competition as one tries to prove to the other that her home is superior. Da-duh shows the young child the wonders of her village, the fruit, the flowers, the canes, while the child tells her about the marvels of New York, the radios, the cars, the electric lights. The competition continues as each gains respect for the other, until one day Da-duh shows her grandchild her greatest wonder, an "incredibly tall palm tree which appeared to be touching the blue dome of the sky." But the grandmother is completely demolished by the child's Empire State Building. From that time on, Da-duh appeared "thinner and suddenly undescribably old." And she dies the day that airplanes fly for the first time over her village, when her gods, her sense of reality, are totally undercut. As is true of Marshall's work, however, the past and the present are interdependent. Neither has precedence over the other, nor can the conflict between nature and technology be that easily resolved. The story ends:

> She died and I lived, but always to this day even, within the shadow of her death. For a brief period after I was grown I went to live alone, like one doing penance in a loft above a noisy factory in downtown New York and there painted seas of sugarcane and huge swirling Van Gogh suns and palm trees striding like brightly-plumed Watusse across a tropical landscape, while the thunderous tread of the machines downstairs jarred the floor beneath my easel, mocking my efforts.[7]

Like Reena, Da-duh seems to be Marshall's sketch of a more fully developed character who appears in *The Chosen Place, The Timeless People*. Neither Leesy, the character in that novel, nor Da-duh can understand the magnetism of American glamour and technology that seduces their grandchildren.

The third of Marshall's short stories, "Some Get Wasted," seems at first glance completely different from the rest of her work. It is a short story about Hezzy, a black boy who is trying to prove his manhood to the

Noble Knights, the Brooklyn gang to which he wants to belong. As such it is an initiation rite. The story takes place within Hezzy's head as he runs from the Crowns, the rival gang who ritualistically fight the Noble Knights on Massacre Hill every Memorial Day. Many Afro-American writers, including Ralph Ellison, Richard Wright, and James Baldwin, have used street gangs as an element in their work. Marshall's point of view on this subject, though, is linked to the rest of her work in that she focuses on one definition of manhood left to those males who are unwanted in the society.

For Hezzy, who could be a second generation West-Indian American, Boy Scouts and war veterans marching to the blare of "America . . . America" have nothing to do with him. Yet he needs to belong to some country, some brotherhood that is a ritualistic expression of his life and is also opposed to the Boy Scouts of that other world. Hezzy yearns to be a man like Turner, who got a bullet crease on his forehead on another Memorial Day and is seen as a hero by his peers. For them, manhood is tinged by rage and arrogance that is rooted in the will to be recognized: "Yeah, that's right, Hezzy. Read about me in the news next week, you dumb squares."[8] But Hezzy gets wasted, ironically by his own People, who mistake him for one of the Crowns in an initiation rite that moves to nowhere. Yet, even as he dies, Hezzy holds onto the idea of his People, for him his only measure of himself. In his desire to be a hero to his peers, to exhibit his threatened masculinity in a dangerous and glamourous way, Hezzy is linked to Vere, another character in *The Chosen Place, The Timeless People*. He too sees masculinity as rooted in the concept of glory. He too is destroyed by that desire.

In its analysis of characters that are inseparable from their particular spatial and cultural context and its insistence on the intersections of the past and present, Marshall's second novel, *The Chosen Place, The Timeless People*, is a culmination of her earlier work. In it Marshall moved from a localized context in which she focused primarily on one character or one family to a portrayal of the entire socio-cultural fabric of Bournehills, a prototypical Caribbean island. Her scope is considerably larger than that of her previous works, yet the people of this novel are psychologically related to the Boyces of *Browngirl, Brownstones*, to Mr. Watford and Gerald Motley of *Soul, Clap Hands and Sing*, to Reena, Da-duh, and Hezzy of the short stories. Because of this, *The Chosen Place, The Timeless People* is continuous with the rest of her work, its characters, themes, and techniques so consistent with *Browngirl, Brownstones* or "To Da-duh in Memorium" that Marshall creates a coherent universe. As Marshall herself matures, her vision does not change dramatically; rather, her emphasis moves from the way the world affects an individual psyche to how many psyches create a world.

How Marshall achieves an enlargement in scope without losing the intensity of character analysis of her previous work has much to do with the philosophical concepts of this novel. Its plot is a familiar story in the underdeveloped world, consisting of the interrelationship between the team members of a philantrophic agency, the Center for Applied Social Research, and the underdeveloped society of Bournehills. The members of this agency believe that they have come to help Bournehills enter the twentieth century. Instead they find that half measures cannot right the wrongs that have been and continue to be inflicted on the people. The novel turns on its epithet, a saying from the Tiv of West Africa:

> Once a great wrong has been done it never dies. People speak the words of peace, but their hearts do not forgive. Generations perform ceremonies of reconciliation but there is no end.[9]

The theme of this novel is the complex series of interactions between the oppressed and those who oppress them, how half-measures cannot substantively change those interactions. Finally it portrays history as an active, creative, and moral process composed by human beings. For Marshall, we as individuals and whole cultures decide upon the moral nature of an act, a series of acts, a history. Marshall sums up the central idea of this novel in one of her essays:

> After struggling for some time, I was finally able in my most recent novel to bring together what I consider to be the two themes most central to my work: the importance of truly confronting the past, both in personal and historical terms, and the necessity of reversing the present order.[10]

The title of this novel, as well as the names of its four parts, "Heirs and Descendants," "Bournehills," "Carnival," and "Whitsun," are indicators of its composition. Marshall constructs the society of Bournehills by using what she considers to be the two most important elements of any society—the contours of individual human beings as they form and are formed by their land and their culture and the relationship between the past and present of a specific community as manifested in its concept of time, in other words by its rituals. Largeness of scope does not result in tedious analysis, for we come to empathize with and understand individual and various members of the society. But neither is the novel individualistic in its approach, for Marshall's careful presentation of rituals and mores, as rooted in a common history, demonstrates the inevitable influence of the society on specific individuals. Because the major characters of the novel span the western world, are black and white, male and female, Jew and Anglo-Saxon, upper, middle, and working class, natives and outsiders, Marshall creates a microcosm representative not only of Bournehills, but of other underdeveloped societies in the Third World, that are held captive *both* psychologically and economically by the metropoles of the West, yet somehow possessed with their own visions of possibility. And because the personal pasts of the various characters intersect and sometimes conflict with the rituals of Carnival and Whitsun, which are embodiments of Bournehills' time and pointers to its own specific vision of the future, Marshall is able to show the necessity for and complexity of struggling to reverse the present order.

Pivotal to the possibility of change in the novel is Merle Kimbona, the Bournehills woman who had studied in London, married an African, relinquished their child to him, and returned to her native land, wounded and fragmented. Throughout the novel, she is identified with Bournehills, that abandoned land that refuses half-measures of change but can only effect revolutionary change if it insists on creating its own history. In struggling to confront her own painful past, Merle grows toward confronting the equally painful history of her people and finally to the point where she must act to reverse *her* present order. Implicit in her development is Marshall's assertion that Bournehills must undergo a similar process. Personal and social change are inextricably linked; in a creative tension of reciprocity, one is virtually impossible without the other.

Marshall's presentation of a black woman as a major actor on the social, political, and cultural issues of her society can be compared only to Alice Walker's major character in her novel *Meridian*, published seven years later. Both Merle and Meridian are new literary characters in Afro-American women's novels, for they are presented as complex women who struggle to understand themselves, precisely as black and female, through their interactions with their community and then use that understanding to try to reverse the present order. In seeking their own personhood, they find they must pursue substantive social transformation. They are female literary characters of a social and political depth seldom seen in either Afro- or Euro-American literature. In developing such a character as Merle Kimbona, within the context of a graphic analysis of her particular society, Marshall announced the major theme of Afro-American women's fiction of the 1970s where black women were finally presented both as complex developing people and active participants in the socio-political world.

Like *Browngirl, Brownstones* and *Soul, Clap Hands and Sing*, *The Chosen Place, The Timeless People* received fine reviews, but was not a commercial success. And since Marshall is solely committed to writing fiction, not to teaching, public performances, or magazine writing, she has had difficulty supporting herself as a writer. As a result she had to rely primarily on grants from institutions such as the National Endowment for the Arts and the Ford Foundation. The financial difficulties of being a writer in America, even more so a black female novelist, have certainly had an impact on her ability to concentrate on her work with the intensity that it deserves. Nonetheless, in spite of Marshall's unwavering commitment to writing as a serious mode of thought and her resistance to commerciality, her work is becoming better known. As Afro-American and feminist thought advances, the depth of her work is more and more appreciated. For years *Browngirl, Brownstones* was out of print, almost impossible to find. In 1981 it will be [and was] reissued by the Feminist Press so that it can again become readily available to another generation of readers. Hopefully, *Soul, Clap Hands and Sing*, which is still out of print, will also be reissued, as the relationship between the metropoles of the West and the colonized people of the Third World is understood by Americans to be the critical issue it is.

Since the publication of her second novel in 1969, Marshall has remarried and lives in both New York City and the West Indies in what she calls an "open and innovative marriage" that allows her the time and freedom to work. During the 1970s she has worked on a third novel, *Praise Song for the Widow*. Its theme, as described by Marshall, is one of her persistent concerns. In her interview in *Essence*, in 1979, she says it is about "the materialism of this country, how it often spells the death of love and feeling and how we, as Black People, must fend it off."[11] Marshall read several chapters of this not yet published work in 1981 when she came to the West Coast for the annual African and Caribbean Writers Conference. From that reading, the novel seems to center on a middle-class, middle-aged black woman who has bought into the materialistic values of America. But on a cruise to the West Indies she experiences a rupture in her consciousness precipitated by a persistent dream about a childhood memory. Years before on her annual visit to the South, her now dead southern aunt used to take her to a place called Ibo Landing where slaves were said to have walked across the water back to Africa. The dream of her aunt, of this place, takes hold of her consciousness in so profound a way that the past and present intersect. As in Marshall's previous work, myth and history, place and consciousness intersect. And, as in her previous work, the black woman as black and female struggles against obstacles to become full. In this novel, however, the emphasis seems to be on the relationship between class, race, and culture, a concern that other Afro-American women writers—most recently Toni Morrison—are also exploring.

Twenty years after the publication of *Browngirl, Brownstones*, Marshall continues to explore the relationship between personal growth and societal change, between the history of black peoples and their future, between their language and their lives, through the form of the novel. Marshall is solely a writer of fiction, as opposed to a practitioner of many forms. For her that form has special qualities rooted in the African and Caribbean tradition of story telling. The modern western counterpart of such a tradition has been the novel, in which a writer can construct a world of her own, affected by her personal vision yet tempered by a reality and informed by social change. Marshall is devoted to this view of the novel:

> I realize that it is fashionable now to dismiss the traditional novel as something of an anachronism, but to me it is still a vital form. Not only does it allow for the kind of full-blown, richly detailed writing that I love (I want the reader to see the people and places about which I am writing), but it permits me to operate on many levels and to explore both the inner state of my characters as well as the worlds beyond them.[12]

It is this aesthetic that permeates the work of Paule Marshall from *Browngirl, Brownstones* through *Soul, Clap Hands and Sing*, the short stories, *The Chosen Place, The Timeless People*, as well as her yet unpublished novel, *Praise Song for the Widow*. At the heart of such an aesthetic is the love of people—their speech, gestures, thought—as expressed in her skillful and often tender characterizations. Underlying this aesthetic is a faith in the ability of human beings to transcend themselves, to actively change their condition, a theme that is at the core of much of Afro-American literature. Paule Marshall's particular contribution to such a tradition is not only her ability to render complex women characters within the context of equally complex societies, linked by their African roots and their experience of oppression and transcendence, but also her creation of worlds in which the necessity of actively confronting one's personal and historical past is the foundation for a genuine revolutionary process.

NOTES

1. Alexis de Veaux, "Paule Marshall—In Celebration of Our Triumph," *Essence* X, no. 1 (May 1980): 96.
2. Paule Marshall, *Browngirl, Brownstones* (New York: Avon Books, 1959), p. 22.
3. de Veaux, "Paule Marshall," p. 98.
4. Paule Marshall, "Barbados," *Soul, Clap Hands & Sing* (1961; Chatham Bookseller, orig pub. 1961, reissued, 1971, p. 4., reprint ed., The Chatham Bookseller, 1971), p. 4.
5. Ibid., p. 9.
6. Ibid., pp. 27-28.
7. Paule Marshall, "To Da-Duh In Memorium," *Black Voices*, ed. Abraham Chapman (New York: New American Library, 1968), p. 214.
8. Paule Marshall, "Some Get Wasted," in *Harlem, USA*, ed. John Henrik Clarke (New York: Collier Books, 1971), p. 352.

9. Paule Marshall, *The Chosen Place, The Timeless People* (New York: Harcourt Brace & World, 1969).
10. Paule Marshall, "Shaping the World of My Art," *New Letters* 40, no. 1 (October 1973): 110-111.
11. de Veaux, "Paule Marshall," p. 135.
12. Marshall, "Shaping the World of My Art," p. 105.

8 Afro-American Women Poets: A Historical Introduction* (1982)

This piece was written for an anthology, Women Poets of the World, *which was clearly an attempt by its editors, Joanna Bankier and Deidre Lashgari, to rescue from oblivion women poets, who, in these patriarchal times, have been neglected, no matter where they are from. Writing this short introduction brought up, for me, certain questions about focus and placement of energy.*

This short piece is the other side of an essay on women writers I might do for an anthology of Afro-American writers. Both groups (women writers and Afro-American writers) have been excluded from "mainstream" exposure; both groups tend to exclude or to minimize the significance of each other. Women of color are the group to suffer most from this exclusion. Thier response, in many areas of endeavor, has been to articulate their own tradition and create their own organizations and collections devoted to themselves, where they are unhindered by tokenism and condescension. This approach, is, of course, absolutely necessary to an articulation of a tradition.

But, I think, it is also necessary to include ourselves whenever we are respectfully requested to (as I was in this anthology) or even sometimes to wage battles for inclusion, since we are a part of, a central part of, the world. The amount of energy we put into such involvements sometimes seem to yield little return. However, if we focus only on building our own separate tradition I think we distort its meaning. For we do not in a bubble live, and our worlds are continually intersecting with other worlds. Black feminist criticism, then, must both reclaim and build a tradition, even as it pressures other points of view to be affected by our own.

Afro-American women have been creating poetry ever since they were brought to America some 400 years ago. The existence of numerous songs and folktales treating the subjects of work, courtship, love, as well as the equally large body of spirituals, testify to the rich, oral tradition collectively created by slave women and men. This tradition clearly ran

*A shorter version of this essay was first published in Joanna Bunkier, Deidre Lashgari, eds., *Women Poets of the World*, New York: MacMillan, 1983.

counter to the accepted norms of European poetry of the seventeenth and eighteenth centuries, for it utilized pervasive African stylistic motifs such as "call and response," which were unfamiliar to European ears, and emphasized the system of slavery, a subject that white Americans wished to avoid. Since slaves were considered to be less then human by the dominant culture, it is not surprising that their expressions were as discredited as they were. It was not until the early part of the twentieth centruy that the spirituals and the blues began to be considered by some to be art. Still, today, forms that are specifically Afro-American in nature, whether poetry, painting, or music, are continually threatened by the dominance of Euro-American aesthetic concepts.

The tension between the unacknowledged art of an oppressed people and the aesthetic forms of the majority culture had critically influenced the development of Afro-American poetry. As early as 1765, a precocious slave girl, Phyllis Wheatley, was well known as a poet throughout the American colonies and the mother country. A "curio," Phyllis Wheatley wrote poetry about love and death in the style of Pope. Her story is, in heightened form, that of all Afro-American writers, for she would not have been published if she had not been approved by whites. It was her ability to imitate European poets rather than the expression of her own sensibility that brought prestige to her otherwise ordinary masters. Her poetry reflects little of her identity either as a black or a woman, except in a few of her poems where she attempted to justify slavery, since through it, many Africans were introduced to Christianity. Yet, as Alice Walker aptly pointed out, the brilliant Phyllis preserved for her descendants "the notion of song" in the only manner she could.

Phyllis Wheatley died poor and malnourished in 1784. Her verse was published again in 1838 by the abolitionists in order to prove that black slaves could write poetry, that is, that they were culturally human. By that time, the institution of slavery was being challenged by an interracial Abolitionist Movement. Women's auxiliaries, a radical innovation of the nineteenth century abolitionists, were the arena for the first intense participation of American women in national politics. As a result of that experience, American women began to forge their own political movement for equality. The sexual abuse of the slave woman and the usurpation by the slavemaster of her role as mother were not only dramatic instances of the immorality of slavery, they were also vivid metaphors for many free women, black and white, of their own condition. It is not surprising, then, that black women activists and writers were central to both the nineteenth century Abolitionist and Women's Rights Movements.

Frances Harper, the most important of nineteenth century Afro-American women writers, protested the society's treatment of black women. She wrote more as a speaker for her race and sex than she did as an individual. Because she measured her poetry by its effectiveness as protest, she tended to write highly melodramatic verse directed toward a popular audience. Since she was primarily an activist with specific goals in mind, she could not devote herself to writing. And, because her reading audience was necessarily white, she did not often use specific Afro-American folk forms. Rather, a change in content was effected as she and other Afro-American poets overtly wrote about social issues.

That the first significant outpouring of Afro-American literature took place within the context of a social movement was extremely important for its development in the twentieth century. The poet was seen as having a responsibility to her racial community, as well as to her own sensibility, *and* the discussion of the condition of women was seen as an integral aspect of black thought and expression rather than separate from it. Throughout much of the nineteeth century, black male leaders like Frederick Douglass supported women's struggle for equality and acknowledged the premise that the prevalent definition of woman was indirectly related to societal norms rather than based on natural law.

Yet, when blacks won emancipation and attempted to become a part of the American nation, they increasingly began to see the nineteenth century American definition of woman as a desirable goal. Increasingly, intelligent and active women were seen as necessary to the struggle for racial equality, but not as a desired ideal, if all things were equal. This view is already implicit in the first published novel by an Afro-American, William Wells Brown's *Clotelle* (1861). Brown's presentation of his mulatto heroine as the ideal black woman is as close as possible to the image of the southern lady.

By the period of the Harlem Renaissance (1917-1929), many blacks felt pressured to demonstrate that black women were as good as white women—that is, that they would be middle-class white ladies if it were not for racism. Only if such an idea was supported, many asserted, would the race be respected. As important, because the Women's Rights Movement of the nineteenth century was split by racism, black women writers were more inclined to formulate their own concepts of the relationship between race and gender outside of white American women's institutions.

While Afro-American poetry of the nineteenth century had been primarily concerned with the gaining of the rights of citizenship for blacks, the poets of the Harlem Renaissance asked what it meant to be both black and an American and what such a combination meant for the black poet. These questions were and continue to be complex ones, since blacks came from Africa rather than Europe, were forcibly separated from their culture as slaves, and continued to be oppressed economically and culturally in America. Most white Americans in the 1920s saw "Art" not even as American but as European upper class, a tradition to which the black poet had little access. Yet, because many black idealogues saw art as a means of proving the worth of the race, the emphasis on racial pride in the period was often expressed in creating an Afro-American art that would match the "quality" of a basically elitist European art tradition. Thus, the most celebrated black poet of the period was Countee Cullen, who imitated Keats and wished to be seen as a poet, not a black poet. On the other hand, Langston Hughes, the major poet of the period from our contemporary perspective, was not then particularly appreciated because of his use of Afro-American folk forms and his articulation of social issues that indicted America. In fact Hughes would be a major force in the articulation of a specifically Afro-American poetic tradition, folk and working-class oriented, in form and content.

The poetry written by black women that was published during the Renaissance must be seen within this context. Although the Harlem Renaissance was a time of enormous Afro-American poetic activity, few black women were known as poets, and none of them were considered major. They were not an integral part of the literary movement itself as much as they were individual talents who wrote conventional verse. And though they sometimes wrote specifically as women, it was primarily to idealize the black women whose image was under attack in the general society. It might be said that the genuine poetry of the black woman appeared not in literature but in the lyrics of blues singers like Bessie Smith. Female blues singers were extremely popular during this period and wrote about the black woman's autonomy and vulnerability, sexuality and spirituality. Perhaps because the blues was seen as "race music" and catered to a black audience, black women were better able to articulate themselves as individuals and as part of a racial group in that art form.

In contrast the major women writers of this period were novelists. Jessie Fauset is sometimes called the midwife of the Harlem Renaissance, for she was certainly one of its creators. She and Nella Larsen wrote novels that countered the prevalent stereotypical image of the black woman as "loose" by creating sophisticated light-skinned middle-class heroines. They attempted to demonstrate that black women had the same values as white middle-class ladies and therefore were no different, except for race restrictions. The result was an adherence to the conventional view of woman.

The most significant woman writer of that period, Zora Neale Hurston, did not publish her important works until the 1930s. However, the effect of her presence on the Harlem Renaissance movement is instructive, for her ebullient personality and free life style did not endear her to the major literary figures of the day. She did not fit the conventional image of woman. Hurston, however, had much influence on Langston Hughes's poetry, for she shared with him her enthusiastic study of Afro-American folk speech and culture. Her classic novel, *Their Eyes Were Watching God* (1937), is a breakthrough in the literature of Afro-American women, portraying a black woman in search of herself in the context of a rich folk culture and innovatively using the folk culture as the basis for its form.

The devastating political and economic impact of the Depression changed the tone of Afro-American writing. In the 1930s and 1940s, Afro-American writers such as Richard Wright increasingly presented the black person as a peculiarly oppressed proletarian, for they explored the relationship between race, poverty, and urban life. As northern ghettos grew larger, the alienating effects of segregation on the personality of blacks became a major theme. Two Afro-American women, Margaret Walker and Gwendolyn Brooks, were the major poets of the 1940s and 1950s. As different as these poets are, they both emphasized the qualities of everyday life in their poetry rather than the sophisticated world presented in the 1920s, and they both presented the impact of racism on the way black women are viewed in America.

"For My People," Margaret Walker's most celebrated poem, combines many of the qualities of the poetic tradition that preceded her. She used the sweep of history to both express the Afro-American folk culture and protest the oppression of blacks. As important as her subject is her definition of the poet at the beginning of this poem, a definition that so many Afro-American poets share, for Walker presents herself as an embodiment of her people's history and culture as expressed through her individual sensibility.

While Margaret Walker tends toward broad historical strokes, Gwendolyn Brooks is a poet of intense concentration. In her many volumes of poetry she uses the seemingly trival images of everyday life to explore intricate ideas and patterns of behavior. Thus, her poems about the complex effect of poverty and racism on ordinary people and their equally complex responses are vivid and concrete rather than rhetorical and abstract. And in pursuing her themes, Brooks has effectively used both Afro-American and European forms.

A major poet, Brooks has always written about women—how they see themselves, as mothers and daughters, wives and lovers, as restricted or fulfilled. And her work has always focused on the sexist expressions of racism in this country. Yet Brooks would not consider herself a woman poet. She does not protest the restrictive conditions of woman's lives so much as she presents the complexity of their existence. Her poetry about women, however, is some of the most poignant in American literature.

Gwendolyn Brooks wrote much of her poetry during the 1940s and 1950s when blacks were vigorously striving to achieve integration into the American social structure. By the 1960s, as whites resisted blacks' dramatic attempts to transform society, the Civil Rights Movement gave way to the Black Power Movement. Brooks's later work published in the late sixties and early seventies reflects that shift. The dominant literary movement of that period, cultural nationalism, focused on the development of black selfhood and nationhood. Afro-American poets like Imamu Baraka (Leroi Jones) eschewed European art forms and explored Afro-American speech, rhythm, and images in their works. There was a renewed interest in African and Afro-American history and culture and a corresponding contempt for whites. Poets saw themselves as revolutionaries in the service of their community.

Many black women poets such as Nikki Giovanni, Sonia Sanchez, and Carolyn Rodgers were part of that cultural nationalist thrust. Their works called upon black women to heal themselves by asserting their pride in black beauty and by reassessing their relationship with black men, a relationship continually distorted by a racist society. However, in the process of unifying black people, cultural nationalists often saw specific women's issues as diversionary and inconsequential. Angered by the Moynihan report, which falsely stated that the black family was matriarchal and therefore deviant, many felt it necessary to assert black manhood. And sometimes the observation that men were taken more seriously than women in white America led to the corollary that black women should subordinate themselves to black men. The ambivalence about comparative sex roles in black and white society was a keenly felt issue during this period, resulting in such poems as Giovanni's "Woman Poem." Yet, ironically, the emphasis on a rediscovery of Afro-American history and on social activism led many Afro-American women poets to reassess the conventional definition of woman.

The poetry of the seventies, of such writers as Audre Lorde, Alice Walker and June Jordan, poets who participated in the movements of the sixties, is evidence of the depth of that reassessment. In the last decade, Afro-American women poets have increasingly focused on themselves as women as well as blacks. The contemporary feminist movement of the 1970s, which had many of its roots in the Civil Rights Movement in much the same way that the nineteenth century Women's Rights Movement sprung from the Abolitionist Movement, raised critical issues about the nature of sexism in this country. For many Afro-American women poets, their search for self must take place within the context of an entire transformation of society, in contrast to many white feminists who see their community as one made up solely of women. Having been subjected to a definition of white womenhood, which because of race and economic oppression they could not possibly attain, most Afro-American poets emphasize the impossibility of freeing one part of the society without freeing all of it.

In attempting such radical social transformation, Afro-American poets like Walker, Jordan, Lorde, and Shange have forged alliances with other Third World and white women in an intense literary activism. Poems about motherhood, female sexuality, sexism, work, political and social action, women's friendship, the relationship of woman and man, and the whole range of women's thought, emotion, and action have become part of the literature. Their themes not only protest and express the lives of women as they are, they also project visions of what might be. And the forms that these poets are using are increasingly based on their cultural expressions as women. Images, language, modes of expression heretofore ignored or trivialized are now being mined for poetic possibilities.

The poetic expression of Afro-American women of the seventies has been at its most intense in the history of Afro-American literature. The questions—whether more Afro-American women poets are being published because of a vocal Women's Movement, as well as whether the issue of race and class will be critical to that movement—may very well determine the visibility and continued development of the poetry. For the history of Afro-American poetic tradition suggests that unless the issues of race, class, and gender are integrated concerns, the black woman poet will not be able to use the full range of her voice. And such an integration will not occur until an American society itself is in a process of committed social transformation. By necessity, then, the poets of this tradition are most intimately in search of that process.

9 Nuance and the Novella: A Study of Gwendolyn Brooks's *Maud Martha* (1982)

When Mary Helen Washington reviewed Black Women Novelists, *she quoted from an interview she had done with Paule Marshall, Marshall's praise for Gwendolyn Brooks's novella,* Maud Martha. *I had, for some time, intended to do an essay on this neglected though important work in relation to the change in the portrayal of Afro-American women characters that was occurring in the 1950s. Mary Helen's reference heightened that desire. And when Gary Smith and Maria Mootry asked if I would contribute to their book on Gwendolyn Brooks, I was already at work on this essay.*

"Nuance and the Novella" is an essay of particular importance to me, not only because of its subject matter, but because of its approach. I show how the hidden sexist biases in the society, how the historical moment at which it appeared, made it difficult for the work to be appreciated. And at the same time I look at the novella itself, its structure and characters. Both elements are, I think, necessary to an understanding of the tradition of Afro-American women novelists.

(1)

Maud Martha, Gwendolyn Brooks's only novel, appeared in 1953, the same year that *Go Tell It On The Mountain*, James Baldwin's first novel, was published. By that time, Brooks had already published two books of poetry, *A Street in Bronzeville* (1945) and *Annie Allen* (1949), for which she won the Pulitzer Prize. But although she was an established poet, Brooks's novel quietly went out of print while Baldwin's first publication was to become known as a major Afro-American novel. Brooks's novel, like Baldwin's, presents the development of a young urban black into an adult, albeit Brooks's major character is female and Baldwin's is male. Her understated rendition of a black American girl's development into womanhood did not arouse in the reading public the intense reaction that Baldwin's dramatic portrayal of the black male did. Yet Paule Marshall

*To be published in Maria Mootry, Gary Smith, eds., *The Art of Gwendolyn Brooks*, University of Illinois Press, Fall, 1985.

(whose novel, *Browngirl, Brownstones* (1959) is considered by many critics to be the forerunner of the Afro-American woman's literary explosion of the 1970s, would, in 1968, point to *Maud Martha* as the finest portrayal of an Afro-American woman in the novel, to date, and as a decided influence on her work.[1] To Marshall, Brooks's contribution was a turning point in Afro-American fiction, for it presented for the first time a black woman not as a mammy, wench, mulatto, or downtrodden heroine, but as an ordinary human being in all the wonder of her complexity.

Why is it that *Maud Martha* never received some portion of the exposure that Baldwin's novel did, or why is it still, to this date, out of print, virtually unknown except to writers like Marshall and a small but growing number of black literary critics? Even within the context of Black Studies or Women's Studies, Brooks's novel is unknown or dismissed as "exquisite," but somehow not particularly worthy of comment. One could say, of course, that *Maud Martha* was not significant enough to receive such attention. However, comments such as Marshall's tend to nullify that argument. Or one could say that Brooks's accomplishment as a poet overshadowed, perhaps eclipsed, her only novel, although the novel shares so many of her poetic characteristics that one would think that it would attract a similar audience. I am inclined to believe that, ironically, the fate of the novel has precisely to do with its poetic qualities, with the compressed ritualized style that is its hallmark, and as importantly, with the period when it was published.

George Kent tells us in his essay "The Aesthetic Values in the Poetry of Gwendolyn Brooks," that her pre-sixties poetry was published at a time when the small number of blacks reading poetry expected that it be "the expression of interest in the universal, but without the qualifications or unstated premises or doubts regarding Blacks' humanity."[2] And that the larger white audience "reflected happiness when they could assure the reading public that the artistic construct transcended racial categories and racial protest . . . and yet paradoxically insisted upon the art construct's informative role, by asserting that the Black artist was telling us what it meant to be a Negro."[3] These observations would, I believe, also apply to the anticipated reading audience of *Maud Martha*, a poetic novel of the 1950s without any of the sensationalism that characterized popular novels about blacks—a novel that would be considered art. But although *Maud Martha* certainly does have these perspectives, it provides another dimension, in that it focuses on a young black girl growing into womanhood without the employment of Afro-American female stereotypes found previously in the novel. While poetry was expected to transcend racial boundaries and aspire toward universality, the novel, by definition, dealt with a specific individual's interaction with her society. The type of interaction that even this small literate audience was used to in the "Negro Novel" was not at all present in *Maud Martha*. In the novels written by black women in the first half of the century, most featured tragic or not so tragic mulattas, as in the Harlem Renaissance novels of Nella Larsen and Jessie Fauset, or the oppressed and finally tragic heroine, as in protest novels like Ann Petry's *The Street* (1945). Dorothy West's *The Living Is Easy* (1949), the closest in time to Brooks's *Maud Martha*, focuses on a central protagonist who resembles the heroines of the Renaissance period, in that an almost histrionic investment in social mobility and decorum is her principal value. And even in that innovative novel of the 1930s *Their Eyes Were Watching God* (1937), Zora Neale Hurston imbues her major character with an extraordinary life. However, Brooks's major character is neither an aspiring lady, the Major's wife, nor a necessarily beautiful and doomed heroic figure. She lives, like so many of us, an ordinary life, at least on the surface. An excerpt from the novel distinguishes its stance from its predecessors.

> On the whole, she felt life was more comedy than tragedy. . . . The truth was, if you got a good Tragedy out of a lifetime, one good ripping tragedy, thorough, unridiculous, bottom-scraping, *not* the issue of human stupidity, you were doing, she thought, very well, you were doing well.[4]

In its insistence on examining the supposed "trivia" that makes up the lives of most black women, their small tragedies and fears notwithstanding, *Maud Martha* ran counter to the tone of "the Negro Novel" that both blacks and whites would have expected in 1953. For Brooks replaced intense drama or pedestrian portrayal of character with a careful rendering of the rituals, the patterns of the ordinary life, where racism is experienced in sharp nibbles rather than screams and where making do is continually juxtaposed to small but significant dreams.

Brooks's portrayal of a black woman whose life is not characterized as "tragic" was perhaps due partly, to two overlapping trends in Afro-American life and thought of the 1950s. One was the integrationist thrust, which culminated in the Supreme Court Decision of 1954. Arthur P. Davis points out the complexity of this thrust in *From the Dark Tower*. On the one hand, black writers like Wright, Hughes, Himes, and Brooks had participated through their literature in the protest movement of the 1940s against racism and poverty, especially its manifestations in the urban ghetto. To some extent, the effect of the literature was the development of an *apparent* climate in the country out of which full integration could develop. Emphasis on the overall black protest movement of that period had been on securing equality through the law, thus the significance of the 1954 Supreme Court decision. On the other hand, "there was surface and token integration in many areas, but the everyday pattern of life for the overwhelming majority remained unchanged. In the meantime he [the Negro literary artist] had to live between two worlds and that for any artist is a disturbing experience."[5]

In the 1940s, black writers like Richard Wright had presented the everyday pattern of life for the overwhelming majority of blacks in as dramatically tragic a form as possible in an attempt to affect the philosophical underpinnings of America toward its black native sons. One unwanted result of this dramatization was white America's tendency to stereotype blacks as creatures entirely determined by their oppression, a tendency that undermined blacks' humanity as much as the previous attitude that they were genetically inferior. Many black intellectuals' reaction to this "protest" stereotype was to emphasize those qualities blacks shared with all other human beings. Thus, the "expression of interest in the universal" could be seen in the major books of the 1950s published by already established writers: e.g., Wright's *The Outsider* (1953), in which he attempted to weave together the impact of racism on the black man with philosophical issues about the existential nature of all men, or Ann Petry's, *The Narrows* (1953), which is set not in the urban ghetto of *The Street* (1945), but in a small New England city and focuses on the relationship between a black man and his white mistress. *Invisible Man* (1952)(perhaps the most influential Afro-American novel of the period, emphasizes this double-pronged approach among blacks, for Ralph Ellison consciously weaves together motifs of both Afro- and Euro-American culture as the foundation of the novel's structure.)Afro-American writers, in other words, were trying out new settings, approaching new subjects. In general, these new approaches attempted to break the image of the black person as an essentially controlled and tragic individual, as well as to dramatize the variety of his or her experience. The political tone of integration and literary striving to portray black people's many-sided experiences went hand in hand.

One aspect of these strivings was a return to the chronicle of the black family that was apparent in some of the Renaissance novels of Jessie Fauset. But while her novels were entirely about the upper middle class, whose conventions supposedly mirrored those of their white counterparts, the novels of the 1950s featured lower middle-class folk set against the background of coherent, specifically black communities. Unlike the conventional novel of the 1920s or the protest novels of the 1930s and 1940s, the novel of the 1950s put more and more stress on the black community as community. Still there were novels like Himes's *The Third Generation* (1954), which traced the maturation of a black boy within a family that attempts to restrict his growth.

In fact many of the novels of the late 1940s and the 1950s put some portion of the blame for the conflicts of the main characters on the black wife and/or mother, who is depicted as a powerful embodiment of white middle-class values. Variations on this theme appear not only in Himes's *Third Generation* but in West's *The Living is Easy* and *The Outsider*, novels that precede the infamous Moynihan Report (1966). In the popular arena, the image of the aggressive, castrating black female who is bent on making the male tow the line was made popular through Sapphire, a major character in the Amos n' Andy radio programs of the late 1940s and 1950s.

Interestingly, this image, a variant of the old plantation mammy, became current at a time when sociology, one of the major image makers of blacks, paid little attention to the black family. As Billingsley points out in *Black Families in White America* (1966), sociology did not discover the black family until the 1930s and by the 1950s had virtually abandoned it. The academic view of the black family, the context within which most studies of black woman were initially conducted, was, during the 1940s and 1950s represented by Frazier's *The Negro Family in the U.S.* (1948) and Cayton and Drake's *Black Metropolis* (1948).[6] Both studies emphasized the strength of the black mother, her coping with poverty, poor housing, and desertion, which, ironically, was interpreted by many to mean that she was more powerful than the black man and therefore too powerful. And though this attitude would not be fully developed or officially authorized until the Moynihan Report, one can in hindsight see the process by which this view gained currency during the 1950s.

But just as Brooks's Maud Martha is not a tragic figure, neither is she a domineering personality. As daughter and then as a mother, she exhibits little of the willfulness associated with Sapphire or even Cleo, the major character of *The Living is Easy*. Her strength is a quiet one, rooted in a keen sensitivity that both appreciates and critiques her family and culture. Brooks's portrayal of an ordinary black girl who cherishes the rituals of her community even as she suffers from some of its mores both conformed to and deviated from the family chronicles of the 1940s and 1950s. Her emphasis on the black girl within the community is a prefiguring of black women's novels of the sixties and seventies, which looked at the relationship between the role of woman in society and the racism that embattled the black community.

Yet a description of *Maud Martha* as a work of such grand intentions would undercut its peculiar quality. In keeping with it smallness, more precisely its virtual dismissal of the grand or the heroic, *Maud Martha* is a short novel. Properly speaking, it should be called a novella, not only because of its length but more importantly, because of its intention. Brooks is not interested in recreating the broad sweep of a society, a totality of social interaction, but rather in painting a portrait in fine but indelible strokes of a Maud Martha. In an interview in 1969 with George Stavras, editor of *Contemporary Literature*, Brooks says of her process:

> I had first written a few tiny stories and I felt that they would mesh, and I centered them and the others around one character. If there is a form I would say it was imposed at least in the beginning when I started with those segments or vignettes.[7]

And Brooks goes on to agree with her interviewer when he says that "the unity of the novel is simply the central point of view of Maud Martha herself as she grows up."[8]

Brooks's comments emphasize two points: the centrality of Maud Martha's inner life, for the novella is a revelation of her thoughts, and her reflections on her limited world. Unlike her predecessors, with the exception of Hurston's Janie Stark, Maud Martha is not just a creation of her external world; She helps to create her own world by transforming externals through her thoughts and imaginings. This is a quality seldom attributed to ordinary folk in previous black women's novels. And yet, in illuminating Maud Martha's specific individuality, Brooks must necessarily show her in relation to other people and her physical environment, the basis for the world she knows, imagines, even extends. The other point of emphasis in Brooks's description is her use of the word *tiny* and how diminution affects the form of this novella, the use of segments or vignettes. In all, the 170-page novella is divided into 34 chapters, many of which are three or four pages long, few longer than ten pages, "the small prose sections fitting together like a mosaic."[9] This double emphasis of the novella is introduced in the first vignette, the "description of Maud Martha." Immediately we are in the midst of Maud Martha's images of fancy and her sense of her own ordinariness and diminutiveness.

> What she liked was candy buttons, and books, and painted music (deep blue or delicate silver) and the west sky altering, viewed from the steps of the back porch; and dandelions. . . .
>
> dandelions were what she chiefly saw. Yellow jewels for everyday studding the patched green dress of her back yard. She liked their demure prettiness second to their everydayness; for in that latter quality she thought she saw a picture of herself, and it was comforting to find that what was common could also be a flower.[10]

As a prose piece, *Maud Martha* is a fusion of these two qualities, the sensitive and the ordinary, not only in its characterization of its protagonist, but also in the moments the writer chooses to include in her compressed rendition of an urban black woman's life. Yet these moments, as they form a whole, both look back to the novels of the 1940s and toward black women's novels of the 1960s and 1970s. Since the time period of *Maud Martha* is the thirties and the forties, it is not surprising that the impact of the Depression on black family life (e.g., in "home" and "at the Burns-Coopers") are some of the moments Brooks chooses to telescope. But there are also vignettes about a dark girl's feeling of being rejected by her own community ("low yellow" and "if you're light and have long hair"), a theme that Toni Morrison would use as the basis for her complex analyses of cultural mutilation in *The Bluest Eye* (1970). There are segments about the relationship between the rituals of a black culture and the development of character ("kitchenette folks" and "tradition and Maud Martha"), a structural technique that Paule Marshall would expand and refine in her novels. There are moments that are particularly female ("a birth," "Helen," "Mother comes to call"), themes that would become increasingly important to black women novelists of the seventies. And there are "universal" moments, in that human beings, whatever their race, sex, or class, muse about the meaning of existence and the degree of responsibility they must take to shape their own lives ("posts," "on 34th Street"), an underlying theme in Walker's *The Third Life of Grange Copeland* (1970).

Maud Martha, then, is a work that both expresses the mores of a time passing and prefigures the preoccupations to come. Georg Lukas in his analysis of another novella, Solzhenitsyn's *One Day in the Life of Ivan Denisovich* (1953), points out that novellas often appear at the end of a historical period or at the beginning of a new period, that often they are "either in the phase of a not yet (noch nicht) in the artistically universal mastery of the given social world, or in the phase of the nolonger (nichtmehr)."[11] His analysis of the genre is one way of locating the elusive significance of this "exquisite" novella. For in its focus on a single character or situation rather than the totality of a society and in its economy of presentation, the novella may summarize the essentials of a period that has just ended and be an initial exploration into attitudes that are just forming. Though not consciously intending to write a novella, the writer may find that in trying to express the moment of transition from one mode of interpreting reality to another, the present cannot be expressed in the novels of the past, nor is the totality of the new reality understood enough to transform it.

I think that it is important to note that the period of the 1930s and 1940s had been written about in many black novels. Wright's *Native Son* (1941) is set in that period as is Petry's *The Street* (1945). What Brooks does is to present another version of black life of that time, as she may have experienced it, but also as she could interpret it through the integrationist thrust of the 1950s. Yet she also pointed to future emphases: the sense of the black community as community and the black reaction to impose white notions of beauty, cultural nationalist concepts of the 1960s; as well as the sensitivity and specificity of the black women's experience as woman, a pervasive theme of the seventies. In effect, the seeds of these themes were sowed in the thwarted expectations of the integrationist thrust. And though Brooks could hardly foresee the Civil Rights Movement, the Black Power Movement, or the Women's Movement and their impact on American literature, her experience as she described it in *Maud Martha* was the outline of some of the reasons for the desires and goals of these movements. When Maud Martha's little daughter, Paulette, is rejected by a white Santa Claus and asks "why didn't Santa Claus like me?"[12] and Maud Martha must try to explain why without saying why, we are witnessing one of the "trivial" but significant reasons for the 1960s black search for nationhood. When Helen, Maud Martha's sister, proclaims to her, "you'll never get a boyfriend, if you don't stop reading those books,"[13] we hear in Maud Martha's sighs the rumblings of the redefinition of woman that would be attempted in the 1970s. Perhaps, as Arthur P. Davis pointed out, because there was an apparent climate of change but little actual change, and the Negro artist of the 1950s was living between two worlds, Brooks's rendition of Maud Martha's life would have to look backward and forward.

Yet Brooks's overt intention in writing *Maud Martha* was not to reinterpret the past or prefigure the future. She tells us that she "wanted to give a picture of a girl growing up—a black girl growing up in Chicago, and of course much of it is wrenched from my own life and twisted."[14] In *Report from Part I* she provides us with a partial list of some of those "twists," how she used her knowledge of her specific community and her perception of her own life and culled from it the essence of "a black girl growing up in Chicago." She also tells us that the first passage she wrote for the novella became the opening of the last chapter.[15] That passage emphasizes Maud Martha's awareness of the bursting life within her and without her; the result of which is her whisper, "What, *what* am I to do with all of this life?" That question, which permeates the entire novella, is both its theme and nuance, both the question of all persons in all times and the question of that specific individual in that specific time. Life was drastically limited for an ordinary black girl in the Chicagos of the 1940s, as it was for most ordinary people. And yet, like most ordinary people, there is so much life in Maud Martha. *Whispering* the question emphasizes its ironic truth, for to most institutions, most authorized social processes, even most literature, neither Maud Martha nor her question is at all important.

In a sense, then, the conflict of the novella is contained in its subject—
that such a person as Maud Martha is seldom seen as imbued with
importance. Thus, the question that permeates the entire novella is based
not so much on the usual "character in a conflict" motif, but in the
gradual unraveling of the life that is in Maud Martha, this ordinary,
unheroic girl. The novella does not have intense dramatic rises and falls,
so much as it presents a typical life as not at all typical in the flat meaning
of the word. Concurrently, the novella is the embodiment of the idea that
a slice of anybody's life has elements of wonder and farce, wry irony and
joy. No fire and brimstone need fly. But since the hero or heroine, the
exceptional person, has been extolled in most societies, Brooks's
orientation is in itself a challenge to a venerated "universal" idea. In
framing her intention as she did and in carrying it through in her "tiny"
novel, Brooks articulated the value of the invisible Many. The social and
literary black movements of the 1960s and 1970s would emerge precisely
because these Many would insist on the value of their "little" lives and
would ask the question: "What, *what* am I to do with all of this life?"[16]

(2)

That *Maud Martha* is partially based on Brooks's own experience as a
young black girl growing up in the Chicago of the 1930s and 1940s
contributes to the authenticity one feels while reading the novel. In other
words, *Maud Martha* is not merely a response to the social images of
blacks that were current in the 1950s, but it is also a manifestation of
Brooks's own philosophy about the relationship between life and
aesthetics. She distinguishes a memoir from an autobiographical novel
by calling the former "a 'factual' account," while the latter is "nuanceful,
allowing."[17] As is true of many novellas, *Maud Martha*, is economical in
its presentation, but there are many styles of economic writing. What
characterizes this novella is not only its precision, but its nuance, and how
these stylistic elements are organic to its underlying theme: the
wonderfulness of a Maud Martha.

As a poet, Brooks is known for her precision of language, for the care
with which she chooses every word and that "concentration, that crush"[18]
in her work. It is not surprising, then, that *Maud Martha* also shares this
characteristic. Brooks says of the poet's unique relationship to language
that:

> the poet deals in words with which everyone is familiar. We all handle
> words. And I think the poet, if he wants to speak to anyone is constrained
> to do something with these words so that they will "mean something," will
> be something that a reader may touch.[19]

Her emphasis on the word as being, not as abstraction, but as sensory and concrete, underlines her choice of words in her novella as well as her poetry. *Maud Martha* is a compression of images from which the prose radiates. So that in the chapter "spring landscape: detail," Brooks's description of Maud Martha's school is concrete, sensory:

> The school looked solid. Brownish-red brick, dirty cream stone trim. Massive chimney, candid, serious.[20]

Most of Brooks's adjectives are certainly concrete. But look at how they move to the words, *candid, serious*, words that are usually abstract but have now become concrete, something you can touch in this spring landscape. And when her description of the solid school is contrasted with the school children whom she describes as "bits of pink, of blue, white, yellow, green, purple, black carried by jerky little stems of brown or yellow or brownblack,"[21] who blow into the schoolyard, Brooks shows us more than the color or line of this landscape. She evokes the touch, the feel of a configuration of attitudes represented by the solid dullness of the school, as opposed to the vibrant playfulness of the children. Hence the words that the reader may touch moves him/her toward the nuances he/she cannot touch. The precision and the nuance work hand in hand.

Not only can one touch Brooks's words, one can hear them. Rhythm and sound are not as important to the quality of prose as they are to poetry. But even though *Maud Martha* is written in the form of prose narrative, Brooks employs many of the techniques she uses in her poetry. The pacing of words through her adroit use of juxtaposition, the alternation of short and longer units, the creation of emphasis through alliteration and imagery, the selection of specific sounds to evoke a certain quality—all these elements are characteristic of the prose of *Maud Martha* and contribute to its quality of nuance. Maud Martha's assessment of her first beau is typical of Brooks's use of rhythm and sound to advance the prose narrative:

> For Russell lacked—What? He was—nice. He was fun to go about with. He was decorated inside and out. He did things, said things with a flourish. That was what he was. He was a flourish. He was a dazzling, long and sleepily swishing flourish.[22]

The emphasis in this two-page chapter is on Maud Martha's recognition of her first beau's grand superficiality, a quality that is not enough to absorb her, though it had vanquished so many others. So that the passage quoted above is not just a description of Russell, but a process of insight for Maud Martha as well as for the reader from which we learn much about her character by feeling her reaction to Russell.

Brooks gives us the nuance of Maud Martha's insight as well as the factual through her choice of words, imagery, and sounds. The dashes indicate reflection, the slowing of the pace, as Maud Martha begins her assessment. "He was fun to go about with" is followed by equally short sentences that use repetition to create a gradual quickening of pace—*He was, he* did *things,* said *things, he was*—until the pace slows down to the moment of recognition "That was what he was." Finally, various elements of language, repetition, imagery, alliteration, assonance, combine in the long sentence that summarizes his essence: "He was a dazzling, long and sleepily swishing flourish," in which the z's, s's, l's and i's evoke Russell as much as the meaning of the words themselves.

Because of her careful use of these poetic devices, Brooks is able to compress the prose narrative, drawing fine outlines of mood, emotions, thought, and events without having to fill in many details. By eliminating the nonessential fact, by creating nuance, we touch, see, and hear the whole much in the same way a few deft lines by an accomplished artist can suggest the entire human body. Abstraction of form is only possible because we recognize, know, *what* is being suggested. But even more than recognizing the mood, emotion, event, we can concentrate on its essence, without the distraction of superfluous details that can sometimes obscure rather than reveal. And because of Brooks's distillation, our experience is more focused, more intense.

But poetic devices are not enough to make a novella. The form, by definition, involves some kind of narrative, some reflection of external as well as internal reality, some development of character, as well as a structure that shows the organic relationship between these elements. So while Brooks employed poetic devices to advantage in *Maud Martha,* she also had to utilize the techniques of fiction. Yet the line between her poetic and prose techniques is not a hard one, for her creation of nuance is especially critical to the overall design of the novella. Not only does each vignette evoke the essence of a specific mood, emotion, thought or event, it contributes to a composition that suggests the essence of Maud Martha's character and the pattern that is her life. Brooks's poetic sensitivity is especially apparent in the novella's structure, for she usually selects only those moments that accomplish two things: reinforce the outline of a pattern that is repeated in many other lives and is being reenacted here, while paradoxically focusing on Maud Martha's individuality. The effect is that of a ritual performed for time immemorial by different actors, who can vary the pattern only slightly—the actor this time being an ordinary girl from Chicago. The tension between these two elements, a pattern that seems prescribed and Maud Martha's transformation of it, moves the narrative.

The pattern of Maud Martha's life is presented in extremely short, condensed chapters, thirty-four in all, which are loosely divided into six phases. While Brooks's creation of nuance suggests Maud Martha's inner life, the chapter divisions are the external structure of the novel. These divisions are stages in the universal process of becoming an adult and therefore an outline of societal configurations of custom, culture, and historical forces which help to shape that individual. Thus the phases of early childhood and school, adolescence, courtship, work, marriage, the beginning of a family, the impact of the Depression of the 1930s and the war in the 1940s are a general outline of life for a young American girl growing up in the 1930s and 1940s. The moments Brooks selects to focus on in these divisions, however, are to a large extent a reflection of her view of that external reality. In concretizing the universal outline, she stresses both the rituals of a black family and community. She outlines the individuality of the girl-woman Maud Martha while emphasizing the impact of the particular concept of beauty, as well as the societal limits of being a woman, upheld by her community, on her personality. She focuses on the ordinary tone of Maud Martha's life while stressing the complexity of her inner character. Because we know, in general, the universal concept of growing up, because we know, in general, about family life and community, because we know, in general, the way that girls and women should be, she can evoke these configurations through nuance while emphasizing the uniqueness of Maud Martha's character and context. Thus, the "racial element is organic not imposed."[23] So is her portrayal of womanhood and of the ordinary person.

At the crux of Brooks's composition is the development of her central actor. Of course, the chronology of the novella is its outer movement, but it is Maud Martha's sensibility, her perception of the world, that enlivens the narration. Yet Brooks does not use the "I," the first person point of view. As is her custom in many of her poems (e.g., "The Rites for Cousin Vit," "Mrs. Small"), the author creates a character for whom she cares intensely, but from whom she is clearly detached. And though the substance of the novel is told through Maud Martha's eyes, Brooks suggests, by her use of the objective third person, that other eyes see what hers see. While the reader feels intimately connected to Maud Martha he/she is constantly aware of the world around Maud Martha as separate from and yet connected to her. Brooks use of an omniscient narrator who sees through Maud Martha's eyes emphasizes the sensibility of her central actor solidly located in a world of many others. The beginning of the vignette "Tim" illustrates how effective this technique is as a means of establishing Maud Martha's relationship to the outer world:

Oh, how he used to wiggle!—do little mean things! do great big wonderful things! and laugh laugh laugh.

He had shaved and he had scratched himself through the pants. He had lain down and ached for want of a woman. He had married. He had wiped out his nostrils with bits of tissue paper in the presence of his wife and his wife had turned her head, quickly, but politely, to avoid seeing them as they dropped softly into the toilet, and floated. He had a big stomach and an alarmingly loud laugh. He had been easy with the ain'ts and sho-nuffs. He had been drunk one time, only one time, and on that occasion had done the Charleston in the middle of what was then Grand Boulevard and is now South Park, at four in the morning. Here was a man who had absorbed the headlines in the Tribune, studied the cartoons in Collier's and the Saturday Evening Post.

These facts she had known about her Uncle Tim. And she had known that he liked sweet potato pie. But what were the facts that she had not known, that his wife, her father's sister Nannie, had not known? The things that nobody had known.[24]

Clearly, Tim and his life exist outside of Maud Martha's head, but it is her language that articulates his individuality. And it is also her language that indicates that she is a woman, is black, and lives in a certain section of Chicago. The way she chooses details that appear trivial on the surface but cumulatively communicate a feeling for and a knowledge of this man, the way she focuses on intimate details that emphasize his relationships with others, are styles of speaking that often indicate a woman's voice. The content of these details tells us that he is a working-class black man who lives in Chicago and is somewhat interested in the world beyond him. And it is typical of Maud Martha's personality that she would ask what was beneath the surface—What were "the things that nobody had known?"

The qualities of Maud Martha's language is, in fact, of considerable importance to the major theme of the novella. Brooks carefully constructs Maud Martha's voice as that of a woman. The images she uses throughout the book are often derived from the world of the home, the world of cooking, of flowers, ferns and furniture, the world of emotional relationships—worlds that have traditionally been seen as woman's domain. And much of what Maud Martha says is not said aloud; it is usually her internal conversation with herself, since her observations, critiques, and musings are not considered important. There is also a way in which her persistent attention to size (which sometimes stems from her own feeling of littleness) connotes "the smaller sex," as well as the ordinary person, a scale that is reflected in the tinyness of the novel itself. And it is often because she understands that there is sometimes so much in what appears to be so little that she gleans many insights about herself and her world.

In fact, the critical aspects of Maud Martha's sensibility are her ability to see beneath the mundane surface of things and to transform the little that is allowed her into so much more than it originally was. As Paule Marshall puts it, "In her daily life, Maud Martha functions as an artist. In that way this novel carries on the African tradition that the ordinary rituals of daily life are what must be made into art."[25] In her adolescence, Maud Martha is able to put this insight into words in the vignette, "At the Regal."

> To create—a role, a poem, picture, music a rapture in stone: great. But not for her.
> What she wanted was to donate to the world a good Maud Martha. That was the offering, the bit of art, that could not come from any other.
> She would polish and hone that.[26]

That awareness of her own being, as valuable, unique, as created by herself yet connected to those around her, marks her personal development. So that she can refuse to be devalued by her potential employer, Mrs. Burns-Cooper, though there is only "a pear in her ice box and one end of rye bread."[27] She can be hurt by her husband's desire to be a social somebody, understand how that is linked to his hidden dislike of her dark skin and heavy hair and yet maintain her own sense of worth, precisely because she has developed her own standards, her own concept of the valuable.

It is the articulation of this value in Brooks's unheroic ordinary black girl from Chicago, a value that is almost always celebrated in the heroic, the extraordinary, the male, that marks the distinctive language, movement, substance of *Maud Martha*. Through her use of nuance, Brooks is able to present this celebration in its essential form, suggesting that Maud Martha is one of any number of ordinary people, who, against the limits of the mundane life, continue to create themselves.

NOTES

1. Paule Marshall, "The Negro Woman Writer," tape of lecture at conference, Howard University, 1968.
2. George E. Kent, "Aesthetic Values in the Poetry of Gwendolyn Brooks," in *Black American Literature and Humanism*, ed. R. Baxter Miller (Lexington: University Press of Kentucky, 1981), p. 84
3. Ibid., p. 85
4. Gwendolyn Brooks, *Maud Martha* (Harper & Row, 1953; reissued in *The World of Gwendolyn Brooks* New York: Harper & Row, 1971), p. 291.
5. Arthur P. Davis, *From the Dark Tower, Afro-American Writers, 1900 to 1960* (Washington, DC: Howard University Press, 1974), p. 138.
6. Gloria Wade-Gayles, "She Who is Black and Mother: In Sociology and Fiction, 1940-1970," in *The Black Woman*, ed. LaFrances Rodgers-Rose (Beverly Hills, CA: Sage Publications 1980), p. 95.
7. Gwendolyn Brooks, *Report From Part One* (Detroit: Broadside Press, 1972) p. 162.

8. Ibid., p. 162.
9. Ibid
10. Brooks, *Maud Martha* in *The World of Gwendolyn Brooks*, p. 127.
11. Georg Lukas, *Solzhenitsyn*, trans. William David Graf (Cambridge, The MIT Press, 1969), p. 7.
12. Brooks, *Maud Martha*, p. 300.
13. Ibid., p. 165.
14. Brooks, *Report from Part I*, p. 162.
15. Ibid., p. 193.
16. Brooks, *Maud Martha*, p. 304.
17. Brooks, *Report from Part I*, p. 190.
18. Ibid., p. 146.
19. Ibid., p. 148.
20. Brooks, *Maud Martha*, p. 130.
21. Ibid., p. 131.
22. Ibid., p. 167.
23. Brooks, *Report from Part I*, p. 146.
24. Brooks, *Maud Martha*, p. 149-150.
25. Mary Helen Washington, "Book Review of Barbara Christian's *Black Women Novelists*," *Signs: Journal of Women in Culture and Society*, 8, no. 1 (August 1982): 179.
26. Brooks, *Maud Martha*, p. 148.
27. Ibid., p. 284.

10 Alternate Versions of the Gendered Past: African Women Writers vs. Illich[1]* (1982)

In 1982, Ivan Illich was chosen as Regent Lecturer at the University of California, Berkeley on the subject of gender, despite women's expertise in this area of scholorship. But it was not so much the fact that a man was being honored for a subject pioneered by women that angered feminists, as much as Illich's conclusions about women's place in society. This talk was written for a symposium on Illich's concept of gender, which Women Studies at the university organized.

As one of the participants in this symposium, which drew a large audience, I felt my role, was to illuminate the falseness of his use of the place of African women in their society as the "primitive" component in his argument against women's world-wide attempt to achieve equality. Literature, my own area, was my primary tool. This talk demonstrates another task that black women critics must often take on—that of actively aligning ourselves with other women against reactionary ideas, even as we maintain the complexity of our position in the world.

I want to begin by reading a passage by the Bardadian-American writer Paule Marshall from her book *The Chosen Place, The Timeless People*, which describes the content of life for so many women, and I might add men, of color who are condemned to Illich's "gendered scythe" (*Gender*, p. 91). My choice of this piece was influenced by Illich's poetic description of haymaking as a ballet (*Gender*, p. 93).

> Behind him Gwen kept pace, gathering together the canes he flung her way into great sheaves which, with an assist from the other women, she then placed on her head and "headed" down to the truck below. And it was a precarious descent, for the ground would be slick underfoot from the "trash": the excess leaves the men hacked off the stalks before cutting them, and treacherous with the severed stumps hidden beneath. One bad slip and the neck would snap. But Gwen moved confidently down, as did

*First published in *Feminist Issues*, 3, no. 1 (Spring 1983), an issue devoted to the entire symposium.

the other women, her head weaving almost imperceptibly from side to side under its load (the motion was reminiscent of those child dancers from Bali, but more subtle, more controlled), her swollen stomach thrust high and her face partly hidden beneath the thick overhang. . . .

Then even as he [Saul] watched Stinger succumb, Gwen passed him on her way down to the lorry. All along she had been carrying on a lively exchange with the other headers, joking and calling out to them as they bent at their work, but now that the morning had crept into noon and that, in turn, into an afternoon to which there seemed no end, she had fallen silent. And suddenly, she appeared less certain of her footing on the steep grade. The almost offhand confidence of the morning was gone, and like Stinger, who remained absorbed in his cutting to the exclusion of everything else, she was only conscious of the dangerous footing down the hill. The set of her back, the way she stepped—first carefully feeling the ground ahead with her foot before placing her weight on it—said she had marshaled her slender forces to see her down.

She passed, and under the waving green forest on her head, Saul saw her face, a face which when she laughed proved she was still a young woman. But in the short time since he had last glanced her way it had aged beyond recognition. A hot gust of wind lifted the overhanging leaves a little higher and he glimpsed her eyes. . . . He tried describing them to himself some days after when he could bring himself to think of them. But he could not, except to say they had had the same slightly turned up, fixed, flat stare that you find upon drawing back the lids of someone asleep or dead.

He fled then, forgetting even to take his leave of Stinger as he usually did. His head pounding, eyes burning, unable to breathe in the choked-off air, he groped his way down the shorn hillside, which, with the dust and smoldering head and the cane trash lying heaped up like so many abandoned swords, resembled a battlefield on which two armies had just clashed. He stumbled past Gwen, her head weaving in its subtle dance as she meticulously picked her way down amid the debris. Her dead eyes didn't notice him.[2]

It is ironic that I should be addressing the incongruities of Ivan Illich's ideas on gender, his major premises being that we are created not of a human species but as male and female, that we live best in separate, gendered spheres and that women lose when they invade men's sphere. Such premises would obliterate my field of study, the literature written by women, especially black women. The pen has not been considered by societies to be an appropriate tool of woman's. Even the origin of the English word *author* means begetter, father, and is related to the word *authority*, which means the power to enforce obedience. As Edward Said points out, "Underneath the meanings of the word *author* is the imagery of succession, paternity, hierarchy." In contrast, women's creativity is supposed to be located in her body, while the creativity of the mind—writing, reading, thinking—has often been seen by many societies as inimical to her nature. It is interesting that the same constellation of attributes was ascribed by whites to blacks. Blacks were often described as natural, emotional, close to the earth, as hewers of wood and drawers of water, as tainted by reasoning if they ever tried to do it. As one of the nineteenth-century American abolitionists put it: "The Negro Race is the feminine race of the world for it possesses that strange instinctive insight that belongs more to women than to men." Put this way, I am studying, as I am often told by established literary institutions, a literature that is not a literature, written by women who could not be writing.

Nonetheless, I will try to address these incongruities, for much of the evidence Illich uses for the superiority of a prescribed gendered world existing today is based on seemingly static Third World societies, while, paradoxically, historical process is located primarily in the changing societies of France and Germany. Since I have little time, there are three points of opposition I'd like to emphasize about his view of gender and mine. They are summarized in the following pairs: enraged silence versus articulation, prescription versus choice, specialized halves versus potential completedness.

There is a sweet seduction (for people of color) in Illich's premise that we should return to a world of gendered spheres, for our domains were broken, not by Economic Sex or industrialization, but by colonialism and enslavement. To return to a past before colonialism and its accompanying terror, oppression, humiliation, and disorder would be to erase a nightmare that has destroyed many of our people. When most of our societies were broken by colonialism, separate gendered spheres existed that were disrupted and broken by the gendered spheres of the colonizers. Before Illich's "gendered scythe" theories, we had created our own myths to erase that nightmare and to reconstruct those past societies. If Illich is interested in improving the content of women's lives, it might be instructive for him to look at some of these reconstructions and their effects on women.

Such a movement was the negritude movement of the 1920s and 1930s, when black intellectuals in their struggle for independence glorified all things African and disdained all things European. The positive aspects of this movement were many, most importantly the articulation of a cultural identity, which had at its core a world view different from the West. But there were also negative effects—primarily the romantic nostalgia it fostered, which meant a turning away from the problems of twentieth-century Africa and a belief that Africans, whatever their class or caste, were necessarily good. The black, male ruling elites of Kenya, Zaire, Nigeria, who oppress their own people,

BFC-K

have muted the power of the negritude myth, so that some African writers today are correcting the untruths of precolonial history that negritude projected and are challenging the class and sex hierarchy it camouflaged. But not before much damage was done.

One major image of negritude was the African woman idealized as mother earth, the source of all life, who in her traditional gendered sphere remained intact, untouched by the West. Revered as mother, powerful in her sphere of magic, she provided a source of cleansing for the men who had ventured out and were tainted by European education, religion, ideas, money. Poetry, novels, treatises, written by men who of course had access to writing (man's domain), stressed that image, embodying it sometimes in the realm of public policy, as in Kenya when Jomo Kenyatta defended clitoridectomies as necessary in order to preserve the culture, or when, in order to preserve the traditional culture, Kenyan policy makers today try to prevent women from leaving their backbreaking life in the countryside to come to the towns. Men do not, it appears, seem to be necessary to the continuance of culture.

But even in works affected by negritude, another image of woman begins to seep through. Here is an excerpt from *The Concubine*, a novel about precolonial Eastern Nigeria by the male writer Elechi Amadi:

> Wonuma soothed her daughter, but not without some trouble. Ahurole had unconsciously been looking for a chance to cry. For the past year or so her frequent unprovoked sobbing had disturbed her mother. When asked why she cried, she either sobbed the more or tried to quarrel with everybody at once. She was otherwise very intelligent and dutiful. Between her weeping sessions she was cheerful, even boisterous, and her practical jokes were a bane on the lives of her friends. . . . But though intelligent, Ahurole could sometimes take alarmingly irrational lines of argument and refuse to listen to any contrary views, at least for a time. From all this her parents easily guessed that she was being unduly influenced by agwu, her personal spirit. Anyika did his best but of course the influence of agwu could not be nullified overnight. In fact it would never be completely eliminated. Everyone was mildly influenced now and then by his personal spirit. A few like Ahurole were particularly unlucky in having very troublesome spirits.
>
> Ahurole was engaged to Ekwueme when she was eight days old.[3]

Ahurole's reaction to the prescribed fate for women of her society is explained by her society as her *agwu*, her personal spirit, which in women seems to be more troublesome than in men. Her society sees her reaction as woman's nature. And since she cannot articulate her fate as restriction, she is silenced by the gender expectations that she also believes in and becomes hysterical and finally destructive. That she is gifted in areas thought to be man's domain, she also judges as being unnatural; that she is curious, adventurous, intelligent, all these are cancelled out by the gender expectations of her society. Instead of contributing to it, her divided self wreaks havoc.

The woman condemned to a realm of inarticulate speech, ragings, and then silence is presented in these male "negritude" novels as the bad woman, the witch, even as the stylized African mother is presented as the good woman.

Articulation occurs for the likes of Ahurole when African women themselves began to have access to the pen. In the sixties and seventies they created an explosion of literature, which nonetheless is kept as hidden as possible by *new* gender constructs, the written word being the proper domain of men, while women are expected to dominate the oral tradition. Writers like Flora Nwapa, Aimee Aatoo, Bessie Head, and Buchi Emecheta condemn the debasement of the African woman and man wreaked by colonialism, but they also protest the mores of the traditional society that condemn women to a prescribed fate of subsistence, subservience, and silence in the political world.

Let me stress that for these women writers the African woman is not merely a victim; she is also an actor, not only in the precolonial period, but also in the colonial and postcolonial world. So there is strength in the traditions of women and adaptability within the inner circle of women. But there is also waste, tragedy, and tremendous loss in this circle. For these writers, some versions of western feminism are ethnocentric, though not because of the stress on equality. Usually they decry the narrowness of the western version, which does not see sexism as related to class exploitation and racism in an established hierarchy of dominance. Deeply committed to their people, African women writers see their societies as crippled by the devaluing of women's ideas and creativity and their sisters as burdened by the anguish of a life akin to that of a mule.

In her novel, *The Slave Girl*,[4] Buchi Emecheta uses the metaphor of slavery in precolonial Nigeria, when most slaves were women, as an analogy for women's traditional status, whether she is slave or free. And in her last novel, *The Joys of Motherhood*,[5] she condemns the over-specialization of gendered spheres (the woman as mother, the man as wage earner or warrior), which results in a tremendous lack of understanding between man and woman. Instead of the asymmetrical complementarity of gender that Illich describes, writers like Nwapa, Emecheta, and Head portray tensions between two spheres of a world in which the subordinated woman through her language, tools, and behavior must constantly and covertly be outmaneuvering the dominant male. These writers stress the woman as scapegoat, called "backward" when she is traditional, called "western" or "immoral" when in an attempt to better her life she is perceived as invading male domains.

For these women, the "gendered scythe" idea, not a new one in emerging African countries, is a denial of the oppression women experienced in precolonial times. It is a denial that colonialism happened not only to men, but also to women, that industrialization is occurring not only for men but for women. It is an attempt to put women in a world that no longer exists except in the heads of some officials or intellectuals. Without access to the political forms of their society, they do become neuters, voiceless figures on somebody's tally sheet.

It is no wonder then that women of color all over the world, in Angola, Nigeria, Cuba, China, Nicaragua, Grenada, Chile, the U.S., are struggling against what they call the two colonialisms, the domination of their people by the West, the domination of themselves by their men. For them, to articulate their own lives, to have choice in the tools they use, the work they do, to move from specialized fractions of a whole to a potential completeness is not to become neuters; it is not to become fragmented men, it is to have the possibility of becoming free and complete women.

NOTES

1. Ivan Illich, *Gender* (New York: Pantheon, 1982). All references in the text are to this edition.
2. Paule Marshall, *The Chosen Place, the Timeless People* (New York: Harcourt, Brace & World, 1969), pp. 161-63.
3. Elechi Amadi, *The Concubine* (London: Heinemann, 1966), p. 128.
4. Buchi Emecheta, *The Slave Girl* (New York: Braziller, 1977).
5. Buchi Emecheta, *The Joys of Motherhood* (New York: Braziller, 1979).

11 Ritualistic Process and the Structure of Paule Marshall's *Praisesong for The Widow** (1983)

I had heard Paule Marshall read a section of her new novel when she came to University of California, Berkeley in 1982, and so was eagerly awaiting its publication. At the same time, the editor of Callaloo, *a black journal, decided to commemorate the publication of Marshall's third novel with an issue devoted to her works. He asked me to contribute an essay.*

"Ritualistic Process" is that essay. In-depth critical analysis of Afro-American women writers is for me the very foundation of the body of criticism we are developing. Often outlets of publication are more interested in issues, problems, general themes, overviews than in this kind of concentrated analysis. Yet, without this approach, our writers will be reduced to illustrations of societal questions or dilemmas, in which people, for the moment, are interested, and will not be valued for their craft, their vision, their work as writers.

Praisesong for the Widow is Paule Marshall's third novel after a silence of thirteen years. Like her other two novels, *Brown Girl, Brownstones* (1959) and *The Chosen Place, The Timeless People* (1969), her short stories, and her collection of novellas, *Soul, Clap Hands and Sing,* (1961) *Praisesong for the Widow* explores the cultural continuity of peoples of African descent, from South to North America, as a stance from which to delineate the values of the New World. Marshall's entire opus focuses on the consciousness of black people as they remember, retain, develop their sense of spiritual/sensual integrity and individual selves against the materialism that characterizes American societies. Particularly in her novels, Marshall demonstrates how the "shameful stone of false values,"[1] can block life's light, and how a visceral understanding of their history and rituals can help black people transcend their displacement and retain their wholeness.

Like her first two novels, Marshall's *Praisesong for the Widow* penetrates society's structures through the illumination of a black woman's experience while extending her protagonist's discovered truths

*First published in *Callaloo*, 6, no. 2 (Spring-Summer 1983).

to an entire community. But while Selina Boyce in *Brown Girl, Brownstones* and Merle Kimbona in *The Chosen Place, The Timeless People* are consciously concerned with their development, the middle-class, middle-aged, seemingly content Avey Johnson appears, at first, to be an unlikely heroine. Yet *Praisesong for the Widow* builds on the world of characters Marshall created in her previous works. Set in the U.S. and the Caribbean, this novel dramatizes the links between myths of both Afro-American and Afro-Caribbean culture and uses them as the basis for the widow, Avey Johnson, and her assessment of her life. And in naming the novel *Praisesong*, Marshall reminds us of the African origin of her characters, while informing the reader that ritual is at the novel's core.

Avey Johnson, a middle-class, middle-aged widow, abruptly leaves the Caribbean cruise she is on with two of her friends. Jolted by a recurring dream in which her long dead great aunt calls her back to Tatum, South Carolina, Avey insists on returning to the security of her suburban home in White Plains, New York. Under the strain of recurring hallucinations, she misses the plane to New York. Stranded in Grenada, she is drawn into the yearly festival in nearby Carriacou, which for island people is *their* annual excursion of spiritual rejuvenation. In contrast to Avey's artificially fatted cruise, this excursion is rooted in the rhythm of the drum and the collective ritual of the dance—similar to the rituals of Tatum and Brooklyn, New York, which Avey has left behind. The widow rediscovers her true name, her true place, obscured for years by her and her husband's pursuit of material security.

That is the plot, but hardly the novel. For Marshall develops Avey Avatara Johnson's journey to wholeness by juxtaposing external reality with memory, dream, hallucination—disjointed states of mind in which the past and the present fuse. And Marshall uses these internal elements to guide Avey back to external reality and back to earth. The recurrent motif throughout the novel, that the body might be in one place and the mind in another, is characterized not as fragmentation but as a source of wisdom, stemming from a history of the forced displacement of blacks in the West. Ironically, how to recognize where one's mind should be, whatever the fate of the body, is presented in the novel as one of Avey's guides to becoming centered, to being restored to the proper axis from which her feet can feel the rich and solid ground. Thus, another motif in the novel, a decidedly African one, is the relationship of one's feet to the earth, so that one can stay the course of history.[2]

The structure of *Praisesong* reflects these motifs. Marshall's novels have always emphasized the relationship between character and context or between shape and space. Some critics have often compared her literary forms to architecture or sculpture. *Praisesong* also shares this quality. The book is divided into four parts: "Runagate," "Sleeper's Wake," "Lave' Tete," and "The Beg Pardon"— titles that not only indicate ritualistic process, but also a change in Avey Johnson's character and context.

The title "Runagate" is taken from Robert Hayden's famous poem of that name, a poem that stresses the slave past of New World blacks and their fugitive escape from bondage. This highly concentrated poem juxtaposes different images of escape as a runaway slave "runs, falls, rises, stumbles on from darkness to darkness," on his or her way to freedom in the mythic North. Like that archetypal slave figure, Avey stumbles from darkness to darkness. Ironically, her unconscious run for freedom takes her south, physically south to the Caribbean, psychically south to Tatem, South Carolina, while consciously she believes her promised land to be the North, her safe, comfortable home in North White Plains. "Runagate" is appropriately set in the ship called Bianca (white) Pride and is concerned with Avey's plans to escape from her physical feeling of bloatedness and her mental discomfort at the recurrent dream of her dead Aunt Cuney. For Avey, the antidote to such dis-ease is another haven of whiteness, North White Plains.

It is in this section that Marshall establishes the pervasive technique of the novel: the juxtaposition of supposed reality splitting Avey's being so that her mind may be in one place while her body is in another. In the first few pages of the book, as Avey suddenly begins packing at night, Marshall tells us that "Her [Avey's] mind in a way wasn't even in her body or for that matter in the room" (p. 10). We later learn that Avey's consciousness has, in fact, been disturbed, disrupted by the dream of her great aunt, who recounts her story of Ibo Landing, emphasizing how *her* old gran' told her the story: "Her body she always usta say might be in Tatem, but her mind was long gone with the Ibos" (p. 39).

Like the Runagate in Hayden's poem, Avey's Great Aunt Cuney recalls history, this time in the form of a ritual, which, like the written poem, has the quality of continuity, for it too can be passed on from one generation to the next. In taking her grand niece to Ibo Landing and to church, *her* religion, Cuney personalizes the oldest of Afro-American stories. Like Toni Morrison's Shalimar, the black man who flew back to Africa in *Song of Solomon*, Marshall's Ibos walked on water back to their home "They feets was gonna take 'em wherever they was going that day. . . Stepping" (p. 39). Neither the slaveship, chains, nor the water could stop them. This story of Africans who were forced to come across the sea—but through their own power, a power that seems irrational, were able to return to Africa—is a touchstone of New World black folklore. Through this story, peoples of African descent emphasized their own power to determine their freedom, though their bodies might be enslaved. They recalled Africa as the source of their being.

But the middle-class Avey Johnson has forgotten this story, the core of the "strong nigger feeling" of Baraka's poem, which also prefaces this section. We know this from the rest of Avey's dream, in which she resists her dead aunt, fearing damage to her clothes, her material possessions. Avey is primarily concerned that the "open-toed patent-leather pumps she was wearing for the first time would never survive that mud flat which had once been a rice field" (p. 40). And it is the dust on her new shoes that causes her to "refuse to take even a single step forward. To ensure this, she dug her shoes heels into the dirt and loose stones at her feet" (p. 41). Unlike the Ibos, Avey refuses to take a step, until her dream of her aunt's assault on her body causes her to change her mind. She suddenly leaves her Caribbean cruise for the safety of her well-furnished dining room.

It is the memory of her past, the memory of a *ritual* in the past, that forces Avey to embark on her own personal ritual of cleansing, healing, and empowerment. Thus, the first step in the ritual of healing is often the felt need for healing, although the cause of disease may be unknown. Often that felt need, as in African ritual, is expressed in the confusion of the senses or of outer and inner reality. While "Runagate" is the first step in the ritual called *Praisesong*, this section, like all the other sections of the book, is a ritual in itself. For at its center is Great Aunt Cuney's ritual expressed in Avey's dream. Ironically, it is a dream that startles Avey from her long unnatural sleep.

The second section, "Sleeper's Wake," is just that—a wake for the past, as well as an awakening from the past. Again the motif of the relationship between mind and body is sketched out. "Sleeper's Wake" is the most introspective section of the novel. The action takes place entirely in Avey's mind while her limp body is stranded, displaced in a Grenadian Hotel. Because her body is cut off from normal routine, Avey's mind is free to roam through time and space.

In reviewing her marriage to Jerome Johnson, Avey both celebrates the joyful rituals of their early life together and begins to understand how they dishonored themselves and lost track of their spirits until their faces were no longer recognizable even to themselves. To my mind, this section includes some of Marshall's best prose in her 25 years of fiction writing. She is one of a few American novelists who respectfully penetrates the complex interaction of black women and men and demonstrates how race and gender fuse to affect the quality of their relationships. In describing the decline of the spirit of a marriage, as she does in *Brown Girl, Brownstones*, she recounts how female and male roles help to determine Avey and Jay's specific reactions to their condition. But while the marriage of Silla and Deighton Boyce in Marshall's first novel is overtly tragic, the Johnson's marriage appears to be successful to the outer world, even to the participants themselves, because they accept the "shameful stone of false values." In accepting and achieving the American dream, they dishonor themselves, as blacks, as woman and man.

The motif throughout this section is Jay Johnson's words to Avey on that fateful Tuesday night: "Do you know who you sound like, who you even *look* like?" (p. 106), words that once spoken are the beginning of Jay Johnson's transformation into Jerome Johnson, a black man of property who leaves his heritage behind. Like Silla in *Brown Girl, Brownstones*, Jay knows poverty and its possible attendants of dehumanization and spiritual death. Ironically, in trying to avoid such a fate, he and Avey commit a kind of spiritual suicide, for they give up their music, heritage, sensuality, their expression of themselves:

> Moreover (and again she only sensed this in the dimmest way), something in those small rites, an ethos they held in common, had reached back beyond her life and beyond Jay's to join them to the vast unknown lineage that had made their being possible. And this link, these connections, heard in the music and in the praisesongs of a Sunday.". . . *I bathed* in the Euphrates when dawns were/young . . ." had both protected them and put them in possession of a kind of power. (p. 137)

And Avey, recalling her great aunt's words, concludes that "a certain distance of the mind and heart had been absolutely essential" (p. 139) if she and her husband were to have retained their sense of self.

But Marshall does not present the Johnsons' failure either as inevitable or as the result solely of weakness. In her narrative, she is able to maintain a tension between black peoples' need to survive and develop in America and their even more important need to sustain themselves. Unlike Morrison in *Tar Baby*, Marshall does not present these two elements of black life as mutually exclusive; rather, she shows how complex and interrelated they are. In her description of the Johnson's early marriage, she points up their common heritage: the music, the poetry of Hughes, Dunbar, James W. Johnson; their rituals that acknowledge their own beauty and richness, elements that are one strand of their culture. But Marshall also presents another strand, the screaming of the woman in the street chasing her no-good husband (the woman whom Jay accuses her of resembling), the beating of a black man by a cop, the racism that bites at their heels and eats into their lives as woman and man. Marshall expresses both the pleasure and pain of being a poor black couple in America and how precarious Avey and Jay's footing is— precarious if they succumb to the poverty, precarious if they lose their footing on "the rich nurturing ground from which [they] could always turn for sustenance" (p. 12).

Avey's mourning of her married life is, as it must be, a raging, a release of anger at the loss of her husband, at the loss of herself. "Sleeper's Wake" ends with Avey peeling off her gloves, hat, girdle, the material trappings over which she and her great aunt fought in her dreams, and with her angry words, "Too Much! Too Much! Too Much! Raging as she slept" (p. 145). It is the release of anger, in this scene of traumatic reawakening, that allows her, this contained widow from White Plains, to "open up the bars of her body" (p. 148) so that her mind and body can be healed.

In "Lave' Tete," the bars of Avey's body do begin to open, as her mind wipes itself clean. This section begins with Avey's dream of a soiled baby who needs changing, a baby who Avey discovers when she awakens is herself. The title of this section refers to the Haitian voodoo ceremony in which one is washed clean.[3] It is an appropriate title for this section, since in reviewing and assessing her past, Avey's mind is "like a slate that has been wiped clean, a *tabula rasa* upon which a whole new history could be written" (p. 151). She is, for much of this section, a child. In dressing herself, she acts like a two-year-old, no longer concerned with how she looks. Her walk down the Grenadian beach is like that of a baby seeing each shell, each leaf, each tree, for the first time. It is this seemingly contradictory state, in which her mind is suspended to her usual reality, yet optimally awake to what really exists around her, that gives her the feeling of being a child. This trance-like state of mind moves her toward the childhood memories of community rituals that form the core of this section and toward her childlike relationship with Lebert Joseph, the dominant person in this section.

After her Great Aunt Cuney, old man Joseph is Avey's guide to the wholeness that she is unconsciously seeking. Like her great aunt, Joseph is "one of those old people who gave the impression of having undergone a lifetime of trial by fire which they somehow managed to turn to their own good in the end. Old people who have the essentials to go on forever" (p. 161). And like Cuney's home in Tatum, his Grenadian "dirt floor under Avey Johnson's feet felt as hard and smooth as terrazzo and as cool." (p. 159). He is an apt parent for the bloated Avey who has lost her footing on the nurturing ground, for, like Aunt Cuney, he revers the Old Parents, and is concerned with identity and its relationship to continuity and regeneration. As Aunt Cuney is her spiritual mother, so this old man is her spiritual father. But these Old Parents have also been able to go beyond gender and conflict to something deeper, more essential. Thus, Cuney strides the field like a warrior in her husband's brogans, and Lebert dances the Juba in an imaginary skirt.

Like a parent, Lebert Joseph gives Avey shelter, sustenance, and rest. Partly because he is an elder, living in a place of special light and silence, partly because of her child-like state of mind, Avey is able to confess her dream of the old aunt. Elders in Africa and in New World black communities are known for their ability to interpret dreams. It is no wonder Lebert Joseph is able to perform this function. But what is important to the novel's ritualistic structure is that Avey must take a step that clearly divides her recent past from her present. In calling her to the excursion in Carriacou, in calling her back to Ibo Landing, Avey's "parents" are guiding her to a deeper state of being that was always potentially hers. Thus, like Cuney, Lebert is willing to struggle with the Avey Johnson this widow imagines herself to be:

> They had reached a final silence. The man who, from his look, had known all her objections before they were even born in her thoughts, sat quietly waiting, his eyes on her. Across the way, Avey Johnson was leaning wearily against the table. She felt as exhausted as if she and the old man had been fighting—actually, physically fighting, knocking over the tables and chairs in the room as they battled with each other over the dirt floor—and that for all his appearance of fraility he had proven the stonger of the two. (p. 184)

Exhausted by her dream of her aunt in "Runagate," by her assessment of her past in "Sleeper's Wake," and soothed by the silence and tempered light of the place, she takes that step.

But in order to truly experience the ritual that awaits her, Avey's body must also be cleansed. Her mind (since it is where it ought to be) triggers this process, for it is her comparison of the Carriacou excursion with that of the memories of her childhood that allows her body to let go. Avey's prominent memories in this section emphasize communal rituals: the New York blacks' annual boat ride up the Hudson and the church of her childhood.

The technique of juxtaposing then fusing past and present that pervades *Praisesong* is strongest in this section of the novel. As Avey watches the people board the *Emmanuel C* (Christ's name) to Carriacou, she relives the boarding of her childhood community unto the *Robert Fulton*, when she imagined "hundreds of slender threads streaming out of her navel and from the place where her heart was to enter them around her" (p. 190). So, too, her childhood experience in church is triggered by the old women on the *Emmanuel C* who protect her in her crossing over. These women could have been the "presiding mothers of Mount Olivet Baptists (her own mother's church long ago)" (p. 194) who also helped the congregation to cross over. As these mothers protect Avey in the passage to land, she remembers a childhood Easter Sunday and the preacher's admonition that "the shameful stone of false values" prevents the bright light of the soul from shining. It is his cry, like "cosmic stones," that releases the bloat of artificial fat in her body. Shored by the sisters, her body is being freed to become as essential in form as her Aunt

Cuney's or Lebert Joseph's. Also, Marshall compares Avey's seasickness and her jettison of nonessentials to that of the Middle Passage. Avey had "the impression as her mind flickered on briefly of other bodies lying crowded in with her in the hot airless dark. Their suffering—the depth of it, the weight of it in the cramped space—made hers of no consequence" (p. 209).

Thus, Avey's body, through nausea and excretion (supposedly shameful, yet thoroughly natural acts), relieves itself, even as her mind grasps her relationship to those around her, through history, memory, experience. And by stressing the similarities between Afro-Caribbean rituals and those of blacks in Tatum and New York, Marshall helps us to see the interrelatedness and depth of the black past. Avey is now the soiled baby, the dream with which this section began. Now she can be washed clean in mind and body and pass on to the final and deepest level of the ritual, "The Beg Pardon."

In a real sense, the rest of the novel is a preparation for "The Beg Pardon," the ritual at the end, which is the natural continuation of Aunt Cuney's ritual that dominates the beginning of the book. Thus, this section begins differently from the other sections—not with a disruption in Avey's consciousness, but with a description of the preparation for the ritual. Peace rather than disruption permeates this section, the shortest one in the book and the one most rooted in the present. In "Runagate," "Sleeper's Wake, " and "Lave' Tete," much of the action takes place in Avey's head and in relation to her person. Though Avey is still focal in "The Beg Pardon," the emphasis is on a whole people, on their expression of the links between the present and the past.

Still Avey is a novitiate and must be prepared for her first Big Drum. When she awakens in Carriacou, her body feels as her mind had felt on her first morning in Grenada: "Flat, numb, emptied, it had been as her mind when she awoke yesterday morning, unable to recognize anything and with the sense of a yawning hole where her life had once been" (p. 214). Like her mind, her body must be healed. The bathing rite, the laying on of hands that Rosalie Parvay performs on Avey is sensual in a pleasurable way, as Avey's expulsion of artificiality is sensual in a horrifying way. Central to African ritual is the concept that the body and spirit are one. Thus sensuality is essential to the process of healing and rebirth of the spirit. Just as the mothers on the *Emmanuel C* shored Avey's body up, so Rosalie washes her body as if she were a new-born, stretching her limbs the way she did those of her own children so that their limbs would grow straight. The bathing ritual also takes Avey through childhood to womanhood. Rosalie kneads her thighs creating the sensation that radiates out into her loins., It is only then that her body becomes thoroughly alive: "All the tendons, nerves and muscles which strung her together had been struck a powerful chord and the reverberation could be heard in the remotest corners of her body" (p. 224). That Avey is now ready to assume her adult role is emphasized by Rosalie's utterance, "Bon" [Good], the same word that the presiding mothers had uttered over the sick widow on the *Emmanuel C.*

The slave "runs, falls, rises, stumbles from darkness to darkness" in Robert Hayden's poem. Darkness that has its own light is the context for the Big Drum in Carriacou, a land that for Avey is "more a mirage than an actual place" (p. 254). Like her dream of Tatum, Carriacou seems to have been conjured up to satisfy a longing, a need. Gone is the sleek whiteness of the Bianca Pride, North White Plains, the white hotel in Grenada, and in its place is a natural darkness. And climb Avey must, with her own feet, if she is to reach the healing circle of The Big Drum.

The ritual that Avey observes, dimly remembers, and then participates in, is a collective process of begging pardon, correct naming, celebration, and honoring. It is also a ceremony that combines rituals from several black societies: the Ring Dances of Tatum, the Bojangles of New York, the voodoo drums of Haiti, the rhythms of the various African peoples brought to the New World. Here elements are fused and pared down to their essentials: "It was the essence of something rather than the thing itself she was witnessing" (p. 240). But it is also specifically the embodiment of the history and culture of New World blacks. Avey hears the note that distinguishes Afro-American blues, spirituals and jazz, Afro-Caribbean Calypso and Reggae, Brazilian music, a music that is almost non-music, which sounds like the "distillation of a thousand sorrow songs."

> The theme of separation and loss the note embodied, the unacknowledged longing it conveyed summed up feelings that were beyond words, feelings and a host of subliminal memories that over the years had proven more durable and trustworthy than the history with its trauma and pain out of which they had come. After centuries of forgetfulness and even denial, they refused to go away. The note was a lamentation that could hardly have come from the rum keg of a drum. Its source had to be the heart, the bruised still-bleeding innermost chamber of the collective heart. (p. 245).

As with the music, the dance is so pared down to its African essentials that it is a non-dance, in which the body is unleashed, but the soles of one's feet must never leave the ground. It is this knowledge of the body as well as of the mind that takes Avey across to the confraternity she had once known in the Robert Fulton, to the Ring Dances of Tatum, the dances she shared with her husband, the essence that had always been there—"the shuffle designed to stay the course of history" (p. 250). That Avey now recognizes herself as Avatara is also essential to the ritual, for in African cosmology it is through *nommo*, the correct naming of a thing, that it comes into existence. By knowing her proper name, Avey becomes herself.

Avey Avatara Johnson must, as we all, Beg Pardon for her excesses if she is to be free in herself and in the world. And yet the Beg Pardon, though a triumph of humility, is not a humiliation. As Alice Walker learns from her mother in the poem, "Good Night Willie Lee," so Avey finally learns from the Old Parents that:

> the healing
> of all our wounds
> is forgiveness
> that permits a promise
> of our return
> at the end.[4]

Marshall's novel is indeed a praisesong: It is an African ritual that shows the relationship between the individual and the community by recounting the essence of a life so that future generations may flourish. It is a praisesong, not only for Avey Johnson, but for the perennial Avey Johnsons in Afro-American history, who succumb to the "shameful stone of false values" only to seek the attunement of body and spirit because of an insistent, seemingly irrational memory of collectivity and wholeness. Unlike Toni Morrison's skeptical *Tar Baby*, Marshall's *Praisesong* insists that New World black rituals are living and functional and that they contain, whether they are in North or South America, an essential truth: That beyond rationality, the body and spirit must not be split by the "shameful stone of false values," that we must feel with humility "the nurturing ground from which [we] have sprung and to which [we] can always turn for sustenance." (p. 12) Thus Paule Marshall, like Avey Johnson, must continue the process by passing on the rituals. And this function is finally the essence of *her* praisesong.

NOTES

1. Paule Marshall, *Praisesong for the Widow* (New York: G. P. Putnam's Sons, 1983), p. 201. Subsequent references are included in the text.
2. For a general study of African cosmology, see John Mbiti, *African Religions and Philosophy* (New York: Doubleday/Anchor, 1970). For a study of ritual in African Literature, see Wilfred Cartey, *Whispers from a Continent* (New York: Vintage, 1969).
3. For a general study of Haitian Voodoo, see Michel Laguerre's works, especially *Voodoo Heritage* (Beverley Hills Sage Press, 1976).
4. Alice Walker, "Good Night Willie Lee, I'll See You In The Morning," *Good Night, Willie Lee, I'll See You in The Morning* (New York: Dial Press, 1979).

12 Creating a Universal Literature: Afro-American Women Writers* (1983)

This short essay is an example of how a seed can become an oak. Written for Pacifica Radio Station's KPFA Folio *commemorating African History Month, it attempts to connect the various struggles within which we must be engaged and demonstrates the centrality of the ideas expressed in contemporary Afro-American Women's literature to these struggles. In using literature as a repository of active ideas, I attempted to apply its insights to our philosophical orientations.*

This piece grew into a longer paper called "The Intimate Face of Universal Struggle," which I gave at the University of Wisconsin's Black Women Studies Conference, then into an even longer essay, "Trajectories of Self-Definition: Placing Contemporary Afro-American Women's Fiction." This original piece, though the kernel of the longer ones, is essentially different from them in its tone and thesis, since it applies the works of four writers to our contemporary mindset.

My life seems to be an increasing revelation of the intimate face of universal struggle.

June Jordan, Civil Wars

Zami, A New Spelling of My Name, the title of poet Audre Lorde's most recent book, is itself an insight. Though the book is definitely Lorde's, its subtitle, "A New Spelling of My Name," is a crystallization of a persistent and major theme throughout Afro-American women's literature—our attempts to define and express our totality rather than being defined by others. One, of course, might say that any literature, at core, is concerned with the definition and discovery of self in relation to the society in which one lives. But for Afro-American women, this natural desire has been powerfully opposed, repressed, distorted by this society's restrictions. For in defining ourselves, Afro-American women writers have necessarily had to confront the interaction between restrictions of racism, sexism, and class that characterize our existence,

*First published in *KPFA Folio*, Special African History Month Edition, February 1983, Front Page.

whatever our individual personalities, backgrounds, talents. Our words, in different shadings, call into question the pervasive mythology of democracy, justice, and freedom that America projects itself to be.

The words by Afro-American women writers that are a part of KPFA's African History Month celebration have their roots in a literary tradition that is as old as any American literature. June Jordan's *Civil Wars* (1981), Gloria Naylor's *The Women of Brewster Street* (1982), Ntozake Shange's *Sassafras, Cypress and Indigo* (1982), and Audre Lorde's *Zami, a new spelling of my name* (1982) are as different as their authors; yet, they share that perspective that comes from a tradition held in common. When June Jordan remembers the words of her childhood New York City church congregation; "by declaring the truth, you create the truth," she is referring to a point of view that echoes backward in time through the words of nineteenth century black abolitionist poet and novelist Frances Harper and in space to the slave narratives of enslaved African Women in Jamaica, the birthplace of her parents. So too, with Shange's southern character, Indigo: "There wasn't enough for Indigo in the world she'd been born to, so she made up what she needed." The counterpoint of these two sounds is a strong rhythmic pattern in this literature that exposes not only the pain, violence, restrictions of being born black, woman and poor, but fashions the tools with which to create another context.

Until recently, for most Americans, including Afro-American women, this literature was unknown, as invisible as working class women, "minority" men and women were in our institutions, history, in the American mind set. When this literature is not neglected, it is denigrated by the use of labels that deny its centrality to American life. It is called "political," "social protest," or "minority" literature, which in this ironic country has a perjorative sound, meaning it lacks craft and has not transcended the limitations of racial, sex, or class boundaries—that it supposedly does not do what "good" literature does: express our universal humanity.

And yet it is precisely because this literature reveals a basic truth of our society, of all societies, that it is central. In every society where there is the denigrated *Other* whether that is designated by sex, race, class, or ethnic background, the *Other* struggles to declare the truth and therefore create the truth in forms that exist for her or him. The creation of that truth also changes the perception of all those who believe they are the norm.

Specifically in America, the definition of the enslaved African woman became the basis for the definition of our society's *Other*. It is now a truism to say that the peculiar history and culture of Afro-American women comes out of the peculiar institution of slavery that left a legacy of racism in its wake. But as important, slavery also helped to shape certain elements of sexism that still persist in American society. Slave women were expected to do both men's work and women's work, though there was division of labor in most of the colonies. In many colonies, white women were not allowed to do field work. The work slave women did, provides us with an insight into the restrictive concept of woman in pre-twentieth century southern American life, for female slaves were both valued and devalued for their capacity to breed slaves and mother their master's children. They were valued and devalued for their supposedly incredible sexuality in a society where a true woman was not supposed to have sexuality. They were valued and devalued for their physical and psychological stength in a society where strength was a masculine word, for their lack of beauty in a society where beauty was equated with woman.

The woman, as enslaved and black, is not included psychologically or philosophically in the pre-twentieth century American definition of woman. Yet without her that definition could hardly have persisted. Without the female slave to assist in the continuous and difficult woman's work necessary to plantation life, without the female slave's body that could be used as a vessel for male sexuality, the nature of the ideal woman could not be defined as fragile, virginal, secondary, and primarily a reflection of her husband's wealth, wisdom, or social position. By Thomas Jefferson's time, for all intents and purposes, the definition of woman was white, free, upper class, while females were another entity altogether.

That the intersection of the colonists' definition of race and gender has affected white women as well as black manifested itself most dramatically in the nature of the Abolitionist Movement and Women's Rights Movement in the nineteenth century—the latter of which began the search for a counter definition, what Angela Davis calls "standards for a new womanhood," standards that would have to confront the exclusivity of race and class embodied in the old definition of woman. The struggle of black women, then, to define themselves rather than being defined (which is the major thread in contemporary Afro-American women's literature) is critical to the struggle of white women, of all American women. As poor, woman, and black, the Afro-American woman had to generate her own definition in order to survive, for she found that she was forced to deny essential aspects of herself to fit the definition of others. If defined as black, her woman nature was often denied; if defined as woman, her blackness was often ignored; if defined as working class, her gender and race were muted. It is primarily in the expressions of herself that she could be her totality. And a result of that expression is also the articulation of the interconnectedness of race, sex, and class as a philosophical basis for the pattern of dominance and hierarchy in this society.

Shange's *Sassafras, Cypress and Indigo* and Naylor's *The Women of Brewster Street* are first novels, while Lorde's *Zami* and Jordan's *Civil Wars* are these poets' first works in the autobiographical prose form. Beyond genre, the foci and forms of these four works indicate the diversity of language in contemporary Afro-American Women's literature. In portraying the limited lives of the women of Brewster Street, Naylor uses a narrative form and derives her language primarily from the metaphors of endurance in Afro-American folk speech. In contrast, *Sassafras* is a potpourri of poetry, dreams, letters, and cooking recipes as Shange draws her language from the healing aspects of African derived ritual/ music and Afro-American women's culture. Though *Zami* and *Civil Wars* are autobiographical, the styles of poets Lorde and Jordan affect their prose. Lorde uses the Grenadian word *Zami*, which means women who work together as friends and lovers, as the central image of her book. Like her poetry, *Zami* combines history, myth, and biography, always with a sense of the power of women's relationships. While *Zami* focuses primarily on Lorde's personal development, Jordan's *Civil Wars intentionally* relates her personal growth as a writer to the national and international political movements in her life. The way she transforms the rhetoric of politics into a personal voice is a powerful example of the feminist concept that the personal and political cannot be separated.

That literature is an integral part of a society rather than "pure" expression is an important point in the story of Afro-American women's writings. Fifteen years ago, we would not be able to call the list (still not long enough) of Afro-American women writers that have been published in the last decade: Alice Walker, Toni Morrison, Audre Lorde, Paule Marshall, June Jordan, Gloria Naylor, Ntozake Shange, Joyce Carol Thomas, Toni Cade Bambara, etc. The social political movements of the 1960s and 1970s have, to a large extent, made it possible for you to hear this month the *published* works of four Afro-American women writers, even as their works have helped these movements to happen. That Ntozake Shange can use for her novel's framework, woman's cultural experiences, from cooking recipes to the bond of three sisters, that Gloria Naylor can focus on the relationships between the women of Brewster Street as central to that community's existence, that Audre Lorde can show the relationship between her Grenadian mother's character and the development of her powerful voice as a radical political poet, that June Jordan can formulate her politics using the words *intimate* and *universal struggle* in the same sentence is a measure of the centrality of Afro-American women's shaping of a vision that overthrows the old white male elitist-centered view of the universe.

Yet the struggle is not won. Our vision is still seen, even by many progressives, as secondary, our words trivialized as minority issues or women's complaints, our stance sometimes characterized by others as divisive. But there is a deep philosophical reordering that is occurring in this literature that is already having its effect on so many of us whose lives and expressions are an increasing revelation of the *intimate* face of universal struggle.

13 The Uses of History: Frances Harper's *Iola Leroy, Shadows Uplifted** (1983)

Catherine Stimpson, the feminist scholar, asked me to partici-pate in a panel on The Uses of History in Relation to Women's Literature for the National Women's Studies Association Con-ference. This essay was written for that occasion. I had been rethinking my analysis of Iola LeRoy *in* Black Women Novelists. *I'd been to a conference at the University of Wisconsin where Frances Foster, a black literary scholar, had given a paper on the autobiographies of nineteenth century black women, which prodded me to think again about the form of the novel as these women used it. I'd also been working on a paper about the definition of self in Afro-American women's fiction, which had grown out of the article I wrote for* KPFA Folio. *The title of Stimpson's panel galvanized my analysis not only of Harper's novel, but on how necessary the use of history is to the development of sound literary analysis.*

In attempting to understand Afro-American women's literature, especially that of the novel, it is practically impossible to ignore its historical roots. I believe (quite unfashionably) that this is true for all literary traditions. In addition, the need to establish the historical origins and context of a literature that emerges from groups of people considered to be marginal or despised is even more critical to its understanding and appreciation. For such literature comes out of needs that are scarcely literary in the esoteric meaning that this society attributes to art. Such literature is not only the product of the individual writer's desire to express herself or to create beauty (though these are significant aspects), but also to affect the historical moment—that is, to help create social change. Nor is this desire a question of the individual writer's perceived intentions or choice. Because the conditions that determine literary worth are also historical, those peoples who are not seen as part of History or Literature must struggle to insist upon their own totality, their own significance in their time. Thus the nineteenth century Afro-American women writers (terms that were contradictory in

*Paper given at National Women's Studies Association Conference, 1983.

that time) *were* seen through historical images, whether they wanted to be or not. They *had* to respond to the images of their race and sex that challenged their ability to even perceive of themselves as creators of literature.

Before looking at specific examples in nineteenth century Afro-American women's literature, I think it is important to define for ourselves the concepts of history and of literature with which we are concerned. Most people are taught to think of history as that which happened in the past. Some of us, because of our insights or education, know that it is one way of organizing human knowledge, the past being raw material. But for those of us who were not in control of our past or our history and are not now in control of our present, we are clear about the fact that history is a selection of significant events, a means of constructing a coherent pattern out of the past. We know that often what is selected as significant is integrally connected to the point of view, values, and intentions of the historian as he or she exists in time. Because of our position, we also almost instinctively understand that whether history is considered science or humanism, it is, at core, a good story.

In contrast to history, which is temporal by nature, literature is often conceived as an art form using words to express the deepest and essential (and therefore universal and timeless) levels of human thought and feeling, which, by necessity are complex. But those of us who have not been in control of definitions of our own cultures see this universality, this essence, as those qualitites that the powerful select to be "human."

Of course, those definitions are not new. They are by now part of the stock and trade of literary scholars and historians involved in creating alternate, coherent patterns, especially Third World peoples and women of all cultures who have had to reclaim their past, their creations. But even as we scholars cite these views as an obligatory part of our approach to literature, we often almost immediately revert to our traditional training when confronted with materials not related to our specialty.

Having been so general, let me become specific. In what ways does history help us to understand and appreciate nineteenth and twentieth century Afro-American women's literature as literature? When I began work on *Black Women Novelists*, I was intrigued by the fact that although Paule Marshall, Toni Morrison, and Alice Walker are very different writers, they focused on similar images of Afro-American women and their work revealed a depth of tradition (whether they consciously knew it or not) that preceded them. In other words, I went on a search in the past for a coherent pattern that might help illuminate the works of contemporary Afro-American novelists.

I found that I had to confront Frances Harper's *Iola Le Roy* published in 1892 and until two years ago considered the first novel written by an

Afro-American woman to be published in this country. I had to contend with it because so many of its characteristics were to remain dominant elements of fiction written by Afro-American women for decades to come.

If read as a novel in our contemporary sense, *Iola LeRoy* could be described as a pious treatise about a neo-black woman, which condemns slavery but otherwise extolls Anglo-American middle-class values, which conceives of the ideal black woman as a middle-class Sunday School teaching octaroon, and which romantically insists on the fulfillment of the American Dream for black people, if only they'd become as moral and thrifty as whites. Like the heroine of *Contending Forces* by Pauline Hopkins, another Afro-American nineteenth century woman writer, Iola LeRoy is so atypical a black woman, one could wonder whether these writers knew any of their sisters.

And yet Frances Harper was probably one of the most knowledgeable persons on the subject of black women during her time, as shown by her journalistic pieces on black women of the Reconstructionist South. As her contemporaries profusely testify, she was a champion for black women throughout her life, had been a leading abolitionist, and after abolition had put much of her energy to improving the dire plight of black women. What is to account for the difference between Harper's characterization of her heroine and the obvious knowledge she possessed about black women? Or is she just a bad storyteller? I discuss in detail in *Black Women Novelists* some of the reasons for Harper's choices. In this discussion, because of the limitations of time, I'd like to focus on one specific problem she faced, that of the genre itself—the novel—the way it was seen at that time and how the form itself fashioned her content.

As we all know, form is not separate from content; it is, in fact, a way of constructing reality. The same "content," when constructed in a different way than it had been before, is altered. In effect, *how* something is seen radically affects *what* is seen.

Frances Harper had constructed the reality of black people's lives throughout her career in the forms of poetry, speeches, and journalism intended to teach white people about the horrors of slavery and to inspire them to do something about it. Though some of her poetry is directed to herself or to other black people, at the core of her work is the intention of teaching and inspiring those others. So, too, with *Iola LeRoy*, written 27 years after the abolition of slavery, (during Reconstruction) when blacks were subjected to a reign of terror calculated to obliterate them or to reduce them to a servile state. That she chose to write a romance novel in 1892, had to do with her perception of what the novel could do that poetry or journalism could not. The 65-year-old Harper tells us in the preface to *Iola LeRoy* that "her story's mission would not be in vain if it awakens in the hearts of our countrymen a stronger sense of justice and a more Christian-like humanity."

What did she think the novel could do that the poem or journalistic piece could not? For one thing, the novel constructed as a romance had been one of the most effective propaganda techniques that abolitionists had used in their fight to change public opinion about slavery. *Uncle Tom's Cabin* had been so successful as propaganda that when President Lincoln met Harriet Beecher Stowe he called her "the little woman that started the war." And William Wells Brown had so aroused public sympathy for enslaved blacks in England as well as America, that Clotel, his heroine's name, had become a household word. Hence the romance novel had popular appeal in a way that political treatise, detailed journalism, or even erudite poetry did not, for it stirred the emotions through the vehicle of a good story.

In addition, the audience to whom the romance novel appealed was primarily women. This kind of literature was seen as not taxing their delicate natures. The novel was edifying and enjoyable, focusing on the mode that convention had bequeathed to them—romance. The form of the novel was a critical choice for Harper, since she well knew that young white women had constituted the ranks of the Anti-Slavery Movement. Moreover, because of the consciousness raising that Women's Rights organizations had effected among certain classes of northern women during the latter half of the nineteenth century, Harper could well surmise that they would be a potentially effective audience who needed only to be inspired by her words. Hence, her choice of the romance novel.

But the romance novel as a form has certain requirements. The most important for this discussion has to do not only with its message, but with the character of its heroine who is the backbone of the form. Romance novels, in the nineteenth century, as today, feature the conventional heroine, the ideal woman as society defines her, and place her in a situation of peril, in conflict with her ideal nature. The anti-slavery heroines, black or white—Eva in *Uncle Tom's Cabin* or Clotel in *Clotel*—embodied the nineteenth century ideal of womanhood. Beautiful in a delicate Anglo-American mold, they were also natural Christians, that is, obedient, pure, refined. The perils with which they are confronted, though physical, are, at core, moral; for what the danger is really about is the assault of the sullied world on their natures. They would rather die than alter their standards. The effect on the reader is edifying, for the fact that such perfection could be destroyed by the world indicates that the world must be changed. Thus, the message, whether it be that men in general are base and must be saved by the refined virgin (as in the conventional romance) or that white men must be led to the path of righteousness by the suffering Christian Octoroon (as in the abolitionist romance), flows from similar images, language, characters.

If Harper were to write a successful romance, one "that would awaken her countrymen to a more Christian-like humanity," she would have to construct such an ideal and discard her knowledge of black women's lives in 1892. One reason for this is that black women were not beautiful according to the norms of the day; another is that most black women, because they had to work, were in contact with the sullied world and could scarcely be "pure" in their attitude toward life. Finally, refinement or the state of being well-bred could hardly be claimed, since the majority of them had been slaves. Yet Harper's message could not be effectively constructed unless the heroine was black in some way, a slave at some time, and subject to the perils of bestial men from which most refined women were protected.

She solved this problem in a rather ingenious way by having Iola LeRoy live much of her childhood and adolescence as a white woman of wealth, refinement, and education. Then she is plunged into slavery during which she must confront rape; after becoming free she must earn a living and deal with racial discrimination. Iola LeRoy, Before and After, represents the ideal as affected by the real. Finally, in order to provide edification for the reader, Harper had to conclude with an ideal woman: thus, her construction of a variation on the image of nineteenth century ideal womanhood—the beautiful Iola LeRoy who is the center of a growing black middle class, and who, together with her handsome doctor-husband, work in their respective spheres for the betterment of the race.

The variations are, however, important. For Harper, a believer in nineteenth century women's rights, insists on Iola's need and right to work; first as a seamstress, an occupation through which lucky black women of the day were able to make a living, and then as a social housekeeper, a woman dedicated to cleaning up society's messes through charity and good works. It is important to note that one of the most pressing problems that nineteenth century black women activists found among black women, the majority of whom were sharecroppers, was their need to be instructed in the "domestic arts." Slave women had not had a home to call their own and could hardly cultivate the art. Moreover, because domestic work, laundering, sewing, were jobs to which black women were relegated, training in these areas was not only "domestic art," but occupational advantage. Nannie Burroughs, one of the activists of the early twentieth century, was to raise this to the level of a successful business in her development of the National Training School for Women and Girls. What, then, may be seen as the feminine ideal in nineteenth century culture was for the black woman an occupational skill, necessary for her survival. And Harper, in stressing Iola LeRoy's involvement with the development of such a school, was constructing a new ideal, based certainly on the prevailing one, but affected by the reality of life for black women.

Because of the romance novel form and its audience, Harper had to construct reality in a different way. She constructed an ideal that hardly meshed with her knowledge of black women's conditions; yet, because of that knowledge and because of the movements with which she was involved, she changed that ideal, so that it had some relationship to reality and to her small audience of literate black women of the day.

The impact of the heroine is but one instance of how the form of the romance novel, its dependence on the reigning view of womanhood, affected *Iola Le Roy* as a novel. There are many other instances. The point here is that history, that way of organizing human knowledge into a coherent pattern, helps us to understand Harper's intentions and dilemmas in writing her novel, and most importantly, how the novel as a literary form is conditioned, to some extent, by history.

This realization becomes even more profound when one contrasts the novel with the autobiographical narrative, not the slave narrative, but free black women's accounts of their lives in the nineteenth century. Frances Foster, a scholar on the autobiography of black women, pointed out in a recent paper that these narratives stressed independence rather than obedience, practicality rather than refinement—rather manly qualities for the day. Unfettered by the novel form, these women could be more truthful about their lives. But she also adds that since these narrators were aware of the cult of True Womanhood, they devised social foils, such as being called by God to do these extraordinary things, so that they might still be accepted as women.

The women who wrote autobiographical narratives, many of which can be found in Bogin and Lowenstein's *Black Women of the Nineteenth Century*, sound more like Frances Harper than does her heroine. But because Harper was not intent on presenting reality or pursuing truth, she used that most popular form, the romance novel, to try to change her audience's view of black women, and in so doing had to conform to the form and its meaning for that time.

14 Trajectories of Self-Definition: Placing Contemporary Afro-American Women's Fiction* (1983)

In many ways, this essay is the culmination of the work I'd been doing on Afro-American women writers since 1980. In it I use the historical analysis I'd done in papers such as "The Uses of History," the insights I'd gained from doing analysis of individual writers, and my growing interest in African women writers. What pulled all these insights together for an overview of the literature was the short piece I'd done for KPFA Folio and the responses I'd received from the longer paper that grew out of that article. At the same time, Hortense Spiller and Marjorie Pryse were planning a volume of Afro-American women writers. Their comments on my original paper certainly sharpened by focus.

The centrality of Afro-American women's literature to a world view that we must assert in order to change our societies sent me on a search for the development of the self in that literature. In conducting that search, certain new patterns in the literature began to emerge. One of these, the lesbian theme, resulted in my writing another essay; another, the influence of Afro-American women and African women on each other, affected the essay on Buchi Emecheta and Alice Walker that I'd been struggling with. "Trajectories" both summarizes and projects some of my own findings about the vitality and significance of Afro-American women's fiction.

(1)

I see a greater and greater commitment among black women writers to understand self, multiplied in terms of the community, the community multiplied in terms of the nation, and the nation multiplied in terms of the world. You have to understand what your place as an individual is and the place of the person who is close to you. You have to understand the space between you before you can understand more complex or larger groups.[1]

— Alexis DeVeau

*To be published in Hortense Spiller, Marjorie Pryse, eds., *Conjuring: Black Women, Fiction and Literary Tradition*, University of Indiana, 1985.

In this straightforward statement, Alexis DeVeau alludes to a dominant theme in Afro-American women's fiction of the last decade, as well as to the historical tension from which that theme has emerged. Of course, many literate persons might say that the commitment to self-understanding and how that self is related to the world within which it is situated is at the core of good fiction and that this statement is hardly a dramatic one. Yet, for Afro-American women writers, such an overtly self-centered point of view has been difficult to maintain because of the way they have been conceptualized by black as well as white society. The extent to which Afro-American women writers in the seventies and eighties have been able to make a commitment to an exploration of self, as central rather than marginal, is a tribute to the insights they have culled in a century or so of literary activity. For Afro-American women writers today are no longer marginal to literature in this country; some of them are its finest practitioners.

But in order to really understand the remarkable achievement of a Toni Morrison, an Alice Walker, a Paule Marshall, or the budding creativity of a Gloria Naylor or an Alexis DeVeau, one must appreciate the tradition from which they have come and the conflict of images with which their foremothers have had to contend. For what Afro-American women have been permitted to express, in fact to contemplate, as part of the self, is gravely affected by other complex issues. The development of Afro-American women's fiction is, in many instances, a mirror image of the intensity of the relationship between sexism and racism in this country. And while many of us may grasp this fact in terms of economics or social status, we often forget the toll it takes in terms of self-expression and therefore self-empowerment. To be able to use the range of one's voice, to attempt to express the totality of self, is a recurring struggle in the tradition of these writers from the nineteenth century to the present. Although this essay could hardly survey the scope of such an inquiry, I am interested in showing some measure of the extent to which the tradition has developed to the point where Alexis DeVeau can make the claim she does, and how that claim has resulted in the range of expression that marks the fiction of the seventies and eighties.

Early Afro-American women novelists indicate, through their stated intentions, their primary reasons for writing their works. Frances Harper, for example, in her preface to *Iola Le Roy*, made clear her purpose when she wrote that "her story's mission would not be in vain if it awaken in the hearts of our countrymen a stronger sense of justice and a more Christian-like humanity."[2] Harper was pleading for the justice due Afro-Americans who in the 1890s were being lynched, burned out, raped, and deprived of their rights as citizens in the wake of the failure of Reconstruction. Iola LeRoy, Harper's major character, does not attempt to understand either herself as an individual or black women as a group. Rather, Iola LeRoy is a version of the "lady" Americans were expected to respect and honor, even though she is black. By creating a respectable ideal heroine, according to the norms of the time, Harper was addressing not herself, black women, or black people, but her white countrymen.

Audience was a consideration, as well, for Jessie Fauset, the most published Afro-American woman novelist of the Harlem Renaissance. She, together with Nella Larsen, wanted to correct the impression most white people had that all black people lived in Harlem dives or in picturesque, abject poverty.[3] She tells us why she chose to create the heroines she did in her preface to *The Chinaberry Tree* (1931). Beginning with the disclaimer that she does not write to establish a thesis, she goes on to point out that the novel is about "those breathing spells in-between spaces where colored men and women work and live and go their ways with no thought of the problem. What are they like then? So few of the other Americans know."[4] And she concludes her preface by identifying the class to which her characters belong: the Negro who speaks of "his old Boston families, old Philadelphians, old Charlestonians."[5]

Both Harper and Fauset were certainly aware of the images, primarily negative, of black people that predominated in the minds of white Americans. They constructed their heroines to refute those images, as their way of contributing to the struggle of black people for full citizenship in this country. Of necessity their language was outer-directed rather than inwardly searching, for their characters were addressed to "the other Americans" who blocked the collective development of blacks. To white American readers, self-understanding for black characters might have seemed a luxury. To the extent that these writers emphasized the gender as well as the race of their heroines they were appealing to a white female audience that understood the universal trials of womanhood. These writers' creations, then, were conditioned by the need to establish "positive" images of black people; hence, the exploration of self, in all its complexity, could hardly be attempted.

To a large extent, and necessarily so until the 1940s, most black women fiction writers directed their conscious intention toward a refutation of the negative images imposed upon all black women, images decidedly "masculine" according to the norm of the times.[6] Nonetheless, from *Iola LeRoy* (1892) to Dorothy West's *The Living is Easy* (1948), there is an incredible tension between the "femininity" of the heroines and their actual behavior. On the one hand, the writers try to prove that black women *are* women, that they achieve the ideal of other American women of their time, that is, that they are beautiful (fair), pure, upper class, and would be nonaggressive, dependent beings, if only racism did not exist. At the same time, they appear to believe that if Afro-American women were to achieve the norm, they would lose important aspects of themselves. The novels, especially those about passing, embody this tension. But even in the novels that do not focus on this theme, the writers emphasize the self-directedness of their heroines, as well as their light-skinned beauty and Christian morality. Thus, Iola LeRoy believes that women should work; Pauline Hopkins' heroine in *Contending Forces* (1900) wants to advance the race; Fauset's characters, though class-bound, have ambition to an unfeminine degree; Larsen's heroine Helga Crane in *Quicksand* (1928), though restricted by conventional morality, senses the power of her sensuality and the lie the image of the lady represents.

The tension between the femininity of these heroines and their "contrary instincts"[7] has its roots, in part, in the fact that Afro-American women, contrary to the norm, could not survive unless they generated some measure of self-definition. If they tried to live by the female version of The American Dream, as pure, refined, protected, and well-provided for, they were often destroyed, as is Lutie Johnson, Ann Petry's heroine in *The Street* (1946). And even if they secured a measure of the Dream, some, like Cleo in West's *The Living is Easy*, become destructive, frustrated, alienated from self.

One notable exception to this trend in early Afro-American women writers' works is Zora Neale Hurston's *Their Eyes Were Watching God* (1937). In this work Hurston portrays the development of Janie Stark as a black woman who achieves self-fulfillment and understanding. It is interesting to note, however, that Hurston was obviously aware that the literature of that time focused on the black woman's drive toward economic stability and "feminine" ideals. She constructs the novel so that Janie moves through three stages that embody different views of black women: In her relationship with her first husband, Logan Killicks, Janie is treated like a mule; she is rescued from that state by marrying Jody Starks, who wants her to become a lady, "The Queen of the Porch."[8] But Hurston critiques the achievement of economic stability through feminine submission in marriage as *the* desirable goal for the black woman. She portrays the disastrous consequences of this goal on Janie— that she becomes, in this situation, a piece of desirable property, cut off from her community and languishing in the repression of her natural desire to be herself. Though Janie's relationship with Tea Cake is not ideal, Hurston does present us with a vision of possibility in terms of some parity in a relationship between a woman and a man, based not on material gain or ownership of property but on their desire to know one another.

It is significant, I believe, that Hurston characterizes this relationship as play, pleasure, sensuality, which is for her the essential nature of nature itself, as symbolized by the image of the pear tree that pervades the novel. It is also critical to an appreciation of Hurston's radical effect on the tradition of Afro-American women's fiction that her language is so different from the language of the "conventional" novel of the times. Rooted in black English, Hurston used metaphors derived from nature's play to emphasize the connection between the natural world and the possibilities of a harmonious social order. And in keeping with her choice of language, she structures her novel as a circle, in which the returning Janie explores her own development by telling her story to Pheoby, whose name means the moon, and who is her best friend and the symbolic representative of the community.

In its radical envisioning of the self as central and its use of language as a means of exploring the self as female and black, *Their Eyes Were Watching God* is a forerunner of the fiction of the seventies and eighties. In general, though, most novels published before the 1950s embodied the tension between the writers' apparent acceptance of an ideal of woman derived from white upper-class society and the reality with which their protagonists had to contend. And most seemed to be written for an audience that excluded even the writers themselves.

But the attempt to present "positive" images of the black woman, to restrict her characterization to a prescribed ideal, did not result in any improvement in her image or her condition. Rather, the refutation of negative images created a series of contradictions between the image that black women could not attain, though they sometimes internalized, and the reality of their existence. That tension increased throughout the first half of the centruy, until the 1940s, when the destruction it created becomes apparent in the fiction written by black women. The heroines of this period, Lutie Johnson in *The Street* and Cleo Judson in *The Living is Easy*, are defeated both by social reality and by their lack of self-knowledge. Self-knowledge was critical if black women were to develop the inner resources they would need in order to cope with larger social forces.

(2)

Beginning with Gwendolyn Brooks's *Maud Martha* (1953), we can observe a definite shift in the fiction of Afro-American women, a shift in point of view and intention that still characterizes the novels written today. Afro-American women writers are, as Alexis DeVeau noted, putting more emphasis on reflecting the process of self-definition and understanding that women have always had to be engaged in, rather than refuting the general society's definition of them. The shift is, of course, not a sudden or totally complete one; there are many phases in the process.

The first phase focused on portraying what the early literature tended to omit, namely, the complex existence of the ordinary, dark-skinned woman, who is neither an upper-class matron committed to an ideal of woman that few could attain, as in the novels of the Harlem Renaissance, nor a downtrodden victim, totally at the mercy of a hostile society, as in Ann Petry's *The Street.*

Gwendolyn Brooks claims that her intention in writing *Maud Martha* was to paint a portrait of an ordinary black woman, first as daughter, then as mother, and to show what she makes of her "little life."[9] What Brooks emphasizes in the novel is Maud Martha's *awareness* that she is seen as common (and therefore as unimportant), and that there is so much more in her than her "little life" will allow her to be. Yet, because Maud Martha constructs her own standards, she manages to transform that "little life" into so much more despite the limits set on her by her family, her husband, her race, her class, whites, and American society. Maud Martha emerges neither crushed nor triumphant. She manages, though barely, to be her own creator. Her sense of her own integrity is rooted mostly in her own imagination—in her internal language as metaphors derived from women's experience, metaphors that society usually trivializes but which Brooks presents as the vehicles of insight. Though Maud Martha certainly does not articulate a language (or life) of overt resistance, she does prepare the way for such a language in that she sees the contradiction between her real value as a black woman and how she is valued by those around her.

Perhaps because *Maud Martha* was such a departure from the usual characterizations of Afro-American women in previous fiction, the novel went out of print almost immediately after it appeared. Nonetheless, it was to influence Paule Marshall, whose *Browngirl, Brownstones* (1959) is a definite touchstone in contemporary Afro-American women's fiction. In a lecture she gave in 1968 Marshall pointed to *Maud Martha* as "the finest portrayal of an Afro-American woman in the novel"[10] to date and as a decided influence on her work. And in characterizing Brooks's protagonist, Marshall notes Maud Martha's process of self-exploration: "In her daily life, Maud Martha functions as an artist; in that way, this novel carries on the African tradition that the ordinary rituals of daily life are what must be made into art."[11] The elements Marshall noted in *Maud Martha*—a focus on the complexity of women characters who are central rather than marginal to the world and the significance of daily rituals through which these women situate themselves in the context of their specific community and culture—are dominant characteristics of her own novels.

Like *Maud Martha,* the emphasis in *Browngirl, Brownstones* is on the black woman as mother and daughter. In an interview with Alexis

DeVeau in 1980, Marshall recalls that she wrote her first novel in the late 1950s as a relief from a tedious job. She wrote the novel not primarily for publication but as a process of understanding, critiquing, and celebrating her own personal history.[12] In understanding "the talking women," who were the most vivid memories of her youth, Marshall also demonstrates through her portrayal of Silla Boyce how the role of *mother* for this black woman is in conflict with her role as *wife* because of the racism that embattles her and her community. Marshall's novel, as well as Brooks's, was certainly affected by society's attitude that black women were matriarchs, domineering mothers who distorted their children who in turn disrupted society—a vortex of attitudes that culminated in the Moynihan Report. In attempting to understand her maternal ancestors, then, Marshall had to penetrate the social stereotypes that distorted their lives.

Few early Afro-American women's novels focused on the black woman's role as mother because of the negative stereotype of the black woman as mammy that pervaded American society. But instead of de-emphasizing the black woman's role as mother, Marshall probes its complexity. She portrays Silla Boyce as an embittered woman caught between her own personality and desires and the life imposed on her as a mother who must destroy her unorthodox husband in order to have a stable family (as symbolized by the brownstone). This analysis of the black mother prefigures other analyses of this theme in the 1970s, especially Toni Morrison's *Sula* and Alice Walker's *Meridian*. And Marshall shows that racist and sexist ideology is intertwined, for Silla's and Deighton Boyce's internalization of the American definition of woman and man runs counter to their own beings and to their situation as black people in American society and precipitates the tragedy that their relationship becomes.

Silla, however, is not an internal being like Maud Martha. She fights, supported by her women friends who use their own language to penetrate illusion and verbally construct their own definitions in order to wage their battle. As a result, Selina, Silla's daughter, will, by the end of the novel, have some basis for the journey to self-knowledge upon which she embarks, fully appreciating the dilemma that her mother and father could not solve.

Like Brooks's novel, *Browngirl, Brownstones* emphasizes how the black community, its customs and mores, affects the process of the black woman's exploration of self. But Marshall's novel also stresses the importance of culture and language as contexts for understanding *society's* definitions of man and woman, veering sharply away from much of the preceding literature, which emphasized advancement for black women in terms of white American values. She portrays the Barbadian-American community both as a rock her characters can stand on and as the obstacle against which they must struggle in order to understand and develop their own individuality. Finally, though, Selina's decision to return to the Caribbean is her attempt to claim her own history as a means of acquiring self-consciousness. In *Browngirl, Brownstones*, an appreciation of one's ethnic and racial community becomes necessary for black women in their commitment to self-development.

The emphasis on community and culture in *Maud Martha* and *Browngirl, Brownstones* as a prerequisite for self-understanding reflected a growing sense among Afro-Americans in the late 1950s and 1960s of their own unique cultural identity. But by 1970, when Toni Morrison's *The Bluest Eye* and Alice Walker's *The Third Life of Grange Copeland* were published, black women writers' stance toward their communities had begun to change. The ideology of the sixties had stressed the necessity for Afro-Americans to rediscover their blackness, their unity in their blackness. As positive as that position was to the group's attempt to empower itself, one side effect was the tendency to idealize the relationship between black men and women, to blame sexism in the black community solely on racism or to justify a position that black men were superior to women.

During the sixties few novels by Afro-American women were published; rather, poetry and drama dominated the literature, perhaps because of the immediacy of these forms and the conviction that literature should be as accessible as possible to black communities. The result of that change in perception about audience was that Afro-American writers consciously began to view their communities as the group to which they were writing. Black communities are clearly one of the many audiences to which Morrison and Walker addressed their first novels, for both works critique those communities and insist that they have deeply internalized racist stereotypes that radically affect their definitions of woman and man. In both novels, the community is directly responsible for the tragedies of the major characters—for the madness of Pecola Breedlove, for the suicide of Margaret Copeland, and for the murder of Mem Copeland by her husband. In *The Bluest Eye*, Morrison emphasizes the women's view of themselves. In *Grange Copeland*, Walker stresses the men's view. In these novels it is not only that an individual heroine accepts the sexist and racist definitions of herself, but that the entire black community, men and women, accept this construct—resulting in the destruction of many black women.

This fiction in the early 1970s represents a second phase, one in which the black community itself becomes a major threat to the survival and empowerment of women, one in which women must struggle against the definitions of gender. The language of this fiction therefore becomes a language of protest, as Afro-American women writers vividly depict the victimization of their protagonists. Morrison, Walker, Gayl Jones, and Toni Cade Bambara all expose sexism and sexist violence in their own communities. But it is not so much that they depict an altered consciousness in their protagonists; rather, it is that their attitudes toward their material and the audience to which they address their protest have changed since the novels of the 1940s with their emphasis on oppression from outside the black community. In the novels of the early 1970s, there is always someone who learns not only that white society must change, but also that the black communities' attitudes toward women must be revealed and revised. Interestingly, in *The Bluest Eye* it is Claudia McTeer, Pecola's peer and friend, who undergoes this education, while in *The Third Life* it is the grandfather, Grange, who must kill his son, the fruit of his initial self-hatred, in order to save his granddaughter Ruth. Both Claudia and Ruth possess the possibility of constructing their own self-definitions and affecting the direction of their communities because they have witnessed the destruction of women in the wake of prevailing attitudes.

By the mid-1970s, the fiction makes a visionary leap. In novels like *Sula* and *Meridian*, the woman is not thrust outside her community. To one degree or another, she chooses to stand outside it, to define herself as in revolt against it. In some ways, Sula is the most radical of the characters of 1970s fiction, for she overturns the conventional definition of good and evil in relation to women by insisting that she exists primarily as and for herself—not to be a mother or to be the lover of men. In other ways, Meridian is more radical in that she takes a revolutionary stance by joining a social movement, the Civil Rights Movement, which might have redefined American definitions of both race *and* gender. Sula stands alone as a rebel; Meridian gradually creates a community of support. It is important that both of these women claim their heritage. Sula and Meridian are who they are because of their *maternal* ancestry and their knowledge of that ancestry; it is from their mothers that they acquire their language. This is also true of Merle Kimbona in Marshall's second novel, *The Chosen Place, The Timeless People*. Though published in 1969, this novel depicts a black woman as both outside and inside the black world, as both outside and inside the West. As such, Merle becomes a spokesperson for her people, both female and male, who do not always understand their own dilemmas.

The heroines of the mid-1970s are socio-political actors in the world. Their stance is rebellious; their consciousness has been altered, precisely because of the supposed crimes they are perceived as having committed against Motherhood, and beyond the constraints society imposes on female sexuality. Yet they are wounded heroines, partly because their communities are deeply entrenched in their view of woman as essentially a mother or as the lover of a man. But although these characters are critical of their own communities, they come back to them and work out their resistance in that territory. Marshall and Walker both extend their analyses to the ways in which white women are also affected by definitions of sex and race. Essentially, though, it is within the context of black communities, rather than in the world of women, that they struggle.

By the mid-seventies, Afro-American women fiction writers, like Paule Marshall, Toni Morrison, Alice Walker, Toni Cade Bambara, and Gayl Jones, had not only defined their cultural context as a distinctly Afro-American one, but they had also probed many facets of the interrelationship of sexism and racism in their society. Not only had they demonstrated the fact that sexism existed in black communities, but they had also challenged the prevailing definition of woman in American society, especially in relation to motherhood and sexuality. And they had insisted not only on the centrality of black women to Afro-American history, but also on their pivotal significance to present-day social political developments in America.

(3)

The novels of the eighties continue to explore these themes—that sexism must be struggled against in black communities and that sexism is integrally connected to racism. The fiction of this period— Morrison's *Song of Solomon* (1978) and *Tar Baby* (1980), Gloria Naylor's *The Women of Brewster Street* (1980), Toni Cade Bambara's *The Salt Eaters* (1980), Alice Walker's *You Can't Keep a Good Woman Down* (1981) and *The Color Purple* (1982), Joyce Carol Thomas's *Marked By Fire* (1982), Ntozake Shange's *Sassafras, Cypress and Indigo* (1982), Audre Lorde's *Zami* (1982), and Paule Marshall's *Praisesong for the Widow* (1983) — cannot be treated collectively, for each reflects a great deal of difference. Yet all of these novels look at ways in which the quality of black women's lives is affected by the interrelationship of sexism and racism. And many of them go a step further. They pose the question concerning what community black women must belong to in order to understand themselves most effectively in their totality as blacks *and* women.

Morrison's novels, of those of the major writers, have moved farthest away from the rebellious woman stance of the mid-seventies, for she has focused, in her last two books, on men as much as women. Still, she makes an attempt in both novels to figure out the possibilities of healing and community for her women characters. In *Song of Solomon*, Pilate is such a character, although she derives her accumulated wisdom from her father and primarily benefits Milkman, her nephew, rather than any other woman in the novel. Jadine in *Tar Baby* is portrayed as the woman who has taken a position so far removed from her community that she becomes a part of the West. In her search for self, she becomes selfish; in her desire for power, she loses essential parts of herself. Thus, Morrison has moved full circle from Pecola, who is destroyed by her community, to Jadine, who destroys any relationship to community in herself.

On the other end of the spectrum, Walker's Celie comes close to liberating herself through the community of her black sisters, Nettie, Sophie, and Shug, and is able to positively affect the men of her world. The motif of liberation through one's sisters is repeated in Shange's *Sassafras* in which the healing circle is that of black women: three sisters and their mother. In contrast to the novels of the early 1970s, because of the presence of a stong woman's community, the major protagonists do survive, some with the possibility of wholeness. Ironically, the lush *Tar Baby* is the most pessimistic; the spare *Color Purple*, the most optimistic. Morrison sees no practical way out of the morass of sexism, racism, and class privilege in the western world, as it is presently constructed, for anyone, black, white, female, or male. Walker, however, sees the possibility of empowerment for black women if they create a community of sisters that can alter the present-day unnatural definitions of woman and man.

Between these two ends of the spectrum, other novelists propose paths to empowerment. In Marshall's most recent novel, *Praisesong for the Widow* (1983), Avey Johnson must discard her American value of obsessive materialism, must return to her source, must remember the ancient wisdom of African culture—that the body and spirit are one, that harmony cannot be achieved unless there is a reciprocal relationship between the individual and the community—if she is to define herself as a black woman. Her journey through myth and ritual, precipitated by the dream of her old great aunt, takes her back in time and space as she prepares to move forward in consciousness. So, too, with Audre Lorde's *Zami* (1982), in that she probes the cosmology of her black maternal ancestors in order to place herself. Lorde focuses more specifically than Marshall on a community of women who live, love, and work together as the basis for the creation of a community that might effect the empowerment of Afro-American women. These fictional works are similar, however, in that the search for a unity of self takes these women to the Caribbean and ultimately to Africa.

In fact, in many of these novels, Africa and African women become important motifs for trying out different standards of new womanhood. In *Tar Baby*, Toni Morrison uses the image of the African woman in the yellow dress as a symbol for authenticity that the jaded Jadine lacks. It is this woman's inner strength, beauty, and pride, manifested in the defiant stance of her body, that haunts Jadine's dreams and throws her into such a state of confusion that she flees her Parisian husband-to-be and retreats to the Isle de Chevaliers in the Caribbean. In contrast, Alice Walker reminds us in *The Color Purple*, one-third of which is set in Africa, that "black women have been the mule of the world there, and the mule of the world here,"[13] and that sexism flourishes in Africa. Audre Lorde begins *Zami* by describing her foremothers in Grenada: "There is a softer edge of African sharpness upon these women, and they swing through the rain-warm streets with an arrogant gentleness that I remember in strength and vulnerability."[14] Like Lorde, Marshall recalls in *Praisesong for the Widow* the uniquely African quality of the women she encounters in her Caribbean sojourn on Carriacou, an Africanness that reminds her of her Great Aunt Cuney who lived in Tatum, South Carolina. The recurring motif of *Praisesong*, itself a distinctly African form, is "her body she always usta say might be in Tatum but her mind, her mind was long gone with the Ibo's."[15] Marshall concentrates more than any of the other novelists of this period on delineating the essential African wisdom still alive in New World black communities. Ntozake Shange, too, uses African motifs in *Sassafras*, focusing on their centrality in U.S. southern culture and especially on the development of sensuality in her three sister protagonists. She quite consciously links African rhythms, dance, and style to a uniquely Afro-American woman culture, which is at the core of this book's intentions and connects it to the style and rhythms of other Third World American women.

What is particularly interesting about these novelists' use of African elements in relation to the concept of woman is their sense of concreteness rather than abstraction. All of the major characters in the books I've just mentioned have moved from one place to another and have encountered other worlds distinctly different from their own. Mobility of black women is a new quality in these books of the early eighties, for black women, in much of the previous literature, were restricted in space by their condition. This mobility is not cosmetic. It means that there is increased interaction between black women from the U.S., the Caribbean, and Africa, as well as other women of color. And often it is the movement of the major characters from one place to another (*Tar Baby's* Jadine from Paris to the Caribbean to the U.S.; *Praisesong's* Avey Johnson from White Plains to Grenada; *Sassafras's* Cypress from San Francisco to New York; *Color Purple's* Nettie from the U.S. South to Africa) that enlarges and sharpens their vision.

Not only is mobility through space a quality of present-day fiction, so also is mobility from one class to another. In contrast to the novels of the twenties, which focused on upper middle-class black women, novels of the forties, which tended to emphasize proletarian women, or novels of the seventies, which featured lower middle-class women, many of the novels of this period present the development of black women who have moved from one class to another as a major theme of work. Thus, Jadine in *Tar Baby*, Celie in *Color Purple*, and Avey Johnson in *Praisesong* have all known poverty and have moved to a point where they have more material security. Still there are many variations in these authors' analyses of such a movement.

In *Tar Baby*, Jadine is able to reap the material benefits of her aunt's and uncle's relationship to Valerian, their white wealthy employer, and becomes, in some ways, an Afro-American Princess. Morrison's analysis of Jadine's focus on security and comfort emphasizes the danger that obsession with material things might have for the ambitious black woman. In pursuing her own desire to "make it," Jadine forgets how to nurture those who have made it possible for her to be successful. She forgets her "ancient properties"[16] as Therese, the Caribbean sage points out, and succumbs to the decadent western view of woman. Paule Marshall also focuses on the dangers of materialism, on how the fear of poverty and failure has affected Avey and Jay Johnson's marriage and their sense of themselves as black, to such an extent that they do not even recognize their own faces. *Praisesong* has, as one of its major themes, middle-aged, middle-class Avey Johnson's journey back to herself, an essential part of which is the African wisdom still alive in the rituals of black societies in the West. While Morrison warns us that our ancient properties can be easily eroded by the materialism of the West, Marshall emphasizes the seemingly irrational ways in which the collective memory of black people has a hold even on the Avey Johnsons of America. Alice Walker approaches the element of class mobility in another way. Celie does not lose her sense of community or her spiritual center as she moves from dire poverty and deprivation to a more humane way of living, perhaps because she comes to that improvement in her life through inner growth and through the support of her sisters.

One effect of such a variety of themes and characters in the fiction of the early eighties is not only black women writers' analysis of the intersection of class, race, and gender, but also their presentation of many styles of life, many different ways of approaching the issues that confront them as blacks, as women, as individual selves.

This expression of a range of experience is nowhere more apparent than in these authors' treatment of their characters' sexuality. One radical change in the fiction of the 1980s is the overt exploration of lesbian relationships among black women and how these relationships are viewed by black communities. This exploration is not, I believe, to be confused with the emphasis on friendship among black women that is a major theme in earlier literature. This new development may have a profound effect on present-day attitudes about the relationship between sex and race and about the nature of women. The beginning of this exploration has already shown that lesbianism is a complex subject, for sexual relationships between women are treated differently in *The Color Purple, The Women of Brewster Street, Sassafras,* and *Zami.*

In *The Color Purple,* the love/sex relationship between Celie and Shug is at the center of the novel and is presented as a natural, strengthening process through which both women, as well as the people around them, grow. Walker also seems to be influenced by Zora Neale Hurston's use of language in *Their Eyes Were Watching God,* a book that she greatly admires, for the lesbian relationship between Celie and Shug is expressed through the metaphors of nature and in the form of black English. In a sense, Walker in *The Color Purple* does for the sexual relationships between black women what Hurston in *Their Eyes Were Watching God* did for sexual relationships between black women and men. In contrast, Gloria Naylor, in *The Women of Brewster Street,* places more emphasis on the reactions of the small community to which the lovers belong, as well as their own internalization of social views about lesbianism. There is more concentration in this novel on the oppression that black lesbians experience. Appropriately Naylor uses metaphors of endurance rooted in Afro-American folk speech. In Shange's *Sassafras,* the sexual relationship between Cypress and her lover is a part of a community of lesbian women who, while affirming themselves, are also sometimes hostile to one another as the outer world might be. The lesbian community in *Sassafras* is an imperfect one, and Cypress's sexual love for another woman is but part of a continuum of sexual love that includes her involvement with men.

In *Zami,* however, the definition of a lesbian relationship is extended, since Lorde beautifully demonstrates how the heritage of her Grenadian mother is integrally connected to her development as a woman-identified woman. In using the word *Zami* as a title, a word that means "women who live, love and work together,"[17] Lorde searches for the connections between myth, poetry, and history that might shift the focus of the definition of humankind, particularly black humankind, from one that is predominantly male. One question that these novels leaves unanswered is whether the bond between women might be so strong that it might transcend the racial and class divisions among women in America and make possible a powerful women's community that might effect significant change.

The emphasis on the culture of women as a means to self-understanding and growth is not only treated thematically in this new fiction, but it is also organic to the writers' forms. Increasingly, the language and forms of black women's fiction are derived from women's experiences as well as from Afro-American culture. The most revolutionary transformation of the novel's form is Alice Walker's *The Color Purple*. It is written entirely in letters, a form that (along with diaries) was the only one allowed women to record their everyday lives and feelings, their "herstory." And of equal importance, Walker explores the richness and clarity of black folk English in such a way that the reader understands that the inner core of a person cannot be truly known except through her own language. Like Walker, Ntozake Shange consciously uses a potpourri of forms primarily associated with women: recipes, potions, letters, as well as poetry and dance rhythms, to construct her novel. In *Song of Solomon* and *Tar Baby*, Morrison continues to expore Afro-American folktales and folklore, the oral tradition of black people, which as Marshall reminds us in *Praisesong for the Widow* is often passed on from one generation to the next by women. Marshall also uses dream, ritual, hallucination, and the metaphors of women's experience in CRITIC composing the ritualistic process of *Praisesong*. This exploration of new forms based on the black woman's culture and her story has, from my perspective, revitalized the American novel and opened up new avenues of expression, indelibly altering our sense of the novelistic process.

Thematically and stylistically, the tone of the fiction of the early eighties communicates the sense that women of color can no longer be perceived as marginal to the empowerment of all American women and that an understanding of their reality and imagination is essential to the process of change that the entire society must undergo in order to transform itself. Most importantly, black women writers project the belief, as Alexis DeVeau pointed out, that commitment to an understanding of self is as wide as the world is wide. This new fiction explores in a multiplicity of ways Alice Walker's statement in a recent interview:

> Writing to me is not about audience exactly. It's about living. It's about expanding myself as much as I can and seeing myself in as many roles and situations as possible. Let me put it this way. If I could live as a tree, as a river, as the moon, as the sun, as a star, as the earth, as a rock, I would. Writing permits me to be more than I am. Writing permits me to experience life as any number of strange creations.[18]

NOTES

1. Claudia Tate, ed., *Black Women Writers At Work* (New York: Continuum Publishing, 1983), p. 55.
2. Francis Harper, *Iola LeRoy, Shadows Uplifted*, 3rd ed. (Boston: James H. Earle, 1895), p. 281.

3. Hiroko Sato, "Under that Harlem Shadow: A Study of Jessie Fauset and Nella Larsen," in *The Harlem Renaissance Remembered*, ed. Arna Bontemps (New York: Dodd Mead, 1972), p. 67.
4. Jessie Redmon Fauset, Foreword to *The Chinaberry Tree* (New York: Frederick A Stokes Co., 1931).
5. Ibid.
6. For a discussion of this question see Barbara T. Christian, *Black Women Novelists The Development of a Tradition* 1892-1976, (Westport, Conn.: Greenwood Press, 1980).
7. Alice Walker uses this phrase most effectively in her essay "In Our Mothers Gardens," *Ms.*, 2 #11 (May 1974), p. 71.
8. Zora Neale Hurston, *Their Eyes Were Watching God* (New York: Fawcett Publishing, 1965 edition; first printed by Lippencott, Co., 1937), p. 42.
9. Gwendolyn Brooks, *Report from Part I* (Detroit: Broadside Press, 1972), p. 162.
10. Paule Marshall, "The Negro Woman Writer," tape of lecture at conference, Howard University, 1968.
11. Mary Helen Washington, "Book Review of Barbara Christian's *Black Women Novelists*," *Signs: Journal of Women in Culture and Society*, 8, No. 1 (August 1982): p. 179.
12. Alexis DeVeau, "Paule Marshall—In Celebration of Our Triumph," *Essence*, X, no. 1 (May 1980): 96.
13. Gloria Steinem, "Do You Know This Woman? She Knows You—A Profile of Alice Walker," *Ms.*, X, no. 12 (June 1982):
14. Audre Lorde, *Zami, A New Spelling of My Name* (Watertown, MA.: Persephone Press, 1982), p. 9.
15. Paule Marshall, *Praisesong for the Widow* (New York: G. P. Putnam's Sons, 1983), p. 39.
16. Toni Morrison, *Tar Baby* (New York: Knopf, 1981), p. 305.
17. Lorde, *Zami*, p. 255.
18. Tate, *Black Women at Work*, p. 185.

15 No More Buried Lives: The Theme of Lesbianism in Audre Lorde's *Zami*, Gloria Naylor's *The Women of Brewster Place*, Ntozake Shange's *Sassafras, Cypress and Indigo*, and Alice Walker's *The Color Purple** (1984)

I'd been struck by the emergence of the theme of lesbianism in the novels by Afro-American women in the last few years. How was this theme related to the literature of the previous decade? What did it mean about the depth of feminist thought in the literature? When Women's Place Bookstore in Oakland asked me to give a talk on Afro-American writers for African History Month, I decided to more fully elaborate on this trend that I'd noted in the essay "Trajectories." I was grateful for this opportunity, since I felt the need for audience response to this still explosive topic in the black community. I was not disappointed. The primarily black lesbian audience at Woman's Place was marvelous in their discussion of the books and of my essay. Such enlivened discussion was reward enough for the writing of this essay and indicated how important reader response is to our understanding of the literature's significance.

There is no question that Afro-American women writers are finally being allowed to openly explore the experience of lesbians in their fictional works. In the first four years of the 1980s, works having black lesbian experience as a central theme—Alice Walker's *The Color Purple* (1982) and Audre Lorde's *Zami* (1982)—have received considerable public attention, and novels that unravel the lives of a series of Afro-American women, such as Gloria Naylor's *The Women of Brewster Place* (1982) and Ntozake Shange's *Sassafras, Cypress and Indigo* (1982), include overtly lesbian characters among their presentation of the varieties of black womanhood.

*Read at Woman's Place Bookstore, Oakland, California, February, 1984.

Lesbian life, characters, language, values are *at present* and *to some extent* becoming respectable in American literature, partly because of the pressure of women-centered communities, partly because publishers are intensely aware of marketing trends. I say, *at present*, because the history of the publication of Afro-American books, of women's books, of books about Third World peoples in America illustrates how long periods of silence often follow literary explosions of second-class American citizens unless that group somehow gains the power to determine what appears in print. And I say, *to some extent*, because, despite the fact that Walker received the Pulitzer for *The Color Purple* and Naylor the American Book Award for *The Women of Brewster Place*, I doubt if *Home Girls*, an anthology of black feminist and lesbian writing that was published by Kitchen Table Press, would have been published by a mainstream publishing company. Nonetheless, "the buried life"[1] of the black lesbian writer, which Gloria Hull writes about in her essay on early twentieth century writer Angelina Weld Grimke, is beginning to be uncovered.

Black lesbians, of course, had written before the 1980s.[2] But seldom, until recently, have they identified themselves as lesbian or overtly written from a lesbian perspective. In her 1979 essay, "The Black Lesbian in American Literature: An Overview," Ann Schockley makes this observation:

> Until recently, there has been nothing written by or about the black lesbian in American literature—a void signifying that the black lesbian was a nonentity in imagination as well as reality.[3]

In tracing the minor lesbian characters that appear from time to time in Afro-American literature, Schockley emphasizes the "stereotypical caricature of black lesbians in the black community—the mannish woman,"[4] so that even when a character such as Ruby in Rosa Guy's 1976 novel of that same name emerges, both the writer's stance and the black literary community's response is based on a code of language that disguises the character's lesbianism.

If, as Audre Lorde so magnificently proclaims in her essay "The Uses of Erotic, The Erotic as Power," the erotic is at the core of self, of creativity, of expression, of communication, how does the dismantling of the code that disguises the lesbian perspective affect the works of the black lesbian writer?[5] How does the consideration of lesbianism as one of the varieties of black womanhood affect the stance not only of lesbian writers, but of non-lesbian women writers? In other words, does this way of seeing the world qualitatively change the literature of Afro-American women writers? How does it affect our language, as one powerful basis for our conception of ourselves? How does being black and being lesbian, in a society that restricts woman, condemns homosexuality, and punishes non-whites, contribute to the writer's understanding of self and community? Does a recognition and exploration of women who sexually love women help us toward the freeing of woman?

These are some of the questions that I am interested in approaching as I look at 1980s fiction that focuses on lesbianism. Before I move to the works themselves, however, I think it is important that I make clear the definition of lesbianism that I am using in this exploration. By *lesbian* I do not mean women-identified women, feminists, or women who are loving and supporting of other women. I specifically mean women who find other women sexually attractive and gratifying. Although I know that this definition may appear to some to be severely limited, even clinical, I think it is a necessary one for delineating these books of the eighties from previous books. Black women writers have always written about friendship between women. There are few novels written by black women (Ann Petry's *The Street* and Walker's *The Third Life of Grange Copeland* are notable exceptions) in which the female protagonist does not relate to a woman friend. Zora Neale Hurston's Janie in *Their Eyes Were Watching God* tells her story to her friend, Pheoby; Nella Larsen's Helga in *Quicksand* has a complicated relationship with her friend Anne; the friendship between Nel and Sula in Toni Morrison's *Sula* is the novel's sound and substance. And as Audre Lorde graphically illustrates in *Zami*, all lesbians are not supportive of women. But what is intriguing about novels of the 1980s is the overt exploration of sexual relationships among women, some friendly, some not so friendly, as an important aspect of black womanhood.

I also believe that in blunting the edge of sexuality between women (a sexuality that so threatens society it denies, even attempts to obliterate it) we might inadvertently miss critical discoveries about why societies seem to need to restrict and repress women, whether they are non-white or white, lesbian or heterosexual, working class or middle class. For example, when one looks at the history of the word *lesbian*, we see how its appearance is related to society's fear of women's increasing independence. The word *lesbian* is a twentieth century word, cited for the first time in 1908 in the Oxford English Dictionary.[6] Before that time, a woman's passion for another woman was often subsumed under terms such as *masturbation* or *the secret sin*. Some scholars suggest that the term *lesbian* appeared at a time when women were questioning sexual taboos, when discussions about birth control were on the rise and that the new term was a means of strengthening the stigmatization of non-procreative female passion as well as a strategy for retarding women's drive toward social independence.[7] The connotation of the word *lesbian*, then, when seen in its social context, seems to me to be critical.

In exploring the literature of the early eighties, I am also interested in emphasizing the spectrum of lesbian experiences that our writers are presenting. For this reason I have chosen these four books to discuss— Audre Lorde's *Zami: A New Spelling of My Name*, Gloria Naylor's *The Women of Brewster Place*, Ntozake Shange's *Sassafras, Cypress and Indigo*, and Alice Walker's *The Color Purple*. As their titles indicate, these works present distinctly different views of lesbian experience, even as they possess some powerful similiarities. *Zami*, Lorde's name for her fusion of autobiography, history, and myth is a Grenadian word "for women who work together as friends and lovers."[8] An overt lesbian poet and political activist, Lorde explores her development as a black/ lesbian/poet in the 1940s and 1950s in New York City and how that development is rooted in her mother's Caribbean homeland. On the other hand, though Naylor's title emphasizes place, she vividly portrays a series of women connected primarily by the fact that they happen to live in Brewster Place, a small black urban northern community of the 1960s. Her section "The Two" is as much about how that community sets two lesbians apart, as it is about the exploration of their characters. Shange's title *is* her novel's focus, for she juxtaposes the adolescence and young adulthood of three sisters, Sassafras, Cypress, and Indigo, who come from the southern U.S. of the 1960s, but whose names are symbolic of their roots in ancient black southern folkloric culture.[9] One of the sisters, Cypress, has a lesbian relationship. But unlike the portrayals of lesbianism in *Zami* and *The Women of Brewster Place*, Cypress's relationship with another woman is part of a continuum of sexual experiences, for she also has satisfying sexual relationships with men and by the end of the novel marries one. The women in *The Color Purple* are also from the South. In contrast to Cypress, however, Walker's Celie is forced to have sex with men, and the brutality she suffers is rooted in the relationship between southern sexism and racism. Both *Sassafras* and *The Color Purple* are concerned with the bonds between blood sisters. However, Walker extends her definition of sisterhood to Celie's sexual love for Shug, their initiation into a vision of sensual spirituality, which is nature's essence as symbolized by the color purple.

The portrayal of the variety of lesbian experience is a characteristic of early 1980s works and a considerable contribution to the literature. As Schockley noted in her essay, stereotypes are a major obstacle to black communities understanding and accepting lesbians as *women*, an obstacle that has been maintained and buttressed too often by silence. By presenting a variety of lesbian characters in terms of their physical appearance, personalities, and backgrounds, these four books refute the falseness and one-dimensional aspects of the stereotypes.

The depiction of physical appearance is not a trivial matter, for it has been used as a societal weapon to restrict woman, reducing her to a physical object whose appearance *is* her primary value, as well as being an indicator as to whether she is literally the right or wrong kind of person. For centuries, heroism for a woman consisted largely in her being physically beautiful and overtly compliant. In keeping with that prescription, Afro-American literary female heroes had to be light-skinned, that is, beautiful according to white standards.[10] In much the same way, the stereotypical body type of a black lesbian was that she looked mannish; in other words she was not so much a woman as much as she was a defective man, a description that has sometimes been applied to any Negroid-looking or uppity-acting black woman. Physical appearance was also supposed to be the reason for the lesbian's sexual preference: She was too ugly to get men; she was disappointed in men; she was a manhater; like men, she was overwhelmingly concerned with sex.[11]

Gloria Naylor's "The Two" emphasizes how stereotypes about the right and wrong kind of woman exist in the small community of Brewster Place. The story begins: "At first they seemed like such nice girls,"[12] as Naylor captures in one succinct utterance the community's evaluation of the right kind of woman as *nice*, as *girl*. She emphasizes how *nice* for single women means appearing to be nonsexual: "no wild parties," "no over-eager suitors," and that one of the two, because she has a "timid mincing walk" and regularly says good morning, was clearly nice. At first the women saw the other girl as a threat because she was "too pretty," with "too much behind," and wore clinging quiana dresses. But because she does not respond to the men's supplications, she too was clearly "a nice girl."

Naylor's use of the word *nice* takes on precious irony when the community decides the two women are lesbians, for there are still no wild parties, one of them still regularly says good morning, and the other is still too pretty. The community cannot claim that they are ugly, mannish, or man-haters. Naylor underscores how denigrating stereotypes are by having the people refer to the two women as "the lighter skinny one" and "the short dark one," their appearances being their means of identification rather than their names. Not until the two move inside their apartment and speak to each other do they become Lorraine and Theresa, distinctive persons with names.

In contrast to Naylor's lone lesbians alienated from their community, Shange gives us voluptuous details about a community of Third World lesbians in New York City called Azure Bosom. Mostly dancers, they delight in their female bodies. In this description of some of them, Shange's emphasis on the word *woman* dispels any confusion with the idea that lesbians are incomplete men:

Some of them were super chic and independent ones like Celine . . . others rounder than Xchell and more bangled than Cypress. Women with moustaches and Camels, more subtle types with Shermans. Women with big stomachs and big tits. Women looking like Smokey Robinson and women looking like Mirian Makeba. Somebody being fiery like La Lupe. And some women who didn't even know this was a Azure Bosom party and women couldn't come as woman but only as women and: women and jewelry and attitude, and talent and ennui and good taste and body.[13]

Rooted in the image of the Haitian voodun, Erzulie, Azure Bosom's dances celebrate female culture, protest the abuse of woman's body, and free "the coquette from the responsibility of breaking men's hearts," allowing "women to linger in their own eroticism, to be happy with loving themselves."[14]

Yet Shange also describes another side of Azure Bosom—that their parties were "more like a slave market where everybody is selling herself,"[15] and that many of these seemingly complete women talk obsessively about men and their terribleness. Shange, then, portrays the appearance of her lesbian characters as lush womanness, even as she questions whether some of them are lesbians because they are so male-oriented that they have internalized the standards of male conquests of females.

Lorde also stresses the variety of physical and personality character-istics of black lesbians in New York City of the 1950s. And she also tells us how clothes were used to signal the sexual role a woman is playing, a custom Lorde abhorred.

Bermuda shorts and their shorter cousins Jamaicas were already making their appearance on the dykechic scene, the rules of which were every bit as cut throat as the tyrannies of Seventh Ave. or Paris. . . . Clothes were often the most important way of broadcasting one's chosen sexual role."[16]

She recounts how she and her friends who refused to identify themselves according to the straight world's standards as to who is dominant and who is subordinate were disparaged with the term "Ky-Ky," a name used for gay girls who slept with johns for money."[17]

In contrast to Lorde and Shange's portrayal of a lesbian subculture or Naylor's story about lone lesbians alienated from their community, Walker's Celie and Shug do not have contact with other lesbians, and their love relationship enhances their entire community, male or female. Shug is described by Celie as a sensual, stylish woman who is direct in her speech and in her desires, a characteristic that Celie at first identifies with men:

"That when I notice Shug talk and act sometimes like a man. Men say stuff like that to women, Girl you look like a good time. Women always talk about hair and health. How many babies living or dead, or got teef. Not about how some woman they hugging on look like a good time."[18]

It is Shug's overt eroticism, her insistence on her right to pleasure, that Celie identifies as a male characteristic; in this society such direct womanishness must be twisted into mannishness. And, in an ironic twist on the stereotype, Walker's Celie initially sees herself as ugly. It is only after she develops a love relationship with Shug that she, as well as others, sees her natural beauty.

Not only do the varieties of physical types in these four works challenge stereotypes about lesbians, the reasons as to why the female protagonists make the sexual choices they do are characterized quite differently. The stereotypic reason—that women who choose women as lovers are disappointed in men—is not totally dispelled. In both *The Color Purple* and *Sassafras*, the sexism that men direct toward women is certainly critical to the women's choices. In contrast to societal views, however, which put the onus on the woman, claiming that they are somehow deficient, Walker and Shange emphasize the deficiencies of men. And, I think consciously and for different reasons, neither author describes her characters' relationship by using the term *lesbian*.

From childhood, Celie's only decent relationships are with other women. Her contacts with men are abusive: She is raped, beaten, totally controlled by them. Only the memory of her sister Nettie's love, her sister-in-law Sophie's resistance to abuse, and her admiration for Shug, the feisty woman her husband loves but cannot have, give her any comfort. Long before Celie meets Shug, she sees her photograph. The downtrodden woman's reaction to the image of this daring woman sows the seeds for the love that will later develop between them:

> Shug Avery was a woman. The most beautiful woman I ever saw. . . . She more pretty than my mama. She 'bout 10,000 times more prettier than me. I see her there in furs. And now when I dream, I dream of Shug Avery. She be dress to kill, whirling and laughing.[19]

To Celie, Shug is the woman she would like to be—assertive, beautiful, in control of her life.

Shug, on the other hand, is certainly attracted to men. Although she has been mistreated by them, certainly by Albert, her first lover, she refuses to be cowed by them even as she continues to enjoy them. As she tells Celie in one of her letters:

> . . . I know how you feels about men. But I don't feel that way. . . . I would never be fool enough to take any of them seriously . . . but some mens can be a lots of fun.[20]

Unlike Celie's response to her first glimpse of Shug, Shug's first reaction to Celie is the jealous retort: "You sure *is ugly*,"[21] as she anticipates hostility from Albert's wife. But Celie, Albert's wife, takes care of Shug,

Albert's lover, like she's a baby, and Shug in turn introduces Celie to the mysteries of female sexuality. In many ways, Shug becomes the mother Celie never had, protecting her from Albert and giving her knowledge about her body and about the essential spirituality of the world. And in some ways, Shug's ability to love Celie reconciles the blues singer to her role as mother, for she later goes and looks for her children whom she had left and insisted she didn't miss. In effect, these two women nurture each other.

Walker's characterization of the sexual love between Celie and Shug is conditioned by two themes that overlap and are both expressed in metaphors of familial relationships. The first is the natural bonding between women, as mother and daughter, as sisters. The other is the sexism that men direct against women unless women generate relationships among themselves and create their own community. Sexism, too, is discussed in the novel in familial language, for incest is the first powerful abuse Celie experienced, emphasizing Walker's point that men, even when they are intimately connected to women, may still be dangerous to them.

Cypress, in Shange's novel also experiences sexism as a prelude to her relationship with Idrina. The reason for her movement into Azure Bosom is the consistent slurs at women she hears while traveling with the dance troupe, The Kushites Returned. Most of its members are men who like men, but it is not their involvement with men so much as their narcissistic behavior that reminds her of the way men have related sexually to her. She begins to yearn for "nothing different from her in essence; no thing not woman."[22] Her relationship with Idrina gives Cypress a strong sense of herself, of the rightness of her body as well as the ability "to see other people as themselves and not as threats to her person."[23] Although Cypress is hurt when Idrina's lover comes back and she must leave, she finally learns that "loving is not always the same as having."[24]

Yet, in a subtle twist, it is Cypress's disappointment in her relationship with a woman that leads her to the after-hours night life of Harlem, where she discovers an old boy-friend, Leroy McCullough. He will become her lover, and later her husband. It is primarily in LeRoy's thoughts that Shange uses terms related to lesbianism, as he worries about the fact that he had heard that Cypress belonged to some "bull-dyke cult."[25] No where in the description of Cypress and Idrina's relationship does Shange use such language. Rather their relationship is described in terms of friendship and love.

In contrast to Walker and Shange, Lorde and Naylor consciously use the word *lesbian* in characterizing their protagonists. Neither Lorde nor the lesbians of Brewster Place have been deeply hurt by men before they choose women as lovers. Rather, their choice goes back to their adolescence, and it is society, both men and women, that hurt *them* because they have chosen to love women. Such societal oppression against their sexual preference does not happen to either Celie and Shug or Cypress and Idrina. They are oppressed primarily because they are black and because they are women, while the lesbians of Brewster Place and Lorde are oppressed because they are black and women and lesbians. The emphasis on the term *lesbian* in *Zami* and in *The Women of Brewster Place* is necessary to these author's discussion of society's condemnation of women who love other women.

"The Two" in *The Women of Brewster Place* come to see themselves as lesbians in quite different ways. Lorraine, the one with the timid walk, had fallen in love with a woman in high school and has never had sex with a man, while Theresa has been with men, some of whom she hoped "would die a slow painful death," but some of whom "were good to her—in and out of bed."[26] In her inimitable way, she makes it clear that she is naturally drawn to women rather than being disappointed in men:

> You can take a chocolate chip cookie and put holes in it and attach it to your ears, call it an earring, or hang it around your neck on a silver chain and pretend it's a necklace—but it's still a cookie.[27]

Both women prefer women to men, but they differ dramatically about what that choice means. Theresa insists that being a lesbian means that you are different, by nature, and that you are outside society, since it punishes you so intensely, while Lorraine detests the word *lesbian*, insisting that she is not different from other people. Interestingly, it is she who has suffered the most from her choice: Her father disowned her; she lost her teaching job in Detroit and fears that this will happen again. While Theresa prefers to ignore the straight world and socializes with lesbians, Lorraine hates to be cut off from the community:

> Why should she feel different from the people she lives around? Black people were all in the same boat—she'd come to realize that even more since they had moved to Brewster Place—and if they didn't row together, they would sink together.[28]

Theresa sees Lorraine's rejection of the label *lesbian* as an expression of her need for constant approval and characterizes her timid lover as a child who leans *on* her rather than standing toe to toe *with* her. Yet, when Lorraine does begin to challenge her, Theresa is angered and jealous because she sees her lover's growing rebellion as a result of her friendship with Ben, an old wino. Lorraine certainly does value Ben, for she says he is the only person who doesn't make her feel different, a slap at Theresa who continually stresses their difference. By juxtaposing these two women's totally opposite reactions to the term *lesbian*, Naylor demon-strates the complexity of being an outcast.

Naylor's presentation of the tensions in their relationship hinges on the community's rejection of The Two. And she emphasizes the fact that their isolation is initiated by *women* in the community. It is Mattie, one of the older and wiser women of Brewster Place, who articulates the fear underlying the hysteria of those around her. When she asks her friend, Etta, what makes the two different, and Etta answers that they love each other the way you love a man or a man would love you, Mattie responds:

> "But I've loved some women deeper than I ever loved any man. . . . Maybe it's not so different," Mattie said almost to herself. "Maybe that's why some women get so riled up 'bout it 'cause they know deep down it's not so different after all." She looked at Etta, "It kinda gives you a funny feeling when you think about it that way, though."[29]

Naylor, then, points up the fears of heterosexual women about lesbians, even as she underscores the violence men inflict upon them. In describing the men who rape Lorraine, she uses terms that express the community's powerlessness as well as the male's values:

> They only had that three-hundred foot alley to serve them as stateroom, armored tank and executioner chamber. So Lorraine found herself, on her knees, surrounded by the most dangerous species in existence—human males with an erection to validate in a world that was only six feet wide.[30]

The attack on Lorraine is not only done by these men, but by the entire community that had created an environment in which she could be seen as an accessible scapegoat, and beyond that by a society whose racism exacerbates the fear and anger powerless men feel against women who reject their only visible sign of manhood—their penis. As they tear up this woman, her previous words that black people are all in the same boat reverberate with horrible irony.

Like Theresa in *The Women of Brewster Place*, Lorde also stresses her lesbianism and her difference. But while Naylor's story is about women who are already adults, Lorde describes her growing up in New York City and in so doing gives us the first history I know about of what it meant to be a black lesbian in the 1950s. She tells us about her sense, from an early age, of her mother's difference, her independence and strength, because she came from a heritage of strong women in Carriacou, a small island off Grenada. She tells us that one of her childhood fantasies was "to acquire [a] little female person for her companion,"[31] to alleviate the loneliness she felt as a little girl. She tells us that in a predominantly white high school, she belonged to a group of girls who called themselves, "The Branded," a "sisterhood of rebels," who even talked about their position as women in a world supposed to by run by men."[32] And she tells us about Gennie, black and different like Lorde, who was the first person she was ever conscious of loving. The section in which she relates Gennie's suicide begins with a list of thing she never did with her friend, as Lorde later realized that they never "let [their] bodies touch and tell the passion that [they] felt."[33]

Lorde recognizes in phases that she is a lesbian. It is not until she moved out of her parents' house (anticipating parental disapproval) that she considers the idea that she might be "gay," the word she used at that time. Even before she gets pregnant and has to have a painful abortion, Lorde finds sex with her boyfriend "pretty dismal and frightening and a little demeaning."[34] Only when she is confronted by another black woman who desires her and believes she is gay, does Lorde say "yes." And it is only when she falls in love with Eudora, a radical white newspaperwoman who dislikes the word *gay* and calls herself lesbian, does Lorde herself acknowledge that she is a lesbian with all the societal implications the word implies.

It is women rather than men who are able to confirm Lorde's preference. Yet, it is women who complicate it. Because of the autobiographical quality of *Zami*, Lorde is able to both celebrate and critique the lesbian community of which she is a part. Like Cypress in *Sassafras*, Lorde's social world is the lesbian community. But while Cypress is a part of a Third World women's collective of the 1960s, Lorde tells us there were "no mothers, no sisters, no heroes"[35] for the young black lesbians of the 1950s, and that "it seemed loving women was something that other black women just didn't do."[36] She analyzes some of the reasons why:

> Most Black lesbians were closeted, correctly recognizing the Black community's lack of interest in our position, as well as the many more immediate threats to our survival as Black people in a racist society. It was hard enough to be Black, to be Black and female, to be Black, female and gay. To be Black, female and gay and out of the closet in a white environment . . . was considered by many Black lesbians to be simply suicidal.[37]

Because of this, the lesbians who did show themselves had to be tough (consider the black community's stereotype of the mannish woman) and were defined by white standards of beauty. Their blackness was as disparaged in the lesbian community as it was in the straight world.

The result was that Lorde, like many other black lesbians, became involved with white lesbians. But such relationships too were problematic, as her love relationship with Muriel, a white women, illustrates. For racism was as ingrained in the lesbian community as it was in society at large. Lorde knows that Muriel is wrong when she insists that "we're all niggers, all equal in our outsiderhood,"[38] for the black woman knows that "it colored our perceptions and made a difference between us in the ways I saw pieces of the world she shared."[39] Nonetheless, Lorde emphasizes the way in which being lesbian brought black and white women together in a community of sorts that would be discussed in the women's movement 20 years later as a brand new concept. "Lesbians," she declares, "were probably the only Black and white women in New York City in the 1950s who were making any attempt to communicate with each other." [40]

Zami is the only one of these four books in which there is discussion of deep relationships between black and white women in which the white world regularly intrudes. Because of this, Lorde's sense of the possibilities and difficulties of sisterhood, across racial lines, is sharp. Walker and Shange describe the sexism of black communities, Naylor, the homophobia of black and white communities. Lorde adds to this complexity the racism in the lesbian community and its tendency to adopt the standards of sex roles in the white male dominated world, *even* as she celebrates the community that women, black and white, attempted to build. Perhaps, because of her probing analysis of the complex life of the black lesbian, she is able to say:

> Being women together was not enough. We were different.
> Being gay girls together was not enough. We were different.
> Being black women together was not enough. We were different.
> Being black dykes together was not enough. We were different.[41]

Lorde reminds us that lesbians, black lesbians, are not all the same, and that we are always in danger of repeating society's pattern, of punishing those within our own group because they do not fall into the prescribed mold. She warns us, then, not only of society's attempt to institutionalize an "easy sameness,"[42] as a means of control, but also insists that those of us who have felt society's condemnation because we are different must recognize that therein lies our strength. In speaking about why there are no single issues, but rather an interlocking of oppressive systems, Lorde states:

> We should use difference as a dialogue, the same way we deal with symbol and image in literary study. Imaging is the process of developing a dialectic, a tension between opposites that illuminates the differences and similarities between things in apparent opposition. It is the same way with people. We need to use these differences in constructive ways rather than in ways to justify our destroying each other.[43]

In celebrating her difference, as a source of her energy and her need to speak her truth, Lorde traces its beginning back to her mother and to the many black women she loved during her years of maturation. In many ways, *Zami* seems to me to be a book about Lorde's reconciliation with her mother, her recognition that her mother was the first of those images of women to whom she owed "the power behind her voice," the "woman she became,"[44] even as she admits her mother's disapproval of her and the differences between them. Lorde ends her meditation on her youth with a return to Carriacou, her mother's home: "There it is said that the desire to lie with other women is a drive from the mother's blood."[45] She, then, attempts to place her lesbianism within the context of black women's culture as does Barbara Smith in her introduction to *Home Girls*.[46]

Society has tended to blame the mother for the daughter's lesbianism. Lorde sees her mother as her starting point, but she turns the analysis on its head. She celebrates her mother's qualities, her strength, her perceptions, her sensitivity, rather than society's view of the lesbian's mother as diseased, as somehow bringing up her daughter in the wrong way. By beginning with her mother's character, then, Lorde does more than present her own development, she attacks one of society's most persistent interpretations of the origin of lesbianism, an interpretation that denigrates all women.

In their different ways, Lorde, Walker, Shange, and Naylor relate lesbianism and feminism. Lorde and Naylor explore how society's attack on lesbianism is an attack on all women, not only because lesbians *are* women, but also because lesbian stereotypes expose society's fear of women's independence of man. Or to be more precise, woman is defined by most societies in a dependent, though necessary relationship to man. Lorraine Hansberry suggested many years ago that:

> There may be women to emerge who will be able to formulate a new and possible concept that homosexual condemnation has at its roots not only social ignorance but a philosophically active anti-feminist dogma.[47]

By being sexually independent of men, lesbians, by their very existence, call into question society's definition of woman at its deepest level. It is the importance of this truth that these four Afro-American women writers, lesbian and non-lesbian, proclaim. Walker and Shange challenge society's definition by presenting women's communities that are sexually and economically independent of men, though not separate from them. And Walker, especially, demonstrates how sisterhood among women benefits the entire black community. Lorde and Naylor underscore the many death-obstacles—silence, malice, guilt, violence—that society places in the way of lesbian relationships that might develop into such communities.

Some of the important contributions that the emergence of the lesbian theme has made to Afro-American Women's literature are: the breaking of stereotypes so that black lesbians are clearly seen as *women*, the exposure of homophobia in the black community, and an exploration of how that homophobia is related to the struggle of all women to be all that they can be—in other words, to feminism.

That is not to say that Afro-American women's literature has not always included a feminist perspective. The literature of the seventies, for example, certainly explored the relationship between sexism and racism and has been at the forefront of the development of feminist ideas. One natural outcome of this exploration is the lesbian theme, for society's attack on lesbians is the cutting edge of the anti-feminist definition of women. As important for black women, the stereotypic qualities associated with lesbian women: self-assertiveness, strength, independence, eroticism, a fighting spirit, are the very qualities associated with us, qualities that we have often times suffered for and been made to feel guilty about, because they are supposedly "manly" rather than "feminine" qualities. These works assert the rightness and naturalness of these qualities for women. And as Alice Walker's definition of womanism makes clear, black mothers have always passed on these qualities to their daughters.[48]

It is not surprising, then, that these books use as one of their unifying themes the relationship of mother and daughter, or of sisters. As Adrienne Rich so beautifully points out in *Of Woman Born*, "the loss of the daughter to the mother, the mother to the daughter is the essential female tragedy"[49] and is at the core of patriarchal values. In beginning to write about "the great unwritten story"[50] the relationships between mothers and daughters, a relationship that precedes even sisterhood— these writers celebrate women's natural bonding, as well as demonstrate the threat it represents to male-dominated societies.

I have already discussed how *Zami* proceeds from Lorde's inquiry into her mother's influence on her. Shange's form is also based on three sisters and their relationship to their mother, Hilda Effanie. Hilda's letters to her daughters, which announce the particular idea Shange will be pursuing in that section of the novel, are direct, witty, erotic, full of "Woman's Wisdom." However they also include many instances of "Woman's Folly."[51] For example, Shange juxtaposes Cypress' relationship with Idrina to a letter of Hilda's:

> Don't forget how I told all my girls that close women friends are always
> more trouble than they are pleasure. You can't ever keep your business to
> yourself or be certain that your own beau isn't the light of your life. Really
> that is how women act.[52]

Hilda, who, by the way, has close woman friends, assumes that all women are in competition for men, an assumption that she backs up with examples. But behind her statement lies the implication fostered by society that the presence of men should quell the possibility of genuine friendship between women, an idea that strikes at the heart of the black community from which she comes. Shange's placement of the letter is ironic comment, since Cypress has lost her beau, who is a woman, to another woman.

It is particularly interesting, too, that Lorraine in Naylor's story is the only protagonist in the four books who is tragic, and that she is also the only character who is given no maternal history. Naylor implies that Lorraine's story ends as it does because the women of Brewster Place, who should have been her mothers or sisters, failed to support her, worse, castigated her. That pattern is also evident in Walker's *The Color Purple*. Celie's mother is destroyed because of her isolation from other womenfolk, and Celie herself adopts destructive attitudes about how "uppity" women should be treated when she encourages Harpo to beat his wife Sophie. It is not until Celie and Shug recognize themselves in each other, rather than as competitors for Albert, that they are able to stave off his brutality and express their own right to pleasure and happiness.

These works, both realistic and visionary, focus on black women's need to consciously continue the heritage of womanism that we have forged in the crucible of extreme adversity. Further, these works insist that womanism is a bulwark not only against sexism, but also against racism, for they all insist on the racism that exists among white women, our potential sisters. Sophie in *The Color Purple* is brutalized and jailed because she refuses to submit to the mayor's wife; Lorde enumerates instances of racism in the lesbian community, and Shange extends her analysis of racism among women into a vivid nightmare. Cypress dreams of a matriarchal world where the powerful women are called The Mothers, white women who do not bear children, and the oppressed are called The Bearers, black and Latin women who are punished for crime by having to give birth. These works imply that because of racism, sisterhood across racial lines in America must first begin with black women's assertion of their own womanist relationships.

Yet lesbian relationships among black women in these books are not only bulwarks against sexism and racism, they are natural, self-fulfilling, sensual, the core of life affirmation. Another remarkable accomplishment of this literature is its focus on natural eroticism among women, from the delight of color, sound, and movement in *Sassafras*, the joyous bantering between Theresa and Lorraine in "The Two," to the sensual happiness in *The Color Purple*, and the erotic evocations of lovemaking in *Zami*. At the core of all life, the experience of its worth and fullness is the erotic, which opens us up to visions of possibility, of change. In contrast to Angelina Weld Grimke's life, whose "days cover[ed] her,"[53] and who "lived a buried life,"[54] black lesbian writers may no longer have to stifle their creativity or disguise it with a code that limits the expression of their visions. Lorde puts it beautifully in an interview with Claudia Tate:

> I believe in the erotic and I believe in it as an enlightening force within our lives as women. I have become clearer about the distinctions between the erotic and other apparently similar forces. We tend to think of the erotic as an easy, tantalizing sexual arousal. I speak of the erotic as the deepest life force, a force which moves us toward living in a fundamental way. And when I say living I mean it as that force which moves us toward what will accomplish real positive change.
>
> When I speak of a future that I work for, I speak of a future in which all of us can learn, a future which we want for our children. I posit that future to be led by my visions, my dreams, and my knowledge of life. It is that knowledge which I call the erotic, and I think we must develop it within ourselves. I think so much of our living and our consciousness has been formed by death or by non-living. This is what allows us to tolerate so much of what is vile around us. When I speak of "the good," I speak of living; I speak of the erotic in all forms. They are all one. So in that sense, I believe in the erotic as an illuminating principle in our lives.[55]
>
> . . . Change will rise endemically from the experience fully lived and responded to.[56]

NOTES

1. Gloria Hull, "Under the Days,: The Buried Life and Poetry of Angelina Weld Grimke," *Conditions, 5, The Black Woman's Issue*, ed. Lorraine Bethel and Barbara Smith, New York, 1979, pp. 17-25.
2. See J. R. Roberts, *Black Lesbians: Annotated Bibliography*, Tallahassee, 1981.
3. Ann Allen Schockley, "The Black Lesbian in American Literature: An Overview," *Conditions, 5*, p. 133.
4. Ibid., p. 134.
5. Audre Lorde, *The Uses of the Erotic: The Erotic as Power*, Out and Out Pamphlet, New York, 1978.
6. Catherine R. Stimpson, "The Lesbian Novel," in *Writing and Sexual Difference*, ed. Elizabeth Abel (Chicago: University of Chicago Press, 1980), p. 245.
7. Ibid.
8. Audre Lorde, *Zami, A New Spelling of My Name* (Watertown, MA: Persephone Press, 1982), p. 255.
9. The names of Shange's sisters are keys to their characters. Sassafras is the name of an indigenous green American plant. It is said that explorers knew they were approaching South Carolina by the scent of this herb used by the

Native Americans and then by blacks as a medicinal tea. Cypress is the name of a blue-green tree that also grows in America. It is also associated with North Africa as a wood that holds water. Indigo is an indigenous American plant, precious in the 16th century for its blue dye. Planters came, originally, to raise indigo in South Carolina before they considered the cultivation of cotton.

10. For a more expansive discussion of this point, see Barbara Christian, *Black Women Novelists, The Development of a Tradition, 1892-1976*, Chapters 1 and 2 (Westport, CT: Greenwood Press, 1980).
11. Schockley, "The Black Lesbian," p. 135.
12. Gloria Naylor, *The Women of Brewster Place* (New York: Penguin Books, 1982), p. 129.
13. Ntozake Shange, *Sassafras, Cypress and Indigo* (New York: St. Martin's Press, 1982), p. 145.
14. Ibid., p. 144.
15. Ibid., p. 145.
16. Lorde, *Zami*, p. 241.
17. Ibid., p. 178.
18. Alice Walker, *The Color Purple* (New York: Harcourt Brace and Jovanovich, 1982), p. 72.
19. Ibid., p. 16.
20. Ibid., p. 220.
21. Ibid., p. 50.
22. Shange, *Sassafras*, p. 139.
23. Ibid., p. 149.
24. Ibid.
25. Ibid., p. 160
26. Naylor, *The Women of Brewster Place*, p. 138.
27. Ibid.
28. Ibid., p. 142.
29. Ibid., p. 141.
30. Ibid., p. 170.
31. Lorde, *Zami*, p. 34.
32. Ibid., p. 81.
33. Ibid., p. 97.
34. Ibid., p. 104.
35. Ibid., p. 176.
36. Ibid., p. 179.
37. Ibid., p. 224.
38. Ibid., p. 203.
39. Ibid., p. 204.
40. Ibid., p. 179.
41. Ibid., p. 226.
42. Claudia Tate, ed., *Black Women Writers at Work* (New York: Continuum Press, 1983), p. 114.
43. Ibid., pp. 101-102.

44. Audre Lorde, *Zami*, pp. 3-4.
45. Ibid., p. 256.
46. Barbara Smith, ed., *Home Girls* (New York: Kitchen Table Press, 1983).
47. Lorraine Hansberry, "Letter to The Ladder," in *Gay American History: Lesbians and Gay Men in the U.S.A.*, ed. Jonathan Katz (New York: T.Y. Crowell, 1976), p. 425.
48. Alice Walker, *In Search of Our Mothers' Gardens* (New York: Harcourt Brace and Jovanovich, 1983), pp. XI-XII.
49. Adrienne Rich, *Of Woman Born* (New York: Bantom Books, 1976), p. 240.
50. Ibid., p. 226.
51. I am using the terms, "Women's Wisdom," and "Woman's Folly" as Alice Walker does in her essay, "One Child of One's Own," *In Search of Our Mothers Gardens*.
52. Shange, *Sassafras*, p. 153.
53. Gloria Hull, "The Buried Life," p. 24.
54. Tate, *Black Women Writers*, p. 115.
55. Ibid., p. 112.

16 The Dynamics of Difference: Book Review of Audre Lorde's *Sister Outsider** (1984)

Another new development in Afro-American women's litera-
ture during the last few years has been the publication of
collections of essays by major writers, essays that articulate the
development of a black feminist perspective. Because Women's
Review of Books *gives a writer the opportunity to write a long*
review, I was able not only to discuss Lorde's brilliant essays, but
to relate them as well to a growing body of essays that Afro-
American writers are producing.

In 1975, a colleague of mine asked me if I knew of any collections of
essays by a contemporary Afro-American feminist writer. She was
teaching a course on feminist theory and was using essays as a pivotal
form in her presentations. She knew of the many brilliant novels and
collections of poetry of Afro-American women that had been published
during the last decade. Nikki Giovanni's *Gemini* (1971) and Gwendolyn
Brooks's *Report from Part I* (1972) had been published but were more
autobiographical than analytical in character. Her mainstay in the course
she had taught the previous year was Toni Cade's edition of *The Black
Woman* (1970), a seminal collection that indicated a black feminist
orientation existed. But she yearned for a collection of essays by one of
our writers that presented ideals central to black feminist views, which
exploded with such power in the novels and poems of the seventies.

Since then, June Jordan's *Civil Wars* (1980) and Alice Walker's "In
Search of Our Mothers' Gardens", Womanist Prose (1983) have been
published. And just recently Audre Lorde, one of our finest contemporary poets, has collected her essays and speeches in a volume called *Sister
Outsider.* As poets, these three writers have contributed significantly to
the charting of "forbidden" paths that contemporary Afro-American
women must travel in order to define ourselves. Jordan, Walker, and
Lorde, each in their distinctive voice, have created a body of work that
expresses the varieties of black womanhood, our gropings, our wisdom
and folly, even as each of them has critiqued the ways in which society
attempts to hinder us, even destroy us. In emphasizing our need to probe

*First published in *The Women's Review of Books*, 1, no. 11 (August, 1984).

our maternal history, all three urgently insist that we are central to our survival, our freedom. As black, poor, woman, our view of the world is central to an understanding of the world.

Their collections of essays present another way of saying, of making felt, what these writers express in much of their poetry. And in all three collections we can see a *process* of self-development, the other side of the more distilled, compressed form that is their poetry—a process that delineates their continual pushing beyond a previously held idea, refining it, changing it—a process that illuminates the movement of their thought. Each collection, too, reveals the individual writer's focus on a specific idea that fuels the energy in her poetry and/ or novels—in all of her work.

The titles of each volume are a pointer to that focus. For Jordan, her growth through the fifties and sixties in New York City took place in the context of this country's civil wars between the powerful and the powerless and is reflected in the civil wars within herself. Black, woman, poor, she gropes toward her fullness as a poet, journalist, Third World activist, and teacher. In her many-sidedness, she learns increasingly the "intimate face of universal struggle." Alice Walker's essays trace her search for an understanding of the creative legacy of our mothers' gardens, a search that gives us back an absolutely necessary resource— our history, our various writers and thinkers, our tradition, so that we might recognize, and more importantly, articulate and expand, the womanist in us. Both Sister and Outsider, Lorde, a black lesbian poet, focuses on her discovery of the importance of the concept of difference in our forming of ourselves, our relating to each other. The understanding of difference, is, for her, a creative charge, an aspect of that erotic power that is undermined by society's attempt to promote an "easy sameness," an efficient means of controlling people.

Unlike Jordan and Walker's collections, which cover a period of some twenty years, Lorde's essays date from 1976 to the present. For much of her writing life, she has exclusively published poetry. She tells us in her interview with Adrienne Rich (which is included in *Sister Outsider*) that she couldn't write prose for many years because "communicating deep feeling in linear solid blocks of print felt arcane, a method beyond [her]." Although the fifteen essays in *Sister Outsider* cover only these last seven years, along with *Zami* (1982), her first published book of prose, they trace important concepts in Lorde's development as a black feminist thinker, primarily her intense concern with repression as a means of control, which is reflected in her emphasis on the erotic and her analysis of the concept of difference.

Some of these deeply felt concepts are compressed in the poem "Sister Outsider," after which this volume is named. The poem appeared in

Lorde's The Black Unicorn (1978), which uses as one of its central motifs the ancient wisdom of the women of Dahomey. Throughout the collection of essays, Lorde probes this ancient wisdom. Many of her essays flow from the last lines of her poem:

now
your light shines very brightly
but I want you
to know
your darkness also
rich
and beyond fear

Whether Lorde is writing about her trip to Grenada (her mother's homeland) or to Russia; whether she is analyzing the sexism and homophobia among black women and men, the racism ingrained in white women, the sexism, racism, homophobia of American society; or whether she is asserting the importance of the transformation of silence into language and action, her words are guided by that ancient tradition that cherishes the "darkness" of feelings as well as the "light" of ideas.

In the first essay she'd written in twenty years, Lorde uses the interaction of light and dark imagery to illuminate her statement that "Poetry is not a Luxury." In a sense this essay is her bridge between her writing of poetry and of prose. Insisting that "the woman's place of power within each of us is neither white nor surface; it is dark, it is ancient, and it is deep," she also emphasizes that poetry is "the quality of light within which we predicate our hopes and dreams toward survival and change, first made into language, then into idea, than into more tangible action." The thrust of this critical essay is Lorde's belief that we must combine the ancient, non-European cherishing of the power of feeling with the European concept that ideas will make us free, and that women have the possibility of this fusion because we still have some respect for that darkness within. Her axiom, "The white fathers told us, 'I think, therefore I am.' The Black Mother within each of us—the poet—whispers in our dreams, 'I feel, therefore I can be free'" is examined in other essays, in "The Uses of Anger" and in her provocative essay, "The Uses of the Erotic, The Erotic as Power."

This essay, for me, is one of Lorde's most significant statements, even as it is one of her most difficult to summarize—partly because it is written in such distilled language, partly because the erotic in this society has been so confused with sex that anyone who uses the word, in its root sense, is in danger of being misunderstood. Yet Lorde uses our persistent misunderstanding of the word, and therefore our loss of an important source of power, to make essential distinctions between the pornographic and the erotic. In so doing she addresses one of the dilemmas of humanity. How do people get to the point where they not only recognize their own oppression but will initiate the changes necessary to free themselves?

In defining the erotic, Lorde goes back to the Greek word *eros*, "the personification of love in all of its aspects—born of Chaos and personifying power and harmony." Each part of this definition is critical to her discussion of the uses of the erotic: the trusting of self, the Chaos not fully understood, but from which creativity and harmony spring, the power that the passion for life has to move us toward action. And in discussing its uses for women, she places this definition in sharp focus. For women are the ones who have been trivialized as "feeling" beings who cannot "think," even as the society gives us the charge of feeling for men. As a result, Lorde asserts that we have come "to distrust that power from which rises our deepest nonrational knowledge," which is our basis for demanding from life all that we know it can be. Out of touch with that disturbing Chaos, from which creativity and satisfaction come, we need not be controlled by external forces, we maintain our own repression. But if we are responsibile to ourselves in the deepest sense, in our work, in our pleasures, in our struggles, "our acts against oppression become integral with self, motivated and empowered from within."

Her articulation of the power of the erotic is also connected to the other critical concept that characterizes her thought—difference as a dynamic force. For Lorde, the erotic is the source of that "sharing of joy," which provides a deep connection between persons, who are, necessarily, different. Thus the erotic is one means by which difference among people can become a source of creative dialogue, rather than a threat.

Difference is, for Lorde, a given in any human situation. What she articulates in essays like "Scratching the Surface, Some Notes on Barriers to Women and Loving," or "Age, Race, Class and Sex: Women Redefining Difference" is that racism, sexism, classism, ageism, homophobia, all stem from the same source—"an inability to recognize the notion of difference as a dynamic human force which is enriching rather than threatening to the defined self." And what she analyzes in essays like "The Master's Tools Will Never Dismantle the Master's House" or in "Learning from the 60's" is how movements like the Black Movement, the Women's Movement, which spring from society's intolerance of difference, tend to be as intolerant of differences among their own constituents. The result is not only the weakening of the movement, for so many are excluded from the inner sanctum, but the loss of the creative function of difference as a source of new ideas, new visions. Thus, if "women" are defined as white, heterosexual, young women whose class position enables them to see certain aspects of life as the only ones that demand change, then what is lost is the knowledge of women of color, of older women, of poor women, of lesbian women. If we succumb to the master's most effective tool, the pitting of people against one another by using the threat of difference, we can never dismantle the master's house. Lorde warns that "in our world, divide and conquer must become define and empower."

Lorde, however, is not so naive as to see the path she advocates as an easy one. It means, as she writes in her poem, "Among Ourselves," that we must "stop killing/the other/in ourselves/the self that we hate in others." It therefore means the exposure of self and the recognition of the terror we have for a particular difference. It means to struggle with those with whom we might have much in common, with whom we might have differences. Such a stance means that most of us must give up something, whether it is class privilege or self-absorption.

Lorde follows her own advise in essays such as "Sexism, An American Disease in Blackface," which was written in response to Robert Staples's article, "The Myth of Black Macho, A Response to Angry Black Feminists;" in her "Letter to Mary Daly," which was her response to Daly's unbalanced treatment of women of color in *Gyn/Ecology*; in her telling about her relationship to her son in "Man Child, A Black Feminist Response;" in her exposure of self to other black women in "Eye to Eye: Black Women, Hatred and Anger."

As a black, lesbian, feminist, poet, mother, Lorde has, in her own life, had to search long and hard for *her* people. In responding to each of these audiences, in which a part of her identity lies, she refuses to give up her differences. In fact she uses them, as woman to man, black to white, lesbian to heterosexual, as a means of conducting creative dialogue. Thus, she asserts that "the results of woman-hating in the Black communities are tragedies which diminish all Black People" and that the black man's use of the label "lesbian" as a threat is an attempt to rule by fear. She reminds white women who fear the anger of black women that "anger between peers births courage, not destruction, and the discomfort and sense of loss it often causes is not fatal but a sign of growth." In "Eye to Eye," she acknowledges the anger that black women direct toward each other, as well as our history of bonding, in a society that tells us we are wrong at every turn. In discussing our condition she reminds black women who attack lesbianism as anti-black of "the sisterhood of work and play and power" that is a part of our African tradition, that we have been taught to see each other as "heartless competitors for the scarce male, the all important prize that could legitimize our existence." This dehumanization of the denial of self, she asserts, "is no less lethal than the dehumanization of racism to which it is so closely allied." And underlying all of Lorde's attempts to have creative dialogue with the many parts of her self is her recognition that the good in this society is tragically defined in terms of profit rather than in terms of the human being.

Lorde's essays are always directed toward the deepening of self, even as she analyzes the ways in which society attempts to dehumanize it. In showing the connections between sexism, racism, ageism, homophobia, classism, even as she insists on the creative differences among those persons they affect, she stresses the need to share the joy and pain of living, through language. In speaking, in breaking the silences about what each of us actually experiences, what we think, in voicing even our disagreements, we bridge the differences between us. Like Jordan and Walker's essays, Lorde's collection "broadens the joining," even as it exemplifies another way in which a black woman interprets her experiences.

Sister Outsider is another indication of the depth of analysis that black women writers are contributing to feminist thought. It is an analysis that stresses the connections between people and critiques a stance of easy separatism. As people who have been excluded, because we are black, woman, poor, lesbian, not correct in some way, black women writers carefully search for the sources of real connections. Particularly when Lorde's collection of essays is seen within this growing body of feminist thought, her assertion that difference is a dynamic force is a powerful one if we are serious about recreating our world.

17 An Angle of Seeing: Motherhood in Buchi Emecheta's *The Joys of Motherhood* and Alice Walker's *Meridian* (1984)

This essay has been gestating for quite a while. Convinced that contemporary African and Afro-American women writers had much in common, I began doing a general essay of comparison. But such an endeavor, it became clear to me, was far too ambitious for an essay. In the process, I decided to do a paper that focused on Alice Walker's and Buchi Emecheta's views on motherhood in their novels for "The Spiritual Strivings" conference on Afro-American literature that U.C.L.A. held in April 1983. Soon my inquiry was limited to The Joys of Motherhood *and to* Meridian.

I did not attend the conference, nor was I satisfied with the paper I'd written. It lacked the historical context I felt necessary for an understanding of the ideologies of motherhood that Emecheta and Walker were analyzing. As a result, I spent more time learning from anthropologists, sociologists, philosophers, historians about what motherhood meant in early twentieth century Nigeria and in the U.S. South. This essay is a culmination of that effort, within which the novels are placed.

But "An Angle of Seeing" is, from my perspective, still incomplete. A book could be done on the subject. And literature student that I am, I was frustrated by the lack of coherence in scholars' analyses of this primary institution. This essay is a beginning inquiry rather than a conclusive one, which may lead to a more illuminating analysis of the experience and institution of motherhood.

(1)

Path-let . . . leading home, leading out
Return my mother to me.[1]

> Stella Ngatho, 1953-
> (Kenya)

momma
teach me how to hold a new life
momma
help me
turn the face of history
to your face.[2]

June Jordan, 1936-
(Afro-America)

I have been exploring the possibility that there may be major points of comparison between contemporary African and Afro-American women writers, my intuition being that their cultural roots in Africa, as well as their experiences of sexism, enslavement, and colonialism, have so affected their lives that they might tend toward similar themes and forms. In reading the fiction of Buchi Emecheta, the Nigerian writer, and Alice Walker, the southern U.S. writer, I am struck by the centrality of the theme of motherhood in their works.

Motherhood is a major theme in contemporary women's literature, the "unwritten story"[3] just beginning to be told as a result of women's struggles to become all that they can be. Since a woman, never a man, can be a mother, that experience should be hers to tell; since we all come from mothers, it is striking that such a story remains secondary in world literature. As important is the fact that the role of mother, with all that it implies, is universally imposed upon women as their sole identity, their proper identity, above all others. The primacy of motherhood for women is the one value that societies, whatever their differences, share.

In the last decade, many women scholars and writers have begun to discuss the meaning of this value, the ways in which motherhood is both a universal experience and a world-wide institution. In *Of Woman Born*, Adrienne Rich emphasizes the historical reality that while motherhood is the experience of women, the institution of motherhood is under male control and that the *potential* of women to be mothers—that is, their physicality—conditions their entire lives.[4] Ironically, the experience unique to women is interpreted for them through male authorities and structures, through religion, myth, science, politics, economics. What happens to these interpretations when women begin to articulate their experience of motherhood and interpret its value accordingly? How does this shift in point of view, this angle of seeing, affect our understanding not only of the experience, but of the institution as well? How does it help us understand our position as women in our respective societies?

I am intrigued by the ways in which Emecheta, particularly in her novel, *The Joys of Motherhood*, and Alice Walker, particularly in *Meridian*, interpret the value of motherhood in their communities as related to the outer society. These two writers' foci emanate from the profound value they place on women and from their belief that a positive change in the quality of their lives would ultimately and substantively transform their societies. Their treatment of the theme of motherhood, however, cannot be effectively examined unless we look at their respective society's view of that role and how it has been manifested in the literature that preceded them. What was the ideology of motherhood in early twentieth century Nigeria, the black communities of the U.S.? How did African writers and Afro-American writers treat this subject in the first half of this century? The concept of motherhood is of central importance in both the philosophy of African and Afro-American peoples, so that the theme has not been ignored; rather it is related to the historical process within which these peoples have been engaged, a process that is an intertwining of tradition, enslavement, and the struggle for their peoples' freedom. The beginning of that process is the traditional root. And since Afro-Americans are African peoples, an investigation of the concept of motherhood must necessarily start with its value in traditional African cultures.

(2)

Who has strangled the tired voice
of my forest sister?
. . . .
No it comes no more, still damp with dew
leashed with children and submission. . . . .
One child on her back, another in her womb
—always, always, always![5]

Noemi a da Sousa, 1927-
(Mozambique)

Africa is, of course, a large land mass with a long and complex history. One concept that has been constant throughout the history of this varied continent is the centrality of motherhood to its many religions, philosophies, ways of life. Diop, the African philosopher, emphasizes the preeminence of the prehistoric Mother Goddess in Africa, and that women, the inventors of agriculture, were the organizers of these earlier civilizations. His descriptions of this period are not so much those of matriarchies; rather, they are of mother-centered civilizations that valued agriculture and collectivity. Broken by the need for warriors to resist invading nomadic peoples, these highly civilized societies still left their mark in myth, custom, tales that celebrate the Mother Goddess.[6] Contemporary African writers, like Armah in his book *Two Thousand Seasons*, have transmitted a largely oral history onto the written page. In his singing of the history of his people, Armah also describes a mother-centered society that was disrupted by invaders, the result of which was the increasing importance of the male warrior and a change in women's status. War also resulted in the exchange of women between factions as a means of securing peace and of cementing kinship ties. That daughters might leave the household also resulted in the rise of the status of sons.[7]

Whether Diop or Armah's accounts of earlier African history are true, there is no doubt that motherhood is for most African peoples symbolic of creativity and continuity. John Mbiti, the African anthropologist, stresses that this concept of motherhood is central to African philosophy and spirituality. Without descendants, an African's spiritual existence is nullified, since, for him, the dead of this earthly plane continue to exist in another dimension—as long as they are remembered and called upon.[8] A man's immortality, then, depends not only on the survival of his progeny as a part of a stream of humanity, but also on whether he has descendants to *remember* him and call upon him. Thus, the mother figure is greatly respected in African societies, buttressed as it is by myth, religion, and custom. African women receive certain practical benefits for being mothers. By having children, especially sons, who could grow up to be warriors and heads of households, a woman contributes immeasurably, not only to her community's survival but also to her well-being,[9] since in her old age she will be taken care of and revered by them.

The value given to sons, however, indicates the ambivalent status of women. Daughters are not as valued, since their primary destiny is to become mothers, a role necessary to the society but certainly not its only requirement for survival. In having her identity prescribed as mother, the women's life is preordained. Being a woman, that is, a mother, means that she must play a subordinate role in the society and must be submissive to her male kin.[10] Marriage and motherhood were the significant events in her life, an assumption strengthened sometimes by myths that focused on how women, the original rulers, abused their authority, transgressed against God or the well-being of society, and hence had to be contained by men.[11] Whatever a woman's skills, desires, or talents, she was prescribed by her "nature" and her society to subordinate herself to her primary function—that of motherhood. The high regard for mothers in African society, then, has both positive and negative effects for women, circumscribing them even as it makes them respected.

This is one view of the status of women in traditional African societies. Recently, however, scholars, especially women scholars, have presented another view in which African women are described not primarily as objects but as actors in their society.[12] This view stresses the importance of economic and social contributions that African women make to traditional societies and as a result their ability to determine, to some extent, their own lives.

The African women's contribution to the needs of her household (particularly in the precolonial era) was indispensable, and her status of mother and wife was higher than that of her European counterpart, whose centrality in production was fast undermined by Europe's Industrial Revolution. Joan Kelly-Godal points out that where: "the means of subsistence and production are commonly held and a communal household is the focal point of both domestic and social life, women's status tends to be more comparable to men's than in a society where the domestic and social sphere are separate."[13] In traditional societies, husbands and wives had separate work and incomes with clearly defined financial obligations to their children, spouse, and lineage. Generally speaking, married women had the "right to own and acquire property that was separate from that of their husbands."[14] In addition to farming, women were often engaged in trade and could keep much of those earnings for themselves. Still, these scholars also indicate that a heavy burden of labor was imposed upon the African woman by the system of the division of labor because she was both responsible for the well-being of her children and was expected to contribute to her husband's household. Her entire identity and material needs, however, were not derived from her husband, as her European counterpart's were ideally supposed to be. And since she was irrevocably joined to her natal family, rather than to her husband's family, she did have a certain sense of security that there was always somewhere she belonged.

That sense of security, of having some control over her life, was furthered reinforced by the bond the African woman shared with other women with whom she had experienced initiation into womanhood and who she could always call upon as sisters. Her social and economic well-being was also buttressed by the women's societies and associations that were an integral part of many traditional societies. Women joined together in organizations such as *mikiri* to aid themselves financially, to affect the political process, to participate in leadership positions in religious and ritual situations, or to "sit on a man," that is, to force him to change his behavior.[15]

Recent studies emphasize the many-sidedness of African women's status. On the one hand, women had "a substantial measure of economic independence and a voice in political affairs in many parts of the continent."[16] Scholars insist, however, that probably matriarchies did not exist in Africa, and that "one queen does not a matriarchy make."[17] On the other hand, "the basic framework was one of patriarchy. As elsewhere men rule and dominate."[18]

Often, women's subordinate role in society was guaranteed by unequal access to resources and cultural restrictions having to do with menustration, puberty rites, marriage, and motherhood. For example, many societies had strict taboos that restricted women during menstruation; often puberty rites for women kept them in seclusion for a long time.[19]

While both men and women went through initiation rites, cliterodec-tomies, to a greater extent then circumcisions, are painful, affect sexual pleasure and can result in serious and extended illness. As important, in many societies the domestication of livestock came to be the domain of men and the basis for the development of private property. Some scholars suggest that the "demands of child care were probably the basis for the initial lack of female participation in animal husbandry."[20] The physicality of women, then, their capacity to bear children, contributed to the cultural restrictions placed on them, even when they exerted some economic and political control.

The bride price is one way of illustrating the complexity of the status of the African woman. Often associated with the European dowry, this African custom is quite different in its thrust, for it was an acknowledg-ment that the woman was not so much property as she was a producer, a contribution to her family.[21] Nonetheless, the transaction of the bride price, even in matrilineal societies, is made between the men of the bride's family and her husband, indicating the importance of men as the primary decision-makers in her life.[22] And in many societies, the bride price was the material sign that the right of the mother to her children was transferred to the father, for without the payment of the bride price, the children would belong to the mother's family. So important was her ability to conceive, that in some tribes, a woman's marriage could be annulled and the bride price returned if she did not become a mother.[23]

Motherhood is so critical to most traditional societies that there is no worse misfortune for a woman than being childless. The "barren" African woman is seen as an incomplete woman. She becomes as Mbiti puts it, "the dead end of human life, not only for the geneological level, but also for herself."[24] Unlike the revered mother, the old barren woman is supported not out of love, but out of charity, and her death is seen as a relief to all.[25]

The ways in which colonialism affected the traditional status of African women are still being documented and are the source of much debate. I will not go into the extensive literature on this subject, except to say that it appears that the African woman often lost the benefits that came along with her traditional status, while suffering from oppression that she, her husband, and her group experienced when Europeans imposed their own system of gender constraints.[26] In being relegated more and more into the "private" sphere, she lost access to the degree of economic independence she was entitled to under the traditional system, while having to suffer the limitations that had always been a part of her role. To some extent, Emecheta's *Joys of Motherhood* portrays the loss of this status while protesting the limits of freedom for mothers in the traditional realm.

The struggle for independence in Africa, which has been relatively successful for some peoples, has necessarily affected the status of African women and the concept of motherhood. The contemporary situation, however, is as varied and complicated as is the African past. Some researchers point out that in many newly independent socialist countries like Mozambique, women's liberation is an important aspect of the struggle for independence, and these nations are consciously pursuing a state policy of attempting to equalize women's status with men. Leith Mullings reports that part of the continuing process of the transformation of the status of women in Mozambique includes:

> analysis of traditional practices thought to be detrimental to women, and political education for adults and children specifically directed toward eradicating stereotyped conceptions of male and female roles that would preclude the achievement of full human potential.[27]

Countries like Mozambique and Guinea Bissau have given the improved status of women such high priority that they have incorporated these advances into their legal structure; however, in other independent countries, like Nigeria, one remnant of colonialism is the virtual exclusion of most women from an emerging money economy. In the essay "The African Women as Entrepeneur," Ruth Simms elaborates on this problem in her discussion of Nigerian women traders. "As a group, women hold highly disadvantageous positions in the economic, educational and political institutions of society,"[28] and hence are locked into areas such as petty trading. In many African nations there is no conscious state policy to equalize women's status with men's. Women in these countries must affect social change for themselves against great odds, not the least of which is their precarious economic situation as mothers in societies that are becoming rapidly industrialized. Undoubtedly the traditional value of motherhood in these countries will be affected.

(3)

Winds that drift over the desert
Dance over the Niger,
Steal perfume from the flowering trees
And from the pretty girls,
Pause for an instant with my mother
Where she sits in the doorway of our house
Her hands between her knees,
Brush against my body and whisper in my ear of Africa.[29]
                              Dorothy S. Obi, Contempory
                              (Nigeria)

Given the importance of the concept of motherhood in African culture, it is not surprising that it is a major theme in twentieth century African literature. Andrea Benton Rushing reminds us of the Yoruba proverb, "Mother is gold," and "that portraits of black women in African poetry seem to radiate from that hub."[30] In *Whispers of the Continent*, Wilfred Cartey tells us that the mother is the symbol of Africa itself— that in the works of many twentieth century African male writers such as Camere Laye and Senghor, the love for Africa is expressed in terms of the love for mother, who is untainted by European culture and is the essence of traditional African culture.[31] In general, these writers present an idealized portrait of woman. In the introduction of his book, *Women Writers in Black Africa*, Lloyd Brown further qualifies this characteristic by emphasizing that most African male writers' presentation of women characters "have ultimately been shaped by a certain limited and limiting idealism that assumes that marriage and motherhood *per se* are unequaled routes to female fulfillment and redemption."[32]

Until recently, most African male writers have portrayed woman as the idealized life force rather than focusing on the reality of her subordinate role in most African societies. Increasingly, however, as Kenneth Little points out in his book *The Sociology of Urban Women's Image in African Literature*, the traditional mother image is being challenged in popular and serious literature by images of young urban women as girlfriends, good time girls, and "free women." In much of the contemporary literature, the emphasis is on the woman's sexuality as a means to children, more bargaining power, or in the acquisition of economic resources.[33]

On one hand, then, the idealized image of the African woman in the male literature has been that of the mother, the embodiment of tradition, while the more "realistic" image is that of woman as manipulative in her sexuality, an image often negatively perceived as an effect of the penetration of decadent western values. Like Brown, Little calls for counter images, for an acknowledgment of images closer to reality. In her essay, "The African Heroine," Marie Linton-Umeh describes the few but important African heroines in contemporary African male literature that do not follow the traditional pattern. Thus, Amos Tutuola's novel *The Brave African Huntress* (1958) presents a heroine who becomes famous as a huntress, and the novels of Sembene, Achebe, and Ngugi include women characters who are "active participants in bringing about a cultural revolution."[34] Linton-Umeh concludes her essay by stating that "the small representation of heroic female figures in African literature merely points to the short-sighted conclusions presented in the accounts of many writers who ignore and minimize the significant contributions African women in traditional African society have made"[35]

Critics like Brown and Little acknowledge the existence of an African woman's literature which is seldom noted in the discussion of the literature and is often rendered invisible despite the fact that their voices are quite distinct from those of their male counterparts. Woman writers like Nigeria's Flora Nwapa, Ghana's Aimee Aatoo, Mozambique's Noemia de Sousa, Kenya's Marina Geshe, Zambia's Kesire, and Botswana's Bessie Head protest sexual inequality in traditional as well as modern Africa, even as they are clearly committed to their own societies. In the process of attempting to strengthen their societies, through critiquing them as well as celebrating them, they all present, in varying degrees, more realistic portraits of the African mother. And perhaps the African woman writer who has concentrated most on realistic portraits of mothers, on the value of motherhood from a woman's point of view is Nigeria's Buchi Emecheta.

(4)

What shall I give my children?
Who are adjudged the leastwise of the land,
Who are my sweetest lepers. . .[36]

> Gwendolyn Brooks,
> (Afro-America) 1915-

As in Africa, the concept of motherhood is critical to Afro-American life and thought. In the Afro-American community, "motherhood represents maturity and the fulfillment of one's function as a woman,"[37] and thus is greatly respected. But Afro-American motherhood is also a battleground for racist and sexist ideology and exists within the context of the prevailing view of motherhood in the United States. Hence three points of view—the Afro-American community's view of motherhood, the white American view of motherhood, and the white American view of black motherhood—intersect to produce a distinctly complex ideology of Afro-American motherhood.

Charles Johnson observed that among plantation blacks, the statement that a woman could not have children was seen as an insult.[38] Nonetheless, the African emphasis on woman as mother was drastically affected by the institution of slavery, since slave women and men were denied their natural right to their children. The idea of the "slave mother" itself exposed one of the basic tenets of the universal institution of motherhood. By ripping off the veil of cultural sanctification within which the concept of motherhood was immersed in most cultures, American slavery revealed one of its most significant elements—that women are valued not for themselves, but for the capacity to breed, that is, to "produce" workers, and for their ability to nurture them until they are equipped to become "producers" for the society. African women were not imported in large numbers into the United States until the intermarriage rate between black men and white women was so high that the planters feared the pollution of their population, and not until the abolition of the slave trade made the production of American born slaves vital.

As slavery developed, the sanctification of the slave mother's role did occur in the figure of the proverbial mammy, slave as mother, who was mythologized in America as the perfect worker/ mother, content in her caring, diligent in her protection of her master's house and children against any who might injure them, whose descendent is the "perfect domestic."[39] In reality, house or field slave, the slave woman mothered her own children. In addition to her work in the fields or in the kitchen, she was responsible for domestic duties, not the least of which was getting enough food for her children. And since families were often separated, her mothering took on tremendous importance in terms of safeguarding her children's spiritual health as well as their physical survival.

Certainly some slave women were so disturbed by the prospect of bearing children who could only be slaves that they did whatever they could to remain childless.[40] Yet the evidence of historical information and folklore suggests that most saw their children as a symbol of hope that black people might some day be free. In any case, most were mothers, since they scarcely had effective or foolproof means by which to prevent conception. Slave narratives of men, as well as women, stress the vital role their mothers played, through sacrifice, will, and wisdom, to ensure the survival of their children.[41] Such a monumental contribution could not help but enhance the respect in Afro-American communities, a respect that continues until today.

The centrality of motherhood in Afro-American culture probably has its roots in African culture. However, this emphasis is certainly reinforced as well as complicated by the precarious position the Afro-American community, and therefore mothers and children, occupy here in America. Thus, an Afro-American child's sense of self-concept and security can hardly be derived from Anglo-American society. A positive self-concept must come from his or her own community, natal family, ultimately from the mother. In the book, *Common Differences*, Gloria Joseph discusses the tremendous emphasis placed on mothers in contemporary Afro-American communities. While stressing the significance of the rituals of Mothers' Day and the Dozens as evidence of the Afro-American community's respect for motherhood, Joseph comments:

> The Black Mother, however, is also a woman and herein lies the great contradiction. The "honored" mother is the same second class citizen who is often regarded and treated as an object to be used, bruised and abused for

years, and who is considered to be used up after 30, 40, or 45 years. The societal attitude toward mother is one of both idealization and degradation. The mother's role in the family is symbolic of contradictions and contrasts.[42]

These contradictions and contrasts are as much a part of the dominant society's attitude toward motherhood as they are a part of inner structures in the black community. On one hand, the white society honors motherhood as a pure sanctified state, and like African religions, buttresses this assumption with religion and myth.[43] On the other hand, it punishes individual mothers for being mothers. By relegating all care and responsibility of the child to individual mothers rather than to the society, it restricts women at every level of the society. And in relation to Afro-American mothers, the society neither cherishes nor respects her offspring; in fact, white society clearly does not value black children.

The cultural patterns surrounding white motherhood are also different from those that Afro-American mothers must contend with. Perhaps because of the rapid industrialization of the West, more and more emphasis was placed on the woman as wife, and therefore mother, rather than on the African model of mother, therefore wife. Women are expected to be the "angel of the home,"[44] the refuge for the man when he rests from his daily labor. Western woman's "work" was seen as her "nature". Ideally she was not a part of the productive forces necessary to the society's well-being, except in the sacred realm of the home.

This schema introduces tremendous contradictions for the Afro-American mother, who usually has to work outside the home in order to survive, and who, as a mother in this society, is not expected (respectably) to do so. In addition, the concept of strength, a womanly attribute in African life, is imbued in American society with unfeminine connotations. As Afro-American women attempted to survive within the poles of these contradictions, a further tension develops, for the Afro-American mother is characterized as strong and is punished for being so. While paid homage for her strength, she is also attacked for being a matriarch, both outside and inside the black community. Moynihan's myth of the black matriarch disguises the Afro-American mother's powerlessness, punishing her for the super-human efforts she makes, punishing her if she cannot make them.[45]

In her essay, "The Black Woman and Family Roles," (1980) Carrie Allen McCray emphasizes that:

In much of the social science and popular literature the Black Woman has either been depicted as the dominating castrating female under whose hand the family and the Black community are falling apart, or as the romanticized strong self-sufficient female responsible for the survival of the Black family and of Black people.[46]

She calls for a more balanced view that neither denigrates nor idealizes Afro-American mothers, and she indicates that some scholars (notably Afro-American sociologists such as Billingsley, Staples, Ladner) are using this approach.

One important element of the new research is to look "at the interdependence of black families with other levels of society."[47] This interdependence of societal levels is nowhere more complicated than on the issues of birth control and population control as it applies to Afro-American motherhood. The history of these two issues is a good example of the complexity of the intersection between the Afro-American view of motherhood and the white American view of Afro-American motherhood.

From the beginning of this country's history, the Afro-American birth rate has been seen as a problem to be watched carefully and supervised. As early as the eighteenth century, Benjamin Franklin feared that the presence of large numbers of Afro-Americans might endanger the character of American settlements as white colonies. The settlers, however, needed Afro-American labor in order to reap their high profits. Faced with growing European resistance to the slave trade and realizing the importance of American born slaves, the settlers enacted laws that prohibited intermarriage and clearly designated the Afro-American woman as the bearer of slaves, while the white woman was charged with the responsibility of race purity. Afro-American motherhood, then, was seen by the planters as a necessity in the continuation of the American economy, an essential part of which was slavery.[48]

Staples reports that during slavery Afro-American women bore an average of almost seven children. Between the end of the Civil War and the Depression, the Afro-American birth rate was reduced by one-half and the average family size reduced to four children.[49] During this time there is evidence to suggest that there was a concerted effort by political and social forces to control the population of Afro-Americans and poor people. Afro-American labor was not as important as it had been during slavery. In her book *Women, Race and Class*, Angela Davis reports on how the budding birth control movement of the early twentieth century was infiltrated by tenets of eugenics—the main argument being that there should be "more children from the fit, less from the unfit."[50] And because it was generally known that by the 1880s the white birth rate suffered a significant decline, "the spector of race suicide," that whites would soon be overrun by people of color, became a political and social problem for people in high political office. By 1932, the Eugenics Society reported that at least twenty states had passed compulsory sterilization laws, and by 1939 the Birth Control Federation of America overtly planned a Negro Project. In their report they stated:

the masses of Negroes, particularly in the South, still breed carelessly and disastrously, with the result that the increase among Negroes, even more than among whites, is from the portion of the population least fit, and least able to rear children properly.[51]

The policy of sterlization of "unfit" people was further exposed by cases in the 1970s of many poor Afro-American women who had been sterilized without their knowledge or permission through federal and state governmental agencies.[52] Further compounding the issue of Afro-American births has been the inordinately high rates of Afro-American infant mortality caused mostly by neglect of the health needs of Afro-American communities, from poor hospital care to bad living conditions.[53] Afro-American life clearly is not valued in the U.S.

Afro-Americans, then, have had a history of having population control imposed upon them, rather than being able to choose birth control. The result has been the tension between the reproductive rights of Afro-American women and the awareness that genocide may be a motivating factor for the advocation of birth control in Afro-American communities. Especially when the pill became accessible to most women, Afro-American male leaders decreed birth control as a genocidal plot.[54] Within the context of this debate, Afro-American women, particularly in lower income brackets, have historically had a tendency to express moral opposition to contraceptives and to abortion. Yet it is clear that they do use contraceptives at a high rate and that they frequently opt to have abortions.

During the last decade, more Afro-American women insisted on their own reproductive rights. They point out that not only are women in the Afro-American community held almost exclusively responsible for preventing pregnancy, but that they are often left to raise children without significant help from either the general society or from beleagured or unwilling mates. In Toni Cade's *The Black Woman* (1970), many of the writers question the desirability of placing emphasis on quantity rather than quality and express the belief that Afro-American women are given the charge of "saving the black race" through numbers.[55] They further question the lack of interest in the quality of their lives as Afro-American persons. Poet June Jordan emphasizes a point of view reiterated by many other Afro-American women advocates. In her "Declaration of Independence I Would Just As Soon Not Have" (1976), she insists that Afro-American men see the liberation of Afro-American women as a priority in our struggles:

How is it even imaginable that Black men would presume to formulate the Black Movement and the Women's movement as either/or, antithetical alternatives of focus? As a Black woman, I view such a formulation with a mixture of incredulity and grief: The irreducible majority of Black people continues to be composed of Black women. And, whereas many Black sons and daughters have never known our Black fathers, or a nurturing, supportive Black man in our daily lives, all Black people have most certainly been raised, and cared for, by Black women: mothers, grand-mothers, aunts. In addition, and despite the prevalent bullshit to the contrary, Black women continue to occupy the absolutely lowest rungs of the labor force in the United States, we continue to receive the lowest pay of any group of workers, and we endure the highest rate of unemployment. If that status does not cry out for liberation, specifically as Black women, then I am hopelessly out of touch with my own preordained reality.[56]

Jordan's sharp assertion is borne out by statistics. She could have added that Afro-American women are the victims of violent crimes more than any other group in this country and that the poorest among poor Afro-American women are mothers. In 1974, over one-third of Afro-American families were headed by women, 52 percent of which were below the poverty level. As La Frances Rodgers-Rose notes: "The data shows that Afro-American women who are heading households are living in or near poverty and rearing children who do not have the basic necessities of life."[57] Afro-American mothers are clearly under attack despite claims of the sanctity of motherhood in both the Afro-American community and American society at large.

(5)

They were women then
My mamma's generation
Husky of voice—Stout of
Step
With fists as well as
Hands[58]

                                        Alice Walker, 1944-
                                        Afro-America

Afro-American motherhood was also a concern of the literature in the first half of the twentieth century, although it was not as important a theme in the novel, which was directed to the general American audience, as it was in poetry, more personal in its thrust. Andrea Benton Rushing tells us in her essay on Afro-American poetry, that "the most prevalent image of black women is the image of mother,"[59] and that "almost all the images of mother revolve around her strength under stress."[60] However, until the 1940s, novels, for social and literary reasons, Afro-American women as mothers were seldom the focus.

From *Clotel* (1850), the first Afro-American novel to be published, until Ann Petry's *The Street* in 1945, the prevailing qualities of black female heroes were their light-skinned beauty and their refinement, rather than their strength and endurance as mothers under pressure. Mothers were sometimes backdrop characters, as the practical refined mother is in Pauline Hopkins *Contending Forces* (1900) or Bigger Thomas's narrow-minded mother in Wright's *Native Son* (1941). Sometimes the heroine might incidentally be a mother, as Irene Redfield is in Nella Larsen's *Passing* (1929), but the focus in the novel is not on the experience of motherhood. Even Zora Neale Hurston in *Their Eyes Were Watching God* (1937) was not able to render her wonderful heroine, Janie Stark, as a mother, since it would severely limit her mobility. Some male novelists did feature strong mother figures, as did Langston Hughes in *Not Without Laughter* (1935), but the few figures who match the image in Afro-American poetry of mothers under stress are interestingly enough grandmother figures who have become elders. In general, not until Petry's portrayal of Lutie Johnson do we have a portrait of an Afro-American woman whose motherhood is critical to the major themes of the novel.

The novel, more than the poem, tended to respond more to the image of Afro-Americans in the dominant American society. Thus, many nineteenth century novels promoted "positive" images of Afro-Americans in an attempt to refute the pervasive negative stereotypes.[61] The image of "the black mammy," the strongest caricature that the South inflicted on Afro-American women, must have made it difficult for an Afro-American writer to create a really penetrating view of black motherhood. As important, black women writers in the early part of this century focused on those qualities that were highly valued in the dominant society. For women, especially in literature, heroism meant beauty, refinement, and finally a "good" marriage.

Motherhood does become a more complicated theme in the novels written between 1945 and 1960. And in this period, the differing views of male and female writers emerge more sharply. Certainly Ellison in *Invisible Man* (1952), Baldwin in *Go Tell It On The Mountain* (1953), and Chester Himes in *The Third Generation* (1954) focus on mothers, as do Dorothy Best's *The Living Is Easy* (1948), Gwendolyn Brooks's *Maud Martha* (1953), and Paule Marshall's *Browngirl, Brownstones* (1959). But the points of view are significantly different. Himes presents the middle-class mother in his novel as the major force that the male protagonist must overcome in order to fulfill his individuality and escape conventionality. Ellison presents Mary, the only Afro-American woman character in his novel, as the stereotypical mother who takes care of his down-and-out hero for a short time in the book, describing her as "a stable familiar force."[62] Baldwin's rendition of Elizabeth Grimes, more developed than Himes or Ellison's characters, is a portrait of a long-suffering female. In her essay "The Politics of Intimacy," Hortense Spiller describes this overriding quality of Baldwin's early women characters:

> The weight of lamentation falls most strikingly on them because they have no language relevant to their specific condition, generating humor, variety and above all personal choice.[63]

West's and Brooks's protagonists also lack a language relevant to their specific condition. But in contrast to Baldwin's women, Cleo in *The Living Is Easy* is presented as a frustrated, dangerous woman who is constrained by her traditional role as wife and mother and articulates her frustration through her wiles to move up the social ladder. Brooks's *Maud Martha* begins to fashion a language, for in the novel, it is Maud Martha's imagination, her groping for her own identity as an "ordinary" Afro-American daughter, mother, and wife that generates the novella. Finally, Marshall's *Browngirl, Brownstones* breaks through the muted language of the mothers in previous books. In her portrayal of Silla Boyce, Marshall creates a multidimensional character in the context of Barbadian-American culture, whose experience of motherhood is in conflict with the prevailing ideology of motherhood in America. In order to succeed materially, Silla must destroy essential parts of herself. Although she is a wounded character, she does have a language to convey her fighting spirit, and she passes unto her daughter, Selina, the knowledge of the intricacies of womanhood and the sense of the struggle necessary to define oneself.

Browngirl, Brownstones is a touchstone in the Afro-American novel's portrayal of motherhood, for it exposes the complexity of the experience and how it is affected by the racism of this society. Yet it, and its predecessors, were not widely known, as Afro-American woman's literature was seldom noted either in mainstream American literature or in the Afro-American literary tradition. Not until the 1970s with the emergence of a strong women's movement in America was the literary tradition of Afro-American women given serious attention. Nonetheless, *Browngirl, Brownstones* created a space within which novelists like Sarah Wright, Toni Morrison, Toni Cade Bambara, and Alice Walker could continue to penetrate the theme of motherhood. Perhaps one of the most complex analyses of this theme, its history and its effects, is Alice Walker's second novel, *Meridian*.

(6)

Children, why do you fear, why turn away? Do
you not know these knobbed, harsh hands are
those that turned and pulled your brothers
from the womb?

These red eyes saw you first. These swollen
feet tramped to fetch water for your father's
comfort. This failing memory was quick to
count shillings to school him with. He'll tell
you how. It is still I.[64]

> Majorie Oludhe Macgoye, Contemporary
> (Kenya)

My grandmothers were strong.
They followed plows and bent to toil.
They moved through fields sowing seed.
They touched earth and grain grew.
They were full of sturdiness and singing.
My grandmothers were strong.

. . . .

Why am I not as they?[65]

> Margaret Walker, 1915-
> (Afro-America)

Through their many novels, both Emecheta and Walker have
challenged prevailing views of motherhood held by their respective
societies. They have also graphically presented their own view of the
experience of motherhood in contrast to the literary tradition that
preceded them. Their critiques of their societies are not located solely in
the particular books on which I will concentrate. Certainly Emecheta's
novel *Second Class Citizen* (1975) is as much an exposé of West African
views on motherhood as is *The Joys of Motherhood* (1979). Walker's
The Third Life of Grange Copeland (1970) as well as her most recent
novel, *The Color Purple* (1982) look carefully at aspects of motherhood
in the southern U.S. that the previous literature had not approached. But
The Joys of Motherhood and *Meridian* have as a dominant theme an
appraisal of the ideology of motherhood within the context of changing
forces in Nigeria of the 1930s and 1940s and the southern U.S. of the
1950s and 1960s, times when these societies were forging strong
movements of liberation. At the same time, these authors dramatize the
changes that affect their mother-protagonists in the context of history, in
the light of a tradition that informs their central characters.

Thus, each author begins her novel in the middle of her character's
story, then takes us back in time, before she brings us into the present.
We meet Nnu Ego, Emecheta's protagonist, as she hysterically runs
through the streets of 1930s Lagos to throw herself into the river. We
have no idea why she is so crazed. Gradually we move from an outside
view of her, a view that sees her as crazy, to an inside view, where her mad
action makes perfect sense within the context of her tradition. Meridian,
too, seems crazed when we meet her, as she leads a motley crew of black
children in 1970 up against a tank in a small southern town so that they

might claim their "right" to see Marilene O'Shay, a mummy of a dead white woman, who was killed by her husband for her adultery, and who now is fraudulently billed by her husband as the Twelfth Wonder of the World. While Walker uses comic slapstick and Emecheta melodrama, both authors initially present their mother/protagonists as outwardly crazy.

Too, the initial scene in each novel not only underscores the irony of their protagonists' situations, but also gives us a sense of their respective societies. As Nnu Ego runs through the streets of Lagos, it is clear that we are in a city and not a village. Yet as we listen to her thoughts she draws us back to her village, Ibuza, and to the story of her *chi*, her personal god, whom she sees as her tormentor. While Nnu Ego is caught between an unfamiliar urban culture and the clearly established patterns of village life, Meridian is, in the 1970s, enacting a ritual of the early 1960s. Truman, her comrade of that period who observes her crazy action, puts it succinctly when he tells her that "When things are finished it is best to leave."[66] Meridian's response—"And pretend they were never started?"[67] —is the prelude to a journey back in time. Like Emecheta, Walker places her analysis of motherhood in the context of a tradition that must be understood before it can be assessed.

The first chapter of *The Joys of Motherhood* is called "The Mother," as Emecheta immediately signals to her readers that Nnu Ego's attempt at suicide is, in some way, related to that condition. Emecheta reinforces that view by calling her second chapter "The Mother's Mother," as Nnu Ego recalls her history through her mother and her mother's mother. Although it is not immediately obvious that one of Walker's major concerns is motherhood, she too moves backward in time through Meridian's recent past to that of her mother and her mother's mother. In both novels, a portion of a history of a people is seen, not through battles or leaders, but through the history of the mothers. This thematic element is an important one in articulating the ideology of motherhood in both societies and how these mothers experience it.

The mothers of both protagonists had a lasting effect on their psyches and on their lives. Central to both novels is how the mother/daughter relationship is critical to the society's continuation of the ideology of motherhood. Ona, Nnu Ego's mother, had been an extraordinary woman in that she refused to marry her father, Agbadi, although he was a great chief and was passionately in love with her. She is described by Emecheta as "a very beautiful young woman who managed to combine stubbornness with arrogance."[68] She does not marry because her father, who deeply cherishes her, vowed that "his daughter was never to stoop to any man."[69] That is, to any man but him. For she is free to have men, but if she bears a son, he would take her father's name, thereby giving him the son he had never had.

Ona them becomes, in a real way, her father's replacement for a son, since her womb might "rectify the omission nature had made."[70] In relating Ona's story, Emecheta immediately gives us a lesson about the values of sons for a woman as well as a man. When she describes Ona as haughty and vibrant, we begin to sense that this woman is allowed to behave more like a man than a woman, for she too does not want to "stoop to any man." Marriage, not sex, is the condition that demands submission. Yet although she will not marry and does have a sexual life, Ona is beholden to her father, thus maintaining the rule of men in her tradition.

Emecheta weaves proverbs throughout her novel to indicate how her characters' sense of life is rooted in time immemorial. It is a tradition so unquestioned that variations on it are possible for haughty women such as Ona. Yet Ona is also subject to the laws of "nature." Caught between her father and her lover's wishes, she comes to stay with Agbadi when he has been critically wounded in a hunt and is seduced by him on the very night that his senior wife dies. It is at this woman's funeral that a slave girl who is destined by tradition to be buried with her mistress, fights back and has to be clubbed into her grave. And it is at this moment that Ona becomes ill. Later, it is discovered that she is pregnant and when her daughter Nnu Ego is born with a lump on her head, the dibia declares, "This child is the slave woman who died with your senior wife, Agunwa."[71] Because Nnu Ego has to pacify her *chi* who was buried in her father's village, her mother Ona finally has to leave her father's house and live with Agbadi, unless she chooses to give up her child. Emecheta adds a further note to the story. Not long after Ona comes to live with Agbadi, she dies from childbirth, making Agbadi pledge that he will allow their daughter "to have a life of her own, a husband if she wants one. Allow her, she tells him, to be a woman."[72]

In this ballad of a tale, Emecheta stresses certain elements essential to the ideology of motherhood in her tradition. Although Ona is allowed to deviate somewhat from tradition, her story is set within the context of a firmly held belief that a woman's primary function is that of being a mother, particularly of sons. Ona must be subject, if not to a husband, then to a father, to whom she might give sons. Another element that appears at first to be contradictory is Emecheta's emphasis on Ona's haughtiness, which attracts Agbadi rather than repels him. Gradually we see that it is her independent spirit that spurs him to make her dependent, to conquer her sexually and to make her a mother. It is her motherhood that forces her to give up her independence and finally kills her. The third element is the emphasis Emecheta places on the slave girl, on women as slaves, which she develops in another of her novels, *The Slave Girl* (1977). That both Ona, her mother, and the slave girl, her *chi*, are women who will not submit easily to the authority of tradition does not auger well for Nnu Ego. It is not surprising, then, that she leads a conflicted life, especially around the issue of motherhood.

In contrast to Emecheta's use of proverbs in her tale about Nnu Ego's mother, Walker does not immediately draw us into Meridian's mother's story. Rather she creates a quilt, a joining of diverse pieces into a coherent pattern, that is both a history of Afro-American mothers in the South, as well as Meridian's personal past. One consistent motif in the pattern is the violence that U.S. society inflicts on its children, especially its black children.

After we observe Meridian's crazy act at the beginning of the novel, we are reintroduced to her. This time she is a student at a black women's college in the early 1960s witnessing one of any number of TV funerals in "a decade marked by death. Violent and inevitable."[73] This short, charged scene is juxtaposed with the college student Meridian's attempt to help The Wild Child, a young girl who had managed to live without parents, relatives, or friends for all of her thirteen years,"[74] and who somehow becomes pregnant. In contrast to the dead national leaders on T.V., this child is an insignificant. Without a mother, no one feels responsible for her, and she, too, dies violently. Within the pattern of the T.V. funerals and this child's funeral, Walker stitches the folktale of the Sojourner, the most beautiful magnolia tree on the campus. This story takes us back to Africa and to the violence of U.S. slavery, for the beauty of the tree is attributed to its root, a slave woman's clipped out tongue that is buried under it.

Louvenia is symbolic of Meridian's original maternal ancestors, for she comes from West Africa and was brought to America a slave. Her West African family's "sole responsibility was the weaving of intricate tales with which to entrap people who hoped to get away with murder."[75] But in America, this gift of storytelling and justice-giving results in the loss of her tongue. In burying it, she preserves her history, for she knows that "Without one's tongue in one's mouth or in a spot of one's own choosing, the singer in one's soul was lost forever, to grunt and snort through eternity like a pig."[76] But even this story of one of our mothers, a history Louvenia literally takes great pains to preserve, is violated. In that decade of death, protesting students at Meridian's campus cut down the Sojourner after the funeral procession of The Wild Child is refused admittance to the school chapel. Only after Walker has demonstrated that it is sometimes black women who deny our own maternal history (often unintentionally) does she introduce Meridian Hill's mother. Unlike Ona's people, this society neither takes care of its children nor its history.

Mrs. Hill's story is both similar to and different from Ona's. There is, indeed, a clearly established tradition in the U.S. that prescribes marriage and motherhood as the primary functions of women. But while the Ibuza have clearly *articulated* precepts, American society is both rigid and indirect in its prescriptions. American women, even Afro-American women, appear to have choice, when they may not.

Meridian's "mother was not a woman who should have had children."[77] Unlike Ona, she "had known the freedom of thinking out the possibilities of her life."[78] But after tasting her independence as a school teacher, she wanted "more of life to happen to her."[79] Unlike Ona, who could, within West African tradition, experience passion and love without marriage, Mrs. Hill began to believe that she was missing something in life, some "secret mysterious life,"[80] which mothers were experiencing. Thus she marries Meridian's father and becomes pregnant, believing that this will add something to her personal life. "She could never forgive her community, her family, the whole world, for not warning her against children,"[81] and for not at least allowing her "to be resentful that she was caught."[82] For this woman, motherhood meant "becoming distracted from herself."[83] Unlike Ona, she does not physically die from motherhood, but she passes onto her daughter that sense of guilt for having "shattered her emerging self."[84] Appropriately, the chapter in which Meridian remembers her mother's experience of motherhood, and her own experience of being a daughter is called "Have You Stolen Anything?" It is no wonder, then, that Meridian, like Nnu Ego, has deep conflicts around the issue of motherhood.

Although Meridian's mother has not been given information about the restrictions of motherhood, both she and her daughter are told about its glory. Thus, Meridian's conflict is further exacerbated by her knowledge of her maternal ancestors — mothers who were slaves and who were often denied their children; mothers who did anything and everything to keep their children. Like Nnu Ego, who is tormented by her *chi*, a slave girl forced to die, Meridian is tormented by the memory of those slave mothers who had to starve themselves to death to feed their children. She feels that these women "had persisted in bringing them all (the children, the husband, the family, the race) to a point far beyond where she, in her mother's place, her grandmother's place, her great-grandmother's place would have stopped."[85]

In her recounting of Meridian's maternal history, Walker emphasizes certain elements characteristic of the Afro-American ideology of motherhood. Like the Ibuza society, motherhood is the prescribed role for women in American society, but this prescription is not so much ritualized as it is enforced by the limited options available to women. Little is known by young women about what motherhood will really mean for them, the most important omission being that they, not the society, will be totally responsible for their children. Further, because of the history of slave mothers, such sanctification surrounds Afro-American motherhood that the idea that mothers should live lives of sacrifice has come to be seen as the norm. Another element that Walker stresses is significantly different from Emecheta's emphasis. For in America, racism results in violence inflicted upon black children in the society, while in Ibuza children are beloved. Both authors, however, show how the women in their respective societies are valued only in relation to the men in their lives and finally because of the children they bear and how this value demands a giving up of their independence, of their personal life.

In both novels, the daughters are left motherless, one, because her mother dies, the other because her mother is psychologically incapable of mothering her. The stories of the protagonists' mothers, interestingly enough, demonstrate not only their lasting effect on their daughters, but also their inability to mother their daughters. They embody Adrienne Rich's assertion that "the loss of the daughter to the mother, the mother to the daughter is the essential female tragedy."[86] Especially poignant in *Joys of Motherhood* and *Meridian* is the way in which Nnu Ego and Meridian characterize their mothers' history as a process that they cannot or will not repeat. Yet, because these motherless daughters will become mothers, they have few clues as to how to positively change those aspects of that history that are unacceptable to them. In both novels, the mothers' daughters are left with fathers who give them the love they need. As a result, they come to identify more with their fathers than their mothers.

After her initial "crazy" appearance in the novel, Nnu Ego is reintroduced to us—this time as an adolescent girl lighting her father's pipe and listening to his friend's traditional greeting: "My daughters, you all will grow to rock your children's children."[87] Even her name symbolizes her relationship with her father, for she is called *Nnu Ego* because she is priceless to her father, even more than twenty bags of cowries. He is so devoted to her that, like Ona's father, he is reluctant to give her to another man and must be nudged by his friends to do so. But although her father gives her in marriage to another man, Nnu Ego does not conceive a child. She is told that "the slave woman who was her *chi* would not give her a child because she had been dedicated to a river goddess before Agbadi took her away in slavery."[88] Finally Nnu Ego's husband takes a second wife, who conceives immediately. Shamed by her barrenness, Nnu Ego becomes ill and is finally returned to her father's house. In trying to appease her *chi*, Agbadi even "stopped dealing in slaves."[89] As Nnu Ego is recovering in her father's house, she reminds him of her mother, Ona.

Emecheta comments:

> In Nnu Ego were combined some of Ona's characteristics and some of his. She was more polite, less abusive and aggressive than Ona, and unlike her, had a singleness of purpose, wanting one thing at a time and wanting it badly. Whereas few men could have coped with, let alone controlled Ona, this was not the case with Nnu Ego.[90]

And in describing Agbadi's reaction to his daughter's plight Emecheta adds:

> Agbadi was no different from many men. He himself might take wives and then neglect them for years, apart from seeing that they each received their one yam a day; he could bring his mistress to sleep with him right in his courtyard while his wives pined and bit their nails for a word from him. But when it came to his own daughter, she must have a man who would cherish her.[91]

Agbadi's effect on his cherished daughter is to render her a suitable wife, submissive and delightful, and because she does not experience the ordinary domestic relationship of her father to her mother, she is not aware of what mettle a wife or mistress must have in order to be cherished. Unlike Ona, who did not wish to stoop to any man, Nnu Ego lights her father's pipe. While he cherishes the daughter whose life he can determine, he neglects his wives, unless, like Ona, they resist his "natural authority." Without the arrogant Ona to guide her, at least by opposing through her haughtiness the traditions of Ibuza, Nnu Ego does not see the contradictions in her position. Thus, when her father arranges another marriage for her, her response is "Maybe the next time I come back, I shall come with a string of children,"[92] as she accepts whole-heartedly the traditions of her society. Her former husband's response to their separation summarizes the difference between Ona and Agbadi's untraditional relationship and Nnu Ego and his. After her bride price is returned, he consoled himself, "Let her go, she is as barren as a desert."[93]

In repeatedly reminding us of Nnu Ego's *chi*, Emecheta makes a further comment on societal contradictions in Ibuza. This slave girl's fate is tragic because Agbadi's senior wife falls suddenly ill and dies. The chief's wife dies, it is said because she hears her husband making love to Ona in their courtyard. Nnu Ego's existence, then, is due to a series of traditionally correct acts that are unjust. In the novel, her *chi's* revenge represents the tangle of human emotions—contradictions in the society around being a mother, a wife, and a slave—states of mind that are intertwined in Emecheta's narrative.

When Nnu Ego meets her new husband in the chapter "The First Shocks of Motherhood," she naturally compares him to her father. Her assessment of Nnaife is not only a personal one, it is based on her people's concept of manhood. But Nnaife does not live in the village; as a black man in Lagos, he can only be a houseboy, "a womanmade man,"[94] in contrast to the proud men of Ibuza who are farmers and hunters. In describing Nnu Ego's reaction to her woman-like husband, Emecheta is not only demonstrating the difference between the father/daughter and the husband/wife relationship, she is also commenting on the shift from traditional rural life to urban life where racism pervades the entire social fabric. All the wives in Lagos see that their husbands accept their status, seeing only the "shining white man's money."[95]

But while Nnu Ego must adjust to these new mores, she is still expected to abide by the traditional prescription that she is an incomplete woman unless she is a mother. While disgusted by her new husband, she consoles herself by hoping that she may become pregnant. Emecheta emphasizes how powerful is this balm by inserting in the narrative Nnu Ego's dream that her *chi* hands her a baby boy by the banks of the stream in Ibuza. Thus Nnu Ego, although she may live in the city, is still compelled by the traditional norms of her village. When she becomes angry with Nnaife because he is not like her father, he reminds her "Remember, though, without me, you could not be carrying that child."[96] Although her father had helped to give her life, it is her husband who allows her to give life. Thus Agbadi, in spite of all his love and concern for his daughter, cannot alter the path of womanhood that the society expects of her, nor can he guide her through its many pitfalls.

Meridian, too, has a loving relationship with her father, who, unlike her mother, has a gentle temperament. Placed next to "Have You Stolen Anything," the chapter "Indians and Ecstasy" focuses on Meridian's relationship with her father, thus providing some comparison between this woman's responses to her parents. Mr. Hill is introduced to us as a man who is tenderly concerned with Indians, the original inhabitants of this continent. He gives the land he "holds," an Indian burial ground called Sacred Serpent, to an Indian as an attempt to right some of the wrongs of history and as an admission that "we were part of it."[97] Meridian's mother's objection to his "foolishness" is contrasted to his humaneness, his ability to mourn the injustices of the past.

Meridian describes her father as "a wanderer, a mourner, a man who could *cry* over the terrible deeds committed against others."[98] But even in this section, devoted to him, Walker emphasizes Meridian's maternal history, for it is Feather Mae, Mr. Hill's grandmother, on whom the chapter concentrates. Through her father, Meridian learns of this woman who refused to eat food "planted over other folks' bones,"[99] who "renounced all religion that was not based on the experience of physical ecstasy,"[100] who "loved walking nude about her yard,"[101] and who "worshipped only the sun."[102] Like their maternal ancestor, Meridian and her father experience physical ecstasy at the Sacred Serpent's coiled tail. This experience is their "tangible connection to the past."[103] Feather Mae is a womanly model, other than her mother, who is accessible to the developing Meridian.

Other than this intense scene, however, Meridian's father barely seems to touch her life. He scarcely appears again in the novel. And even in this instance, he is unable to effect any change, for the government moves the Indian off the land and turns it into an amusement park. Despite their experience at Sacred Serpent, he is not able to alter Meridian's movement into womanhood, so that she might resist the limited societal patterns prescribed for women. Thus "English Walnuts," the chapter that follows "Indians and Ecstasy," which is about Meridian's initiation into sexual relationships with men, is also a comment on her relationship with her father.

Meridian always has to have a boyfriend, because "mainly it saved her from the strain of having to respond to other boys or even noting the whole category of men. This was worth a great deal, because she was afraid of men."[104] In contrast to the physical ecstasy she experienced with her father, sex for her is "not pleasure, but a sanctuary"[105] from the social behavior expected of an unattached woman. Unlike her father, Eddie, the man she marries, has little depth; like her father, he treats her with "gentleness and respect." When their marriage has fallen apart, Meridian describes Eddie as someone who "would always be a boy. Not that she knew what a man should be; she did not know."[106] She sees all of her male peers as boys who would never grow up, who would always be "fetching and carrying and courteously awaiting orders from someone above."[107] Just as racism affects the black men of Lagos, so that they do the work of slaves, so it affects the young men of Meridian's generation. Both Nnu Ego and Meridian react to their condition in the same way, perceiving their mates as less then men, not only because of the work they do, but because the attitude they exhibit is one of acceptance without protest.

The men Meridian comes to know do not have her father's depth, nor even his capacity to "mourn" the injustices of the society. The sexual relations she experiences with them grow out of the sordid character her society attributes to sex and are essentially different from the sacred experience she had with her father in Sacred Serpent, when "the body seemed to drop away and only the spirit lived, set free in the world."[108] Only with Truman, in the early days of the Civil Rights Movement, does Meridian come close to this experience, for she felt "they were absolutely together,"[109] "that they were at a time and place in History that forced the trivial to fall away."[110] But even her experience of unity with Truman, a man she describes as "unlike any other black man she knew, a man who fought against obstacles, a man who could become anything,"[111] is changed when they become sexually involved. Although she experiences physical sensation with him, their sexual relationship is a coming apart, rather than a coming together, as she is reduced, even in her own mind, to a physical object. Although their relationship, as well as her relationship with her husband Eddie, results in the conception of a child, Meridian does not experience physical ecstasy nor union with them as she had with her father. Having experienced that knowledge, she, like her maternal ancestor Feather Mae, understands that freedom and union are simultaneously possible. Thus, it is through her father, ineffectual though he might be, that the seeds for her pilgrimage toward wholeness are sown.

Like Nnu Ego's father, Meridian's father gives her love and tenderness—even more, the possibility of vision. Like Agbadi, Mr. Hill cannot guide her through the precarious path of womanhood. It is from their mothers that these young women must receive that knowledge, otherwise they must chart their own paths, stumbling over the same ruts that might have hindered their mothers, possibly never being able to rise from the fall, nor understand where they are. Both Emecheta and Walker infer through the narrative and structure of their novels that the knowledge their young mothers need has been denied them because prevailing thought about motherhood is couched either in mystical language or in terms of endurement.

Meridian's and Nnu Ego's first experiences of motherhood are both similar and different, in much the same ways that their cultures are similar and different. In contrast to Nnu ego, who marries in order to have children so that "her old age would be happy, that when she died, there would be somebody left behind to refer to her as "mother"[112] the teenage Meridian marries because she gets pregnant. Without marriage, mothers are socially unacceptable in U.S. society. Sex for Meridian is a sanctuary from social pressure, which unfortunately results in pregnancy; sex for Nnu Ego is a sanctuary, because it leads to pregnancy. For neither woman is sex pleasure or self-fulfilling, nor does it bring them closer to their husbands. After Nnu Ego becomes pregnant she and her husband started "growing slightly apart. Each was in a different world."[113] Eddie complains that after their marriage, Meridian's legs are "like somebody starched them shut."[114] Her disinterest in sex leads him to find a woman who loved sex, even as his wife thinks of motherhood as a "a ball, and chain."[115] For Nnu Ego's society, the purpose of sex is children, while in Meridian's world, pleasure is the expectation. But she is unable to experience that pleasure, since it also is characterized for a woman as "giving in." Thus, constraints about sex in both societies affect these two women's experience of it. Sex's primary effect, wanted or not, is a child.

The initial experience of mothering has a different value for these two women. For Nnu Ego it is her fulfillment as a woman, while for Meridian it is the means by which she becomes further cut off from life. In the chapter "The Happy Mother," Walker describes the teenager Meridian's experience of motherhood as "slavery." Although she was told by everyone that she was an exemplary young mother, it took "everything she had to tend to the child."[116] In rejecting the possibility that she might resent her child, Meridian begins to think of suicide as a possibility— blaming herself for her inability to enjoy the hassles of "happy motherhood." She is cut off from the world, left alone with her baby's needs and the T.V. set. On the other hand, Nnu Ego's delivery of a baby boy, a son, inspires her to vow that she will "start loving her husband for he had made her a real woman."[117] She becomes a part of a community of women who help her deliver the baby, although Nnanife was not awakened on the night that the baby was born. But in contrast to the patterns of her village, she must immediately go back to her petty trading, coming home to feed her baby at lunch. It is on one of these days that she finds her son dead and runs through the streets of Lagos to throw herself into the river.

Although each woman puts a different value on motherhood, they both experience the same feelings of guilt about their inability to perform its duties correctly. Both women are driven to thoughts of suicide— one, because she is locked out from the world as a result of her responsibility for her child's need; the other, because she believes her child dies since she must leave him to work in the world. Ironically, although no one is aware of Meridian's thoughts of suicide, Nnu Ego's people find her attempt at suicide understandable when they hear her child has died. "They all agreed that a woman without a child for her husband was a failed woman."[118]

While Nnu Ego waits for the day when she might again bear a child, Meridian becomes more involved in the world as a participant in the Civil Rights Movement. It is through this involvement that she receives a scholarship to college, an event that precipitates the decision that will affect her entire life. She must choose between keeping her child and going to college, since mothers are not allowed there, their fate in life having already been decided. The chapter "Battle Fatigue," in which Meridian and her mother confront each other on this decision, is at the core of Walker's discussion of the ideology of motherhood in the Black South.

"Battle Fatigue" begins with our introduction to Truman Held, "the first of the Civil Rights workers to mean something to Meridian"[119] and continues with a description of their unifying experience in a demon- stration against the town's segregated hospital facilities. Juxtaposed to their attempt to improve the health of the community is Mrs. Hill's castigation of her daughter for wasting her life in this way. Mrs. Hill's comments, which invoke tradition—that things should be as they have always been—are a subtle preparation for the climactic action in this chapter—Meridian telling her mother that she will give up her son so that she can go to college.

It is important that in order to confront the mother, Meridian brings two women with her: Delores Jones, a movement worker, and Nelda Henderson, an old classmate. Meridian needs these sisters, of distinctly different orientations, to support her. The intrepid Delores is clear, her voice an indication of change: "You have a right to go to college,"[120] she tells Meridian. On the other hand, Nelda Henderson's voice is from the past. Her history informs the discussion, for she had borne the burden of helping her mother care for her five younger brothers and sisters and was herself pregnant at 14. She'd had little information, if any, about sex and pregnancy; she resents Mrs. Hill, her neighbor, for not giving her the information she needed to get through her adolescence. Despite her awareness that Meridian has an opportunity to open up her life, Mrs. Hill is adamant in her condemnation of her daughter:

> "It's just selfishness. You ought to hang your head in shame. I have six children," she continued self-righteously, "though I never wanted to have any. And I raised everyone myself."[121]

Meridian's confrontation with her mother is followed by her own conflicted thoughts about her decision. She gave her son away "believing she had saved a small person's life."[122] But although she knows he is better cared for by others than he would have been by her, she feels "condemned, consigned to penitence for life,"[123] for she has committed the ultimate sin against black motherhood. She knows that freedom for black women had meant that they could keep their own children, while she has given hers away, and she therefore feels unworthy of her maternal history. The chapter ends as she goes to college, where she begins to hear "a voice, that cursed her existence; an existence that could not live up to the standard of motherhood that had gone before."[124] The appearance of this voice is the first indication of the spiritual degeneration that will, a year later, result in her "madness."

What Walker does in "Battle Fatigue" is to present in a succinct way the essence of Afro-American motherhood as it has been passed on. At the center of this construct is a truth that mothers during slavery did not have their natural right to their children and did everything, including giving up their lives, to save them. From this truth, however, a moral dictum has developed, a moral voice that demands that Afro-American mothers, whatever the changed circumstances of their lives, take on the sole responsibility of children. One result of this rigid position is the guilt that permeates parent/child relationships. For although some women like Mrs. Hill raised their own children, they did not want them and thus poisoned their development. Although Meridian saved her own child from those thorns of guilt, she cannot save herself. Only her mother or a mother figure can save her from her own judgment. But both women are trapped by the myth of motherhood and cannot help each other. The moral choice that Meridian makes saves her child, but not herself. Ironically, although she believes she has sinned against her maternal history, she belongs to it, for she is willing to die on account of her child. Her spiritual degeneration results in a kind of madness as well as the deterioration of her body.

Nnu Ego also goes "mad" when she loses her child, and her body also begins to deteriorate. "She had to face the fact that not only had she failed as a mother, she had failed in trying to kill herself and had been unable even to do that successfully."[125] Her husband continually calls her a "mad woman," and she herself begins to believe in her madness. She is saved from her deterioration by two events: a visit from one of her sisters, a woman with whom she was initiated, who supports her and lifts her spirit, and by a dream of her *chi*.

This dream is significantly different from her first dream, when she had just arrived in Lagos. In it her *chi* hands her "dirty chubby babies," tells her "You can have as many of those as you want. Take them," and laughs as she disappears.[126] Nnu Ego realizes that she may be pregnant and that she should be happy. But the dream also makes her ponder her fate, for it challenges her desire to want children without question. Motherhood, her *chi* seems to say, will be my ultimate revenge on you, the woman whose father caused my death. She responds to her own fear with the traditional recipe: to have a son, like her father, "who would fulfill her future hopes and joys."[127]

Nnu Ego does have a son, but this time she does not trade, fearful that something terrible might happen to him. Although she suffers from her lack of money, she consoles herself with the belief that "never mind, he will be grown soon and clothe you and farm for you, so that your old age will be sweet."[128] What she gives up in this new urban setting is her traditional right to earn her own income. She recalls that "in Ibuza women made a contribution, but in urban Lagos, men had to be the sole providers; this new setting robbed the woman of her useful role."[129] But Nnu Ego resolves to accept this new way of life, since it is the only guarantee she has that she can look after her son. Thus, Nnu Ego, in contrast to Meridian, becomes increasingly cut off from the world and becomes more dependent on her husband. Her "madness" manifests itself in her acceptance of her condition, the years of self-sacrifice for her "dirty chubby babies" that comprise her entire life.

As a result of their circumstances, Nnu Ego and Meridian cope with the restrictive aspects of motherhood in totally different ways. Meridian has the option to go to college. But in order to expand her life, she must give up her child, not only physically buy psychologically. She must be a virgin, with no knowledge of sex, if she is to become a part of that community of learners. The knowledge of sex for women in U.S. society is seen as undesirable, unless tempered by the institution of marriage. Motherhood outside marriage is a sign of transgression rather than fulfillment. Mrs. Hill invokes this point of view when she tells Meridian, "I always thought you were a *good* girl and all the time you were fast."[130] This precept is adhered to, even as men of all types and ages pursue sex with women. Thus, at her college, Meridian must be seen as a virgin, "as chaste and pure as the driven snow."[131] In spite of the attention she receives from Truman, a sophisticated black man, she knows that "had she approached him on the street dragging her child with her by the hand, he would never have glanced at her. For him she would not even have existed as a woman he might love."[132]

Meridian's motherhood puts her beyond the pale—of advancement or of love. But so does the use of birth control, for it involves knowledge about sexuality. In the novel, no adult, not even Mrs. Hill, gives Meridian information about sex or the prevention of pregnancy—even as the mother knows the drastic changes that motherhood will impose on her daughter. Her attitude, as well as society's, is summarized in her words—"Everybody else that slips up like you did *bears* it."[133] Even the doctor who performs an abortion on Meridian when she becomes pregnant by Truman concludes that if such an operation is needed, his patient must be "fast." "I could tie your tubes," he chopped out angrily, "if you'll let me in on some of all this extracurricular activity."[134]

Nnu Ego's society relates to a woman's knowledge of sexuality in a different way. Agbadi says of his virgin daughter, "There is nothing that makes a man prouder than to hear that his daughter is virtuous." But he adds, "When a woman is virtuous, it is easy for her to conceive."[135] Virginity, then, is linked to the capacity to conceive. and when Nnu Ego does not conceive a child, the fault, of course, being hers, her father can return her bride price and she can be engaged to another man. The fact that she is not a virgin does not interfere with her new marriage. But if she had conceived a child, her marriage would not have been so easily dissolved. Thus, motherhood, not sexual intercourse, is the seal of marriage in Ibuza society. It is *the necessary* state of being for a woman.

Because children are the primary reason for marriage, prevention of conception, regardless of the family or of the woman's situation, is not important. Emecheta stresses the rigidity of this position by emphasizing the economic precariousness of Nnu Ego and Nnaife's family. When Nnaife's white boss leaves Lagos, he loses his job and must depend upon Nnu Ego's tiny income from trading. Ironically, at this time she becomes pregnant. Nnaife's response indicates that motherhood is not as blessed as tradition might decree: "What type of *chi* have you got when you were desperate for children, she would not give you any; now that we cannot afford them, she gives them to you."[136] Nnu Ego is blamed for becoming pregnant, just as she had been blamed for not becoming pregnant. Her children might starve, but she will continue to have more, seeing them as a mother's "investment." She will deny herself everything, will almost die from giving birth, but she will continue to have children. Nnaife will take on other wives so that he might guarantee himself even more children. Nnu Ego's reaction to the arrival of Nnaife's second wife underscores the toll that motherhood has taken:

> Nnu Ego felt that she should be bowing to this perfect creature—she who had once been acclaimed the most beautiful woman ever seen. What had happened to her? Why had she become so haggard, so rough, so worn...[137]

But she knows she cannot protest even to her father, for he would respond with the proverb, "What greater honor is there for a woman to be a mother and now you are a mother."[138] Motherhood for Nnu Ego, then, regardless of what toll it takes, is an honor and is to be endured at whatever cost. When she and her co-wife cannot get enough money from Nnaife to run the house—for women are dependent on men in Lagos—it occurs to her that she "was a prisoner, imprisoned by her love for her children."[139] Ironically, her honor, her investment becomes her imprisonment.

Meridian, too, for a time, is imprisoned by her love for her children, the one she gives away, the one she aborts. Obsessed by her guilt, she thinks constantly of her mother, as "Black Motherhood personified and of that great institution she was in terrible awe, comprehending as she did the horror, the narrowing of perspective for mother and for child, it had invariably meant."[140] She loses her hair, has severe headaches and terrible dreams, until finally she temporarily loses her sight and becomes paralyzed. Only then does she experience ecstasy, this time from suffering rather than from pleasure. She does not recover from her illness until she is absolved by Miss Winter, her music teacher. A symbol of Meridian's mother, Miss Winter responds to Meridian's statement when she is in a dream-like state—"Mama I love you. Let me go."—with the necessary words, "I forgive you."[141] This absolution give Meridian the permission to go on the quest that will occupy the rest of the novel, a quest that will take her beyond the society's narrow meaning of the word *mother* as a physical state and expand its meaning to those who create, nurture, and save life in social and psychological as well as physical terms.

The points of view of Emecheta and Walker on the possibilities of change available to their mother/protagonists are completely different. While Meridian perceives herself as having sinned against her maternal tradition, she is able, in the context of the Civil Rights Movement, to probe the meaning of motherhood. Nnu Ego, on the other hand, is trapped in herself by traditional norms and by the lack of a social movement that might give her insight into her own condition.

Thus, Nnu Ego's life deteriorates, until by the end of the novel she ends her life alone, expecting to hear from her sons in America and Canada. Because her family is dispersed, she goes back to her village, Ibuza, where she becomes slightly mad and, until one night, "she died quietly there with no child to hold her hand and no friend to talk to her."[142] Emecheta quietly adds that "Nnu Ego had been too busy building up her joys as a mother,"[143] to indulge in friendship. The novel ends ironically as her children come home and build her a shrine. Although many people agreed that she had given all to her children, they mitigate this sacrifice by pointing out that "the joy of being a mother was the joy of giving all to her children."[144] Because of this, her family and tribeswomen are angry that she never answered the prayers of people who called upon her. In death as well as life, Nnu Ego does not fulfill the prescriptions of motherhood.

Although Emecheta's novel ends tragically, she indicates that some change is taking place in relation to the status of women. Nnu Ego's daughter, Kehinde, goes against her father's wishes, runs away to marry a man from another tribe, and seems to build a life for herself. But even here, Nnu Ego is the one who suffers, for her husband, angered by the loss of his daughter's bride price, assaults the young man and is hauled off to jail. Because they do not understand the laws of their country, Nnaife and Nnu Ego effectively condemn themselves. In honestly recounting her years of sacrifice, the years her husband spent in the army, the money she saved to send her sons to school, her insistence on her husband's ownership of their family, she exposes the tragedy of her own life. Her confusion is succinctly contained in one of her last statements; "Why were they all laughing at me. Things surely have changed, but Nnaife still owns us, does he not?"[145] A "backward woman," she is blamed for the destruction of her family, for Kehinde's bad behavior, for her husband's imprisonment, her son's departure to the West. Kehinde's farewell to her mother is true irony: "Mother, pray for us, that our life will be as productive and fertile as yours."[146]

In contrast, Meridian does not follow the traditional pattern of her mothers. Within the context of the Civil Rights Movement, a movement opposed to the fragmentation of violence and committed to the wholeness of creativity, she is able to probe the meaning of motherhood, not solely in a biological context, but in terms of justice and love. As she struggles through her own atonement, she becomes a "man/ woman person with a shaved part in close-cut hair, a man's blunt face and thighs, a woman's breast,"[147] who owns nothing and wanders through the land, listening to the people, being close to them and helping them "to get used to using their voice." In the final chapter of the novel, "Release," she becomes *strong* enough to return to the world, not strong in the sense of her mothers' sacrifices, but in the sense of her understanding of the preciousness of life. She passes on her struggle to Truman, who understands that the "sentence of bearing the conflict in her own soul which she had imposed on herself, and lived through must now be borne in terror"[148] by us all. In passing this struggle for understanding to a man, Walker infers that the need for understanding of creativity and life in both men and women is a prerequisite for revolutionary change.

Although Meridian's journey is a painful one, she is able, partly because of the existence of a social movement among her people, to struggle in order to rise up and bring back the truth of her personal discovery. In that sense, she is a hero in the classical sense. Unlike the antiheroes of much contemporary literature who are alienated from self and society, Meridian "sloughes off the victim role to reveal her true powerful and heroic identity."[149]

On the other hand, Emecheta's rendition of Nnu Ego's life is that of a victim who has yet to articulate her victimization, a necessary step for change. She is destroyed by this lack of consciousness and by the silence in her society where the personal lives of women and wider social change have yet to be related. *The Joys of Motherhood* protests the lack of value Nnu Ego's society places on her life; Walker's *Meridian* both protests Meridian's powerlessness and traces her journey to spiritual health. Although similar in their thrust against the restrictions placed on mothers, these two novels are extremely different in the presentation of the particular state of women's development, the particular historical moment in their respective societies.

(7)

They told us
Our mothers told us
They told us[150]

                                   Aimee Aatoo, 1944
                                   (Ghana)

. . . when we speak we are afraid
our words will not be heard
nor welcomed
but when we are silent
we are still afraid.[151]

                                   Audre Lorde, 1934-
                                   (Afro-America)

Emecheta's *Joys of Motherhood* and Walker's *Meridian* substantiate much of the ideology of motherhood in their societies, even as they illuminate their effects on women. Both authors clearly preceive that motherhood is the primary function expected of women—that women are often reduced to this function, are not seen as complex human beings, and as a result have inferior status in their societies. They both insist that such reductionism occurs because women have little knowledge of or control over societal structures that interpret this aspect of their potentiality. As a result, women themselves internalize these values without being aware of the dire effects they will have on their lives. Both writers also agree that motherhood is not an issue of the individual; it is an ideology that is interwoven into every aspect of society's basic structures. The forms of these two novels reiterate the power of these structures, even as they emphasize the value of women's culture.

By weaving proverbs into the narrative of *Joys of Motherhood* Emecheta shows us how tradition had decreed that motherhood is a necessary state for African women. The novel has the qualtiy of an oral tale; its plot and characters are subordinated to a world view incorporated in the proverbs, an oral form of transmitting values. In compiling the innumerable succinct statements on motherhood in Ibuza tradition, Emecheta also juxtaposes them to the reality of the new urban life to which they have little applicability. But in literally separating these sayings from the societal layers of Ibuza life, Emecheta also heightens the way they restrict women's lives in traditional societies as well. Thus, the saying on which the book is centered—"The joy of being a mother is the joy of giving all to your children"—is set in such relief in the novel that we feel the impact of religion, custom, myth, economics, and politics in its formulation. And we understand how important it is for the novelist to break through the many layers of the societal language about motherhood because of the power of these often repeated statements. Thus, Emecheta does not include in the novel coping mechanisms, such as women's organizations, that might obscure the primary tenets of motherhood as she perceives them.

The question of whether the oral tradition, represented by the proverbs, is the domain of all the folk, the property of men, or the remnant of a post mother-centered society is not dealt with in this particular novel of Emecheta's. There is, however, some indication in her other novels, especially in *The Bride Price* (1976), that the oral tradition was partially created by women in a context that, at one time, was of some benefit to them.

Just as Emecheta uses an indigenous African form in the construction of her novel, in *Meridian*, Walker uses the form of the quilt, the southern Afro-American women's creation of functional beauty out of the discarded pieces of their society. She connects the many aspects of the experience and ideology of motherhood in the South and shows how complex is the design. Her restructuring of the design emphasizes the way in which certain motifs of maternal history, the focus on sacrifice as a means to goodness, disguise other motifs, that unjust sacrifice may also be a means to death, to stifling self-righteousness and to guilt. The tension between a maternal history when "extreme purity of life was compelled by necessity" and the present era, "an age of choice"[152] for which mothers fought, is one of the major axes of *Meridian*.

But Walker goes a step further. She sees the waste inherent in a society that is fragmented at every level by hierarchical concepts of gender, race, and class, concepts that result in violence and are opposed to the unifying truth that is Nature. Thus, *Meridian* is a novel dedicated to the need for making connections between the many aspects of society, if "One Life" is to be cherished. Like Emecheta, Walker does not condemn motherhood, rather she respects it so much that she condemns society's use of mothers for its own ends, even as it takes no responsibility for their lives.

Both Emecheta and Walker are mothers. Their own personal experiences of motherhood has surely sharpened their insights into the ideology of motherhood that restricts women. One feels Emecheta's urgency in her novels, some of which are dedicated to her children, to expose the plight of African mothers. Most of her work is concerned with the dilemma of young girls becoming mothers, either in traditional settings as in *The Slave Girl* and *The Bride Price*, or in the transition from traditional to modern life, as in *In The Ditch* (1972), *Second Class Citizen*, (1975), *Joys of Motherhood*, and *Double Yoke* (1983). And in most of her novels, she also demonstrates the impact of colonialism, whether the characters understand it or not, on mothers, even as they are restricted internally by their own culture.

Walker's three novels also focus on mothers. In the *Third Life of Grange Copeland* (1970), both Margaret and Mem Copeland are violently destroyed by the incredible burden of motherhood that black and white society imposes on them. Her third novel, *The Color Purple*, presents many types of mothers: Celie, a child who has children conceived in rape that are taken away from her; Shug, who leaves her children partly because of her lover's treatment of her; Sophie, who is taken away from her children when she is unjustly imprisoned by whites; Nettie, to whom Celie's children are given. In all of Walker's novels, violence is inflicted upon black mothers and children precisely because they are powerless in black and white society, have little control over their lives, and are clearly not valued.

Although the state of motherhood restricts women in these authors' novels, it also give them insight into the preciousness of life. In her essay *"One Child of One's Own,"* Walker tells us that her daughter's "birth was the incomparable gift of seeing the world at quite a different angle then before and judging it by standards that would apply far beyond my natural life."[153] And as she points out in her review of Emecheta's *Second Class Citizen*, "Emecheta is a writer and a mother and it is because she is both, that she writes at all."[154]

While both writers clearly see the experience of motherhood as a profound one, they protest its use by society as a means to ends other then the value of human life, including and especially their own. Because women are reduced to the function of mother, which often results in their loss of a sense of self, the gift of seeing the world from that angle is lost to them and their communities.

So Emecheta stresses in *Joys of Motherhood* the inherent waste of Nnu Ego's life *and* the contribution that such an awareness of self might have been to her society. Walker attempts to demonstrate the struggle of her protagonist to penetrate the death-producing ideology of motherhood in which her society is embedded so that she might "judge the world by standards that would apply beyond her natural life." Nonetheless, that personal struggle occurs within the context of a societal struggle for freedom, suggesting that Meridian's quest cannot, if it is to be successful, be a purely individualistic one. This point becomes even more clear if one looks at Walker's first novel, where Mem Copeland resembles Nnu Ego in that she initially internalizes her society's value system. But when, out of pure necessity, she begins to question and resist those values, she is destroyed. Like Nnu Ego, she is a victim without awareness, without a language through which she can forge understanding with others like herself.

Thus, the importance of societal change, rather than solely individual awareness, in transforming society's ideology of motherhood is one of the major themes of these novels. Both Walker and Emecheta establish the relationship between slavery, racism, and the oppression of women in constructing their novels. Emecheta makes clear distinctions between an indigenous African slavery and the racism that the European colonialists inflicted on all Africans. In both phenomena, the slave or the African is reduced to a function, to a thing for use, in much the same way that her protagonist is reduced to the function of mother. In all three states of mind, the people in power construct myths as to why slaves or Africans or women should enjoy being a function. *Joys of Motherhood* protests the interrelationship between these states of mind and the language within which they are embedded, which result in a sense of inferiority in the slave's mind, the African's mind, the Ibuza woman's mind. Her novel focuses on breaking through this state of mind — hence her presentation of Nnu Ego as a woman whose tragedy is her lack of self-awareness, her loss of *her* sense of her right to life.

Walker also shows the relationship between slavery, racism, and the oppression of women. But because of the particular history of Afro-Americans, she gives Meridian historial models to which she can turn, as well as cultures that have consistently opposed fragmentation. Her use of Native American culture as well as Afro-American culture emphasizes the need for a point of view that values *all life* rather than some life. But even within these cultural contexts, women who have resisted the norm are compelled to a "purity of life." While celebrating her maternal ancestors' strength and sacrifice, Walker also insists that mothers have a right to a fullness of life and that sacrifice should be a means to more life rather than an end in itself. Further she demonstrates that if the ideology of motherhood in Afro-American culture does not value women, that culture loses the particular gift of seeing the world from the angle of continuation, a necessary attitude for any meaningful struggle toward health and freedom.

These two novels express, in their different ways, two fundamental ideas. While acknowledging the respect for motherhood that African and Afro-American cultures proclaim, the authors insist that women be valued for themselves and not reduced to a function, a thing. On the other hand, both writers see that motherhood provides an important insight into the preciousness, the value of life, which is the cornerstone of the value of freedom. They are also clear about the fact that this particular way of seeing the world does not necessarily proceed from being a biological mother; rather, it is a state of mind that women can lose if biological motherhood is legislated or forced upon them as their necessary state, a state in which they are restricted by being responsible for society's children. It is the entire society that must take on that angle of seeing the world, of judging its development from the standard of the value and continuity of all life.

It is this truth that Emecheta and Walker, among other African and Afro-American women writers, express about the value of motherhood. Thus, motherhood includes not only the bearing of children, but the resistance against that which would destroy life and the nurturance of that which would support and develop life. For them, feminism is inseparable from the struggle of the living to be free, and freedom cannot exist unless women, mothers or not, are free to pursue it.

NOTES

1. Stella Ngatho, "Footpath," in *Women Poets of the World*, ed. Joanna Bankier and Deidre Lashgari; (New York: Macmillan, 1983), p. 289.
2. June Jordan, *Things That I Do in The Dark* (New York: Random House, 1977), p. 37.
3. Adrienne Rich, *Of Woman Born* (New York: Bantam Books, 1976), p. 45.
4. Ibid., p. 49
5. Noëmia da Sousa, "Appeal," *Women Poets of the World*, p. 286.
6. Cheikh Anta Diop, *The African Origin of Civilization*, ed., and trans. Mercer Cook (Westport: Lawrence Hill & Co., 1974), pp. 143-145.
7. Ayi Kwei Armah, *Two Thousand Seasons* (Chicago: Third World Press, 1979), pp. 16-29.
8. John Mbiti, *African Religions and Philosophy* (New York: Doubleday Anchor, 1970), p. 33.
9. Ibid.
10. Denise Paulme, ed., *Women of Tropical Africa* (Berkeley: Univ. of California Press, 1971), summarizes the research presenting this point of view. See also: Filomina Chioma Steady, ed., *The Black Woman Cross-Culturally* (Cambridge, MA: Schenkman, 1981).
11. Nancy J. Hafkin and Edna G. Bay, *Women in Africa: Studies in Social and Economic Change* (Palo Alto: Stanford University Press, 1976), p. 9.
12. Ibid., p. 5.
13. Joan Kelly-Godal, "The Social Relations of the Sexes: Methodological Implications of Women's History," *The Signs Reader*, ed., Elizabeth Abel and Emily K. Abel (Chicago: University of Chicago Press, 1983), p. 20. See also: Niara Sudarkasa, "Female Employment and Family Organization in West Africa," *The Black Woman Cross-Culturally*.
14. Hafkin and Bay, *Women in Africa*, p. 6.
15. Ibid., p. 5.
16. Ibid., p. 8.
17. Ibid., p. 4.
18. Ibid.
19. Ibid., p. 9-11.
20. Leith Mullings, "Women and Economic Change in Africa," *Women in Africa*, p. 245.
21. Jacques Maquet, *Africanity, the Cultural Unity of Black Africa*, trans. Joan R. Rayfield (New York: Oxford University Press, 1972), pp. 70-72.
22. Ibid.
23. Ibid.
24. Mbiti, *African Religions and Philosophy*, p. 144.
25. Ibid.
26. Mullings, "Women and Economic Change," pp. 246-256.

27. Ibid., p. 261.
28. Ruth Simms, "The African Woman Entrepeneur," *The Black Woman Cross-Culturally*, p. 150.
29. Dorothy S. Obi, "Winds of Africa," in *Women Poets of the World*, p. 288.
30. Andrea B. Rushing, "Images of Black Women in Modern African Poetry: An Overview," in *Sturdy Black Bridges*, ed., Roseann Bell, Bettye Parker and Beverly Guy-Sheftall (New York: Anchor Press/ Doubleday, 1979), p. 19.
31. Wilfred Cartey, *Whispers of the Continent* (New York: Vintage, 1969).
32. Lloyd W. Brown, *Women Writers in Black Africa* (Westport, CT.: Greenwood Press, 1981), p. 7.
33. Kenneth Little, *The Sociology of Urban Women's Image in African Literature* (London: Macmillan Press Ltd., 1980), p. 152.
34. Marie Linton-Umeh, "The African Heroine," *Sturdy Black Bridges*, p. 45.
35. Ibid., p. 51.
36. Gwendolyn Brooks, "The children of the poor #2," *Selected Poems* (New York: Harper & Row, 1963), p. 53.
37. Robert Staples, *The Black Woman in America* (Chicago: Nelson Hall, Inc., 1973), p. 153.
38. Charles S. Johnson, *Shadow of the Plantation* (Chicago: University of Chicago Press, 1934), p. 100.
39. Barbara Christian, *Black Women Novelists: The Development of a Tradition* 1892-1976 (Westport, CT.: Greenwood Press, 1980), pp. 7-12.
40. Angela Davis, *Women, Race and Class* (New York: Random House, 1981), pp. 204-05.
41. Ruth Bogin and Bert Lowenthal, eds., *Black Women in 19th Century American Life* (University Park: Pennsylvania State University Press, 1976).
42. Gloria I. Joseph and Jill Lewis, *Common Differences: Conflicts in Black and White Feminist Persepectives* (New York: Doubleday Anchor, 1981), p. 92.
43. Rich, *Of Woman Born*, p. 31-32.
44. Ibid.
45. Staples, *The Black Woman in America*, pp. 27-28.
46. Carrie Allen McCray, "The Black Woman and Family Roles," in *The Black Woman*, ed. LaFrances Rodgers-Rose (Beverly Hills: Sage Publications, 1980), p. 67.
47. Ibid., p. 74.
48. Christian, *Black Women Novelists*, p. 5-8.
49. Staples, *The Black Woman in America*, p. 135.
50. Davis, *Women, Race and Class*, pp. 209-215.
51. Ibid., p. 214.
52. Ibid., p. 215-216.
53. Staples, *The Black Woman in America*, p. 138.
54. Staples, *The Black Woman in America*, pp. 139-141.
55. Toni Cade, ed., *The Black Woman* (New York: New American Library, 1970).

56. June Jordan, "Declaration of Independence I Would Just As Soon Not Have," *Civil Wars* (Boston: Beacon Press, 1981), p. 118.
57. La Frances Rodgers-Rose, "Some Demographic Characteristics of the Black Woman: 1940-1975," *The Black Woman*, p. 39.
58. Alice Walker, *Revolutionary Petunias* (New York: Harcourt Brace Jovanovich, 1973), p. 5.
59. Andrea Benton Rushing, "Images of Black Women in Afro-American Poetry," *The Black Woman Cross-Culturally*, p. 404.
60. Ibid.
61. Christian, *Black Women Novelists*, pp. 32-33.
62. Ralph Waldo Ellison, *Invisible Man* (New York: Random House, The Modern Library, 1953), p. 196.
63. Hortense Spiller, "The Politics of Intimacy: A Discussion," *Sturdy Black Bridges*, p. 90.
64. Marjorie Oludhe Macgoye, "For Miriam," *Women Poets of the World*, p. 293.
65. Margaret Walker, "Lineage," *Sturdy Black Bridges*, p. 339.
66. Alice Walker, *Meridian* (New York: Harcourt Brace Jovanovich, 1976), p. 13.
67. Ibid., p. 13.
68. Buchi Emecheta, *The Joys of Motherhood* (New York: George Brazillier, 1979), p. 11.
69. Ibid., p. 12.
70. Ibid., p. 12.
71. Ibid., p. 27.
72. Ibid., p. 28.
73. Walker, *Meridian*, p. 21.
74. Ibid., p. 23.
75. Ibid., p. 31.
76. Ibid., p. 34.
77. Ibid., p. 39.
78. Ibid.
79. Ibid.
80. Ibid., p. 40.
81. Ibid.
82. Ibid.
83. Ibid.
84. Ibid., p. 41
85. Ibid., p. 121.
86. Rich, *Of Woman Born*, p. 240
87. Emecheta, *The Joys of Motherhood*, p. 29.
88. Ibid., p. 31.
89. Ibid., p. 35.
90. Ibid., p. 36.
91. Ibid.
92. Ibid., p. 39.
93. Ibid.

94. Ibid., p. 42.
95. Ibid., p. 51.
96. Ibid.
97. Walker, *Meridian*, p. 47.
98. Ibid., p. 46.
99. Ibid., p. 49.
100. Ibid., p. 50.
101. Ibid.
102. Ibid.
103. Ibid., p. 51.
104. Ibid., p. 54.
105. Ibid., p. 55.
106. Ibid., p. 64.
107. Ibid.
108. Ibid., p. 51.
109. Ibid., p. 80.
110. Ibid.
111. Ibid., p. 96.
112. Emecheta, *The Joys of Motherhood*, p. 54.
113. Emecheta, *The Joys of Motherhood*, p. 52.
114. Walker, *Meridian*, p. 57.
115. Ibid., p. 63.
116. Ibid.
117. Emecheta, *The Joys of Motherhood*, p. 53.
118. Ibid., p. 62.
119. Walker, *Meridian*, p. 79.
120. Ibid., p. 83.
121. Ibid., p. 86.
122. Ibid., p. 87.
123. Ibid., p. 88.
124. Ibid.
125. Emecheta, *The Joys of Motherhood*, p. 72.
126. Ibid., pp. 77-78.
127. Ibid., p. 79
128. Ibid., p. 80.
129. Ibid., p. 81.
130. Alice Walker, *Meridian*, p. 87.
131. Alice Walker, *Meridian*, p. 89.
132. Walker, *Meridian*, p. 141.
133. Ibid., p. 84.
134. Ibid., p. 112.
135. Emecheta, *The Joys of Motherhood*, p. 31.
136. Ibid., p. 91.
137. Ibid., p. 118.
138. Ibid., p. 119.
139. Ibid., p. 137.
140. Walker, *Meridian*, p. 123.

141. Ibid.
142. Emecheta, *The Joys of Motherhood*, p. 224.
143. Ibid.
144. Ibid.
145. Ibid., p. 218.
146. Ibid., p. 223.
147. Walker, *Meridian*, p. 217
148. Ibid., p. 228.
149. Carol Pearson and Katherine Pope, *The Female Hero in American and British Literature* (New York: R. R. Booker, 1981), p. 13.
150. Aimee Aatoo, "Cornfields in Accra," *Women Poets of the World*, p. 295.
151. Audre Lorde, "A Litany for Survival," *The Black Unicorn* (New York: W. W. Norton & Co., 1978), p. 32.
152. Walker, *Meridian*, p. 123.
153. Alice Walker, *In Search of Our Mothers Gardens: Womanist Prose* (New York: Harcourt Brace Jovanovich, 1983), p. 369.
154. Ibid., p. 67.

Index

Aatoo, Aimee (contemporary African woman poet and playwright), 147, 219, 243
Abolitionists, black women in the works of: 3, 4, 161, 168–69
Achebe, Chinua (contemporary African male writer), 218
"Advancing Luna" (short story, Alice Walker), 83–92. See also: *In Love and Trouble*; Walker, Alice; *You Can't Keep A Good Woman Down*
African motifs in: *The Color Purple*, 94, 181–82; *In Love and Trouble*, 32, 45; Lorde's works, 207, 209; *Maud Martha*, 139–40; *Meridian*, 230; *Once*, 83; *Praisesong for the Widow*, 149–57, 181–82; recent works of Afro-American women writers, 181–82; *Song of Solomon*, 151; *Soul Clap Hands and Sing*, 108; *Tar Baby*, 68.
African Religion and Philosophy (Mbiti) 214, 216. See also: Mbiti, John
African women: idealized, 145–46; motherhood, in relation to, 213–17, 217–219; negritude, in relation to, 145–47
African women writers, 147–48, 219. See also: Emecheta, Buchi
Amadi, Elechi (twentieth century African male writer), 32, 45, 87, 146. See also: *The Concubine*
Antebellum southern literature, 2
Armah, Ayi Kwei (contemporary African male writer), 213, 214
Audience for, definition of: Alexis de Veaux, 171; contemporary Afro-American women writers, 178–85; Frances Harper, 169–70, 172–73; for early twentieth century Afro-American women writer, 172–75; Alice Walker, 185

Baldwin, James (contemporary Afro-American male novelist, essayist and playwright), 15, 104, 127, 225
Bambara, Toni Cade (contemporary Afro-American woman fiction writer) 28, 162, 179, 180, 205, 223, 226

Baraka Imamu (LeRoi Jones) (contemporary Afro-American male poet, playwright, essayist, novelist), 16, 84, 104, 152
Birth control, in relation to black women, 222–223, 240
Black culture in works of:
Afro-American woman poets, 119, 122–23; Emecheta, 229–30, 233–34; Hurston, 175; Marshall, 16–17, 103–04, 108, 113–14, 149, 152–58; Morrison, 65–69; Alice Walker, 82, 85–87, 192–94, 230–32. See also: Community
Black female images: See Conjure woman image; Mammy image; Motherhood; Mulatta image
Black girl as focal character in: *The Bluest Eye*, 25, 75; *Browngirl, Brownstones*, 17, 106, 177; *The Color Purple*, 94; *The Joys of Motherhood*, 232–33; *Maud Martha*, 127, 132–33, 135, 138, 176; *Meridian*, 234; *Sula*, 25; "To da-duh in Memoriam," 111
Black males poets, black women in the works of: 15–16
The Black Woman (ed. Cade), 107, 223
Black women as: artists, 86; matriarchs, 104, 124, 131, 177, 221–22; slaves, 2–3, 86, 219–20, 229, 231, 233, 238, 246–47. See also: Black female images; Motherhood; Sexuality; Womanhood, definition of.
Black Women Novelists (Christian), 1, 47, 165
Black women poets, discussion of, 119, 125
The Black Unicorn (poetry, Lorde), 207. See also: Lorde, Audre
The Bluest Eye (Morrison), discussion of, 25–26, 47–49, 52–53, 56–58, 62–63, 73–75, 178–79:
_____ Characters, black girl as focal character, 25, 75
_____ Structure: language, in relation to, 25, 57; Nature, in relation to, 47–49, 52–53, 56–58, 62–63
_____ Themes: class, 73–75; inversion,

About the Author

Barbara T. Christian is Associate Professor in the Afro-American Studies Department at the University of California, Berkeley (the first black woman to receive tenure at the university). She received her B.A. from Marquette University and her M.A. and Ph.D. from Columbia University, where she was the first woman in the contemporary British and American literature program. While at Columbia, she became extensively involved in teaching and administrating SEEK at City College of N.Y., a program designed to bring disadvantaged, and supposedly uneducable, black and Puerto Rican students into advanced and higher educational studies.

She is the author of *Black Woman Novelists: The Development of a Tradition*, which received the Before Columbus American Book Award in 1983. Her other works include *Teaching Guide to Black Foremothers* in 1980, as well as numerous essays and, *In Search of Our Past*, a multi-ethnic program for junior high school, to which she was a contributor—the program winning the American Educators Award for the Best Curriculum, in 1982.

In recent years, she has been engaged in continued activities for the Women's Studies and Afro-American Departments at Berkeley, as well as special projects directed toward education in the black and women's communities of the East Bay/Berkeley areas. She presently lives with her daughter in Berkeley where she continues her work as a black feminist critic.